TRANSPORT
AND
URBAN
DEVELOPMENT

TRANSPORT AND URBAN DEVELOPMENT

Edited by David Banister

E & FN SPON
An Imprint of Chapman & Hall

London · Glasgow · Weinheim · New York · Tokyo · Melbourne · Madras

Published by E & FN Spon, an imprint of Chapman & Hall, 2–6 Boundary Row, London SE1 8HN, UK

Chapman & Hall, 2–6 Boundary Row, London SE1 8HN, UK

Blackie Academic & Professional, Wester Cleddens Road, Bishopbriggs, Glasgow G64 2NZ, UK

Chapman & Hall GmbH, Pappelallee 3, 69469 Weinheim, Germany

Chapman & Hall USA, 115 Fifth Avenue, New York, NY 10003, USA

Chapman & Hall Japan, ITP-Japan, Kyowa Building, 3F, 2-2-1 Hirakawacho, Chiyoda-ku, Tokyo 102, Japan

Chapman & Hall Australia, 102 Dodds Street, South Melbourne, Victoria 3205, Australia

Chapman & Hall India, R. Seshadri, 32 Second Main Road, CIT East, Madras 600 035, India

First edition 1995

© 1995 David Banister

Typeset by Best-set Typesetter Ltd., Hong Kong

Printed in England by Clays Ltd, St Ives plc

This book was commissioned and edited by Alexandrine Press, Oxford

ISBN 0 419 20390 7

A catalogue record for this book is available from the British Library

∞ Printed on permanent acid-free text paper, manufactured in accordance with ANSI/NISO Z39.48-1992 and ANSI/NISO Z39.48-1984 (Permanence of Paper).

CONTENTS

The Contributors   viii

Acknowledgements   x

Chapter 1.   The Key Issues in Transport and Urban
Development
DAVID BANISTER and NATHANIEL LICHFIELD   1

Chapter 2.   Transport Infrastructure Investment and
Economic Development
JOSEPH BERECHMAN   17

Chapter 3.   ISTEA: Infrastructure Investment and
Land Use
ROBERT E. PAASWELL   36

Chapter 4.   The Economic Debate: Theory and Practice
RONALD McQUAID   59

Chapter 5.   A European Perspective on the Spatial
Links between Land Use, Development
and Transport
PETER HALL   65

Chapter 6.   Transport Planning, Energy and
Development: Improving Our Understanding
of the Basic Relationships
MICHAEL BREHENY   89

Chapter 7.   The Channel Tunnel: The Case for Private
             Sector Provision of Public Infrastructure
             ROGER VICKERMAN   96

Chapter 8.   Critical Issues in Regional Rail
             Investment
             MICHAEL EDWARDS   123

Chapter 9.   Technopole Development in Euralille
             FRANCIS AMPE   128

Chapter 10. Development Impacts of Urban Transport:
             A US Perspective
             BOB CERVERO and JOHN LANDIS   136

Chapter 11. Accessibility and Development Impacts
             MICHAEL WEGENER   157

Chapter 12. The Coming of Supertram: The Impact
             of Urban Rail Development in Sheffield
             PETER TOWNROE   162

Chapter 13. Urban Rail Development and the
             Measurement of Impacts
             TOM WORSLEY   182

Chapter 14. Development Effects at Airports:
             A Case Study of Manchester Airport
             JIM TWOMEY and JUDITH TOMKINS   187

Chapter 15. Development Effects at Airports
             SEAN BARRETT   212

Chapter 16. Sea Ports, Land Use and Competitiveness:
             How Important are Economic and
             Spatial Structures?
             EDDY VAN DE VOORDE   218

Chapter 17. Transport Terminals, Interchanges and
             Economic Development
             KENNETH BUTTON   241

Chapter 18. Private Toll Roads in the United States:
             Recent Experiences and Prospects
             Jose A. Gomez-Ibanez and John R. Meyer   248

Chapter 19. Private Sector Investment in Roads:
             The Rhetoric and the Reality
             David Banister   272

Chapter 20. Summary and Conclusions
             Peter Hall and David Banister   278

Index   288

THE CONTRIBUTORS

Mr Francis Ampe
Directeur General
Agence de Development et
d'Urbanisme de la Metropole Lilloise
2, Place du Concert
549043 LILLE
France

Professor David Banister
The Bartlett School of Planning
University College London
Wates House
22 Gordon Street
LONDON WC1H 0QB

Dr. Sean Barrett
Department of Economics
Trinity College Dublin
DUBLIN 2
Ireland

Professor Joseph Berechman
The Public Policy Program
Faculty of Social Sciences
Tel Aviv University
RAMAT AVIV 69978
Israel

Professor Alain Bonnafous (Chairman)
Laboratoire d'Economie des
Transports
MRASH – 14, Avenue Bertuelot
69363 LYON Cedex 07
France

Professor Michael Breheny
Department of Geography
University of Reading
Whiteknights PO Box 227
READING RG6 2AB

Professor Ken Button
Centre for Research in European
Economics and Finance
Department of Economics
Loughborough University
LOUGHBOROUGH LE 11 3TU

Professor Robert Cervero
Department of City and Regional
Planning
University of California
BERKELEY
California 94720
USA

Mr Michael Edwards
The Bartlett School of Planning
University College London
Wates House
22 Gordon Street
LONDON WC1H 0QB

Professor Jose Gomez-Ibanez
Kennedy School of Government
Harvard University
79, Kennedy Street
CAMBRIDGE MA 02138
USA

Professor Peter Hall
The Bartlett School of Planning
University College London
Wates House
22 Gordon Street
LONDON WC1H 0QB

Professor John Landis
Department of City and Regional
Planning
University of California
BERKELEY
California 94720
USA

Professor Nathaniel Lichfield
Dalia and Nathaniel Lichfield
Associates
13, Chalcot Gardens
England's Lane
LONDON NW3 4YB

Professor Ron McQuaid
Department of Industrial and Social
Studies
Napier University
Merchiston
10 Colinton Road
EDINBURGH EH10 5DT

Professor John Meyer
School of Government
Harvard University
CAMBRIDGE
Massachusetts MA02138
USA

Professor Chris Nash (Chairman)
Institute for Transport Studies
University of Leeds
LEEDS LS2 9JT

Professor Robert Paaswell
Director, University Transportation
Research Center
City College of New York
NEW YORK 10031
USA

Ms Judith Tomkins
Department of Economics and
Economic History
Manchester Metropolitan University
Mabel Tylecote Building
Cavendish Street
MANCHESTER M15 6BG

Professor Peter Townroe
Centre for Regional Economic and
Social Research
Sheffield Hallam University
Pond Street
SHEFFIELD S1 1WB

Dr Jim Twomey
Salford University Business Services
Ltd.
Enterprise House
31, Salford University Business Park
SALFORD M6 6AJ

Professor Roger Vickerman
Centre for European, Regional and
Transport Economics
Keynes College
The University
CANTERBURY CT2 7NP
Kent

Professor Eddy Van de Voorde
Universiteit Antwerpen (UFSIA)
Faculteit tew. Valgroep Transporten
Ruimte (SESO)
Prinsstraat 13
B-2000 ANTWERPEN 1
Belgium

Dr Michael Wegener
Institut Fur Raumplanung
University of Dortmund
Postfach 500500
D-4600 DORTMUND
Germany

Mr Tom Worsley
Department of Transport
2, Marsham Street
LONDON SW1P 3EB

ACKNOWLEDGEMENTS

This book has been made possible through the cooperation of the authors of the chapters and all the participants at the symposium held in London in 1994. The symposium was funded by the UK Economic and Social Research Council as part of their research programme on Transport and the Environment.

Chapter 1

The Key Issues in Transport and Urban Development

David Banister and Nathaniel Lichfield

1.1. Introduction

Transport has a major impact on the spatial and economic development of cities and regions. The attractiveness of particular locations depends in part on the relative accessibility, and this in turn depends on the quality and quantity of the transport infrastructure. At a general level, it seems that these links are well established, but as this book argues, the methods we have available for the analysis of the links between transport and urban development are not adequate, particularly in the context of the changing nature of cities and the globalization of the world economy. It is some 40 years since Mitchell and Rapkin published their seminal study, *Urban Traffic – A Function of Land Use* (Mitchell and Rapkin, 1954) where the links between land use and transport were first analysed in depth. Here it was argued that if activities associated with particular land uses could be measured, then quantitative estimates of the levels of traffic associated with those land uses could be made. The levels of traffic in the urban area were directly related to the land uses.

However, the continuation of a 40-year debate is not in itself a reason for a book. At present there is a set of important conceptual, theoretical, analytical and empirical issues which need to be addressed as there is intense discussion and controversy in the field. The new debate is also international in its scope, and the primary purpose of this book is to pool the best available knowledge from the United States and Europe so that the agenda for the end of the millennium can be established. This introductory chapter presents some of the key issues in transport and urban development and acts as a context within which the contributions in the rest of the book should be placed. Its second purpose is to introduce the reader to the structure of the book and to give some flavour of the arguments and evidence presented.

1.2. THE LINKS BETWEEN TRANSPORT AND DEVELOPMENT

Cities are changing with the movement of people and businesses out from the centre, increased suburbanization and the desire for lower residential and job densities. Suburbanization of employment has followed, and the simple local journey-to-work pattern or the public transport based movement to the strong central area employment location has been replaced by more complex longer distance car based movements. The exodus from cities is partly caused by a lack of affordable housing in the city centres, but also because of higher income levels, higher car ownership levels and the desire for more space. Investment in new roads to accommodate the new demand patterns may only result in further suburbanization and the abandonment of the city centre.

In the past, further transport investment in cities has been argued firstly on the basis of how to allocate growth, and subsequently on the main means to promote economic development and the revitalization of depressed areas (Banister, 1994). Yet the evidence seems to suggest that in advanced Western economics, the addition of new road links means that more traffic will be generated, making the environment more polluted and increasing the mobility problems for those without access to a car. In addition to housing and employment migrating out of the city, shopping centres, science and industrial parks and leisure facilities, have all moved to green field sites where the densities of development are much lower and access is made primarily by the car. The net result has been an unprecedented growth in car based travel with longer journey lengths, yet the transport infrastructure has not been expanded at the same rate. As Blonk (1979, p. 331) concluded some 15 years ago, 'transport is a catalytic force; it is both an agent vital for industrial growth and an agent for decline where economic resources and conditions and human endeavour are insufficient to meet competition of outside areas.'

In many cities there has been a strong reaction to the realization that more urban road construction has led to increased levels of congestion. The unconstrained growth in the demand for travel, particularly by car, is not desirable and there are substantial external costs imposed on people, cities and the environment. A range of policy levers has been used to internalize these costs, including substantially raising the price of petrol, limiting the access of cars to city centres, and making much more positive use of the planning system to direct new development. In the US, the Intermodal Surface Transportation Efficiency Act (ISTEA) has changed the approach to the evaluation, financing and planning processes for new projects (see Paaswell, this volume). In the UK, the new plan-led system is encouraging town centre management schemes, packages of measures to deal with transport strategies in cities and new planning policy guidance to limit out of town development and the need to travel, particularly by car (Department of the Environment, 1994).

It is argued that these new measures are necessary to maintain town centre viability and to reduce the impact that the car has on the use of resources and atmospheric pollution. It is only through a combination of strategies that progress can be made towards sustainable development objectives. But here is the dilemma. It is difficult to see how the conflicting objectives of providing policies which give consumers the freedom to secure the maximum choice, can be reconciled with the desire to protect the viability of town centres and give opportunity to those who do not have access to the car.

To complement the reductions in the need to use the car, it is necessary to promote cities as desirable places in which to live, with a high quality of life. An important component is a high level of local accessibility and good quality public transport. Here again, transport investment in urban rail infrastructure is seen as a major instrument in shaping city structure and in promoting economic development. Changes in accessibility resulting from new rail infrastructure should encourage new development around stations. Many cities have invested in new rail systems and some of the associated development has been privately funded. Offices, shops and commercial centres have formed an integral part of that development. As redundant land around railway stations has become available, new development has also taken place. This compact and high density development is a direct result of changes in accessibility and land being released, and much of the recent new prestige office development in city centres has been of this form. Similarly, in many historic cities not designed for the car, and other medium sized cities, smaller scale bus, tram and pedestrian oriented changes have taken place. A generally better matching of transport facilities with mixed land uses and careful urban designs have resulted in an improved local environment, based on public transport, the bicycle and walking.

At the regional scale, the links between transport and development are also evident. Major transport infrastructures, such as international rail links, airports and ports, all have a substantial effect on local traffic, employment and the local economy. Apart from the direct employment in transport activities, these major transport infrastructures have substantial multiplier effects as they have to be served by a range of firms and industries. For example, Heathrow airport employs about 40,000 people directly, but there are nearly 100,000 people who depend upon it indirectly for employment or who supply services to those who are employed at the airport (e.g. local schools and shops).

Planners, economists and urban policy-makers have been concerned about the growth in urban traffic, particularly the increase in journey lengths and the reliance on the car. As noted above, part of the explanation for this increase in travel has been the decentralization of cities, the development of local centres of activity within the expansive city, and the concentration on particular functions (e.g. specialization in banking and financial services). However the links between transport and urban development are not well known, even in a physical sense. In addition to the physical relationships (e.g. density), there are important economic factors (e.g. rent levels and land prices), social factors (e.g. equity and distributional factors) and environmental factors (e.g. quality of life). In each case, transport has an important influence, which is well accepted at the general level, but at a more detailed level both the methodologies for analysis and the empirical evidence is limited.

1.3. QUESTIONS AND ISSUES FOR DEBATE

What then are some of the main issues which need to be discussed, debated and understood in a book on transport and urban development?

1.   It is widely argued that major new transport infrastructure has a substantial impact on the local economy and the development potential of an area. The logic is based on changes in accessibility which give one area a new competitive advantage over other areas, which in turn results in greater levels of efficiency and higher productivity. However, there are several complications ranging from the evidence on changes in land values and rent levels resulting from new investment, to the debate over whether the new activity is actually new activity or a transfer of activity from one location to another. The relative competitive position of one location is enhanced, but at the expense of another location. Even if there is a measurable impact, the scale and area over which it is experienced may be quite limited. The shift may also result in longer travel distances, more frequent trips and an increase in car based movements associated with low density development. If these new movements are replacing shorter trips by walk and public transport, typical of higher density locations, then the environmental and energy costs may be substantial.

2.   At the regional level, much infrastructure investment is justified on the basis of regional development benefits which accrue directly from improved accessibility. These benefits include a greater attractiveness for new firms who might move to the area, cheaper distribution of goods and a general expansion of the labour market areas. However, there are counter arguments, in particular as to whether major investments, such as high speed rail links, actually increase centralization and the benefits to peripheral regions are minimal. Where local benefits are found, they are very highly localized and small in scale. The high speed rail network in

Europe has been used to argue the case both for and against the regional impacts of transport infrastructure.

3.   Locations of most potential occur where two or more transport modes come together at an accessible interchange point (e.g. Charles de Gaulle/ Roissy in Paris). It is at these points that the greatest commercial interest has been shown and airport locations have proved to be attractive lo- cations for science parks, distribution centres, international conference and hotel facilities, as well as for activities directly related to the airport. These major new international locations are complemented at the city level by the new technopole developments and satellite cities, again with high speed rail connections to the city centre (e.g. Lille – see Ampe, this volume). However, the benefits at these smaller scale developments are more modest, particularly if they take place within an existing urban area. The shifts in development, which could potentially lead to compact growth and higher densities, may be overwhelmed by stronger regional trends towards decentralization with lower densities (see Cervero and Landis, and Townroe, both in this volume). Nevertheless, in each of these situations, the quality of the new transport infrastructure has been instru- mental in encouraging new development.

4.   Traditionally, it has been argued that transport costs form only a small part of total production costs. In Western economies, where there is already a dense network of routes, any additional link in the network is only likely to improve accessibility marginally. Other factors such as labour supply, access to markets, availability of land, government grants and incentives are all more important factors in the location decision. The logic of this argument is that the transport infrastructure is not a primary factor in determining where a firm or household should locate, but that it is a secondary factor, at least in developed economies. Yet it is often cited as a major reason to justify investment in peripheral regions, and in locations where there is high unemployment or where restructuring of the economy is necessary. Infrastructure investment must be subject to de- creasing marginal productivities, as additional links in an already exten- sive network make more industries footloose and its potential influence as a location factor is decreased. Even if there are decreases in transport costs, these may be absorbed through higher profits or rents, or through higher wages, or through lower prices to the consumer. Most analysis is aggregate and not concerned with the distributional issues.

5.   Most transport infrastructure has been funded through the public sector. But if there are substantial benefits to companies from locating near to new road, railway or airport facilities, there should be some means by which the added value can be captured through development taxes and

other forms of exactions – otherwise there will always be a 'free rider' problem. This occurs where developers benefit from the increased accessibility resulting from a new infrastructure project without actually contributing directly to that project. This issue is becoming increasingly important as public finance for infrastructure projects becomes less readily available, and as national and international governments look increasingly to the private sector for finance, either through projects which are completely financed in the private sector (e.g. the Channel Tunnel — see Vickerman, this volume) or through jointly funded projects (e.g. the Jubilee Line extension in London). However, the opportunities for projects funded entirely by the private sector may be limited, as the scale of many transport projects is substantial with a high level of perceived risk (e.g. cost overruns, long payback periods, uncertain levels of demand). Most potential is to be found in partnership projects, particularly where there are associated development opportunities (Banister *et al.*, 1993; and Gomez-Ibanez and Meyer, this volume).

6. Fiscal and taxation policies also influence transport, land development and location. There are many distortions within the market and these all lead to artificially high levels of housing consumption, free use of the car through subsidies to company drivers and parking concessions, and speculative office development in many cities. In some cases cities are very restrictive on the types of development allowed, but in other locations all types of development will be welcomed as they bring employment and increases the economic base of the local economy. Exactions and impact fees may help, but these costs may be transferred to the final user thereby worsening housing and office quality in the city centre. This in turn may lead to pressure for more development on greenfield and peripheral locations.

7. Allocation of resources between different transport modes has always caused problems. To achieve a fully integrated transport market where all modes operate in harmony could be seen as one means to achieve the maximum development benefits from the transport system. Conversely, it could be argued that each transport mode operates in a separate submarket and the greatest overall benefit could be achieved through competition in the market. However, the direct benefits to the supplier and consumer of the transport service need to be balanced against broader social, development, environmental and other costs which may be imposed. The fundamental message of Mitchell and Rapkin (1954) seems to have been overlooked, namely that evaluating proposals only on transport criteria, without evaluating their impacts on land use and development, is not sufficient. There are methods available which can combine evaluation of the transport and land-use impacts, including all relevant

costs and benefits relating to the natural, economic, social and cultural environment. Community Impact Evaluation is one method which achieves these objectives (Lichfield, 1988 and 1994). This method advances evaluation beyond simple transport assessment and would test the degree to which the designers of proposals had or had not taken into account the land-use and development implications. Similarly, multicriteria analysis methods can be used to assess the impact that transport will have on economic and social development (Nijkamp and Blaas, 1994).

8.   There are many theories which have been used to examine the links between transport and urban development. The most important has been classical location theory, based on assumptions from land economics of optimality and equilibrium in land allocation. The basic causality assumed in the process is as follows. Accessibility determines the value for different uses at different locations, and as transport costs change, so do the rent levels, and as land uses and rents are linked by market processes, land uses and development also change. Reduced transport costs have allowed cities to spread as consumers have traded off the cheaper housing costs at the periphery against the higher transport costs. This has in turn reduced residential densities, a process reinforced by real increases in income levels. The same basic arguments have been applied to business locations. As transport costs have been reduced firms can become more competitive and expand or relocate at these accessible locations (see Berechman, this volume). Evolution theory argues that the initial growth of industry took place at particular locations (e.g. ports), and this in turn attracted associated activity related to the trade. Small scale activities in many locations were gradually replaced by concentration and dominance of a few locations which have particular competitive advantages. These dominant locations have easier links to their hinterlands, natural resources, a good transport infrastructure, but they must keep up with technological and other changes within the industry to maintain their position (see Van de Voorde, this volume). Models have been developed for location analysis, but not for evolution theory. In all cases they have been criticized on their narrow range of explanatory variables, their simplification of time, their assumptions on the nature of the household, and their base in market economics (Lee, 1973 and 1994; and Deakin, 1991).

More recent models have combined location and transport choice in a comprehensive and sophisticated manner (Wegener, 1994). Allocation of jobs and housing within a region is seen as a function of land availability, population and employment by category, household income and other factors. A second group of models has focused on a greater behavioural justification for location decisions, and has incorporated a wider range of detailed socio-economic and lifestyle descriptors. Transport is seen as only one of several decision variables. Substantial progress has been made in the development of models which more accurately reflect the complexity of the location and development issues. But this greater complexity has perhaps reduced their impact. There are still very few operational urban models which link transport and development, and even fewer have been validated in more than one application. Alternative, complementary approaches to problem solving and understanding the land-use, development and transport linkages are still required.

9.   One of the basic methodological problems still remaining is that of causality between transport, urban and economic development. The specification of the counterfactual, or what would have happened if there had been no investment, is difficult. The treatment of time in analysis of transport and urban development is also weak as it has proved difficult to isolate the impacts over time, particularly where many of the factors being monitored change continuously by small amounts. There are specification and measurement problems, but the basic difficulty is in determining what one is comparing with what.

10.   Similarly, where a major investment has taken place, new distribution networks have been established. This is particularly true with respect to the European motorway network where the high quality road network has combined with technologies which allow just in time delivery, computerized stock control and material requirements planning. The net result has been a substantial reduction in stock levels with much of the goods being in transit to the final consumer rather than being stored at the factory or in warehouses. Deliveries are now targeted far more accurately with production runs being shorter and responsive to immediate requirements. Substantial cost savings have been made by companies through the use of modern technology in combination with a reliable high quality road network which minimizes delivery time.

1.4.   THE STRUCTURE OF THE BOOK

It is against this background of a widening debate over the nature and extent of the links between transport and urban development that this book is set. The arguments have moved on from the simple conceptual and empirical links between traffic and land use identified by Mitchell and Rapkin (1954). Concerns over traffic have been broadened to cover all forms of transport. The range of land use considered has also been extended to include new types of activities (e.g. technopoles and business parks). More important, however, has been the widening of the debate to include important factors such as the role of the public sector in financing infrastructure, partnership possibilities between the private and public sectors, impacts on employment, the local economy, land values and rents, as well as the necessity for new methods of analysis and evaluation. The links between transport and urban development have fundamentally changed as illustrated by the physical, economic, social and distributional, and financial arguments outlined in this introduction.

But the planning framework has also changed with the fundamental move away from strategic approaches typical of the 1960s and 1970s to the dominance of market forces in the 1980s. This has been particularly apparent in the US and the UK, but to a lesser extent in other European countries. However, particularly in the urban arena, there has now developed a renewed interest in the role that the plan-led system has in determining the location of new development and limiting the impact of the car on the urban environment.

The forms of planning are different and do not rely on the long-term strategic development of the city supported by a comprehensive data-based analysis. The methods used now are simpler, and the guidance is softer, often starting with a statement of a vision for the city. The concerns are now over the quality of life and wide range of employment, social and cultural opportunities which the city can offer. This means planning for accessibility of all residents and others who depend on the city, maintaining a vibrant local economy, minimizing the environmental disbenefits of urban living, and offering a wide range of opportunities for participation. Planners can now act as promoters of change in the city and they have a much more positive role to play.

The book is split into two parts. This first part is scene setting and examines the theoretical and analytical issues from economic and spatial viewpoints. Its purpose is to establish the basic theoretical and empirical links between transport and urban development. The second part explores a range of case studies of transport and development concentrating in turn on all forms of transport – rail, air, water and road. Each of the major chapters is intended to review and to challenge the basic assumptions implicit in much of the research on transport and urban development. The aim here is to identify where the research agenda should be moving at the end of the twentieth century. The major chapters are supplemented by shorter commentaries. These commentaries are designed to interpret and comment on the major substantive chapters from a different disciplinary, cultural or national perspective. The debate can therefore be made both richer and broader.

In chapter 2, Berechman reviews the main issues associated with the modelling and empirical measurement of the impact of transport infrastructure investment on economic growth. At the macro level the focus is on the overall contribution of public capital investment to general economic growth and improved factor productivity. Here he builds upon the work of Munnell (1993) and Aschauer (1989) which provides insights into the mechanisms which link public capital stock with economic growth and job creation. The micro level analysis is concerned with the evaluation of the accessibility, environmental and location impacts of specific transport capital projects in well-defined regions. These form the basis of the case study chapters, later in the book. The principal results from the micro level indicate that, in evaluating the economic development effects of a transport infrastructure investment, it is necessary to consider the travel and socio-economic characteristics of the particular area where it is being implemented, the transport attributes of the project and its relationships with the wider transport network.

In the US, the Intermodal Surface Transportation Efficiency Act (ISTEA) is the most significant piece of transport legislation for nearly 50 years. Put into effect in 1991 to reinvigorate a deteriorating, inefficient and congested highway and transit system, ISTEA departs from previous laws in the types of objectives it sets, in the constraints it places on new investments, in the methods of financing that are available for new investment, and in the inclusion of a much broader group of participants at all stages in the planning process. Paaswell's chapter provides an overview of the main components of that legislation, and reviews those components in terms of the strong environmental mandates imposed. Reviewing the new regulations for planning and a new set of necessary management systems, it is suggested that a range of new concerns must be addressed by those evaluating new investments. These include conflicting objectives, changing demographics, new land uses, attempts to change travel behaviour, new approaches to financing, and changing institutional structures. The possibilities for new types of links between transport and urban development have been addressed by the ISTEA, and there may be important lessons for other countries.

This theme is taken up by McQuaid who argues that there have been similarities between US and Europe in investment priorities, concerns over the environment, and even increased private ownership of transport enterprises, although Europe still lags behind the US in this particular policy. The novelty of ISTEA is that it is multi-modal in its approach together with clear environmental objectives and greater community involvement in decision making. However, the driving force is its comprehensive approach and the relationship between the use of resources and increases in efficiency of the existing infrastructure. When considering the more theoretical arguments, McQuaid identifies four main areas for debate: the question of scale; the key variables linking transport and economic activity; the different impacts; and the time period considered. All this evidence adds to the complexity of the issues and the need for explicit analysis.

The economic issues, together with the legal framework necessary to implement such a policy, are complemented by a chapter which presents a wide ranging European perspective of the spatial issues. Hall covers the changes which have taken place in European cities, first through centralization and then through decentralization, and the current debates over the importance of density as a key determinant of sustainable development. He also covers the full range of policy responses, particularly as it related to transport, including investment in different forms of public transport and restraints on the car. Having discussed the theoretical arguments on sustainability and concluded that there are no clear parameters which adequately define even the characteristics of a sustainable city, Hall then returns to the most recent examples of initiatives on urban development which are closely related to new transport infrastructure. Using examples from France, the Netherlands and Japan, the close relationship between key transport interchanges and terminals and new high quality development is clearly visible and measurable. The question raised then becomes how many of these new transport accessible nodes should be created in total. But here a problem occurs, as there seems to be considerable disagreement on the means to assess development potential and the actual numerical output produced by researchers and consultants. It seems that the potential is there, but the uncertainties of the development, the scale of investment required, perceived problems with public-private partnerships, all make the final decision problematic.

Two major issues are picked up by Breheny, one relating to the debate on sustainable development and the merits of the compact city, and the other on the role that transport investment plays in promoting local economic development. The weaknesses of the research base are exposed together with the lack of understanding of the basic relationships between transport, planning and urban energy consumption. Breheny suggests the introduction of three simple tests of veracity, feasibility and acceptability to establish the case for compact cities. Similar concerns are expressed over the assumed links between transport and local economic development, and the range of possible development impacts are again tested through a simple typology. In both cases the conventional wisdom is questioned. Perhaps new approaches, similar to those used in the Netherlands and France, should be more widely adopted.

The second part of the book takes these issues further by examining in greater depth particular modes and investments. Vickerman takes the Channel Tunnel as the prime example of private sector investment on a substantial scale (over £10bn) to establish whether it can be seen as a success and how far predictions of the Tunnel as an instrument of generation or relocation of economic activity can be validated. The chapter covers the fascinating history of the Tunnel, together with the financial and legal frameworks, different on the two sides of the Channel. It is a great engineering feat, but an organizational and financial nightmare. The complexity of the construction process has hindered the achievement of wider policy aims but it has helped ensure the project's completion. Its economic impact will be felt at all scales (local, national and international), so economic analysis is required at all of Berechman's levels. However, Vickerman concludes that it is also necessary to consider transport infrastructure investments in terms of networks. This is particularly true if impacts are ever likely to be more than local in their effects.

These questions and others are raised by Edwards in his commentary. There is an inherent difficulty, and maybe impossibility, in measuring the actual impact of infrastructure investment schemes, even on the scale of the Channel Tunnel. This is because of the widely distributed nature of the impacts throughout the network. Consequently, it is also unrealistic to expect these benefits to be captured through fares or even increases in land prices around the stations. Much broader based approaches need to be adopted and this is where the English approach differs fundamentally from the French approach. Ampe's chapter suggests that the prospect of rising land and property prices in the Euralille development is to be avoided. Yet in the justification of many schemes in Britain it is the anticipated increase in land and property prices that is used as a lever for private sector investment. The Euralille project provides an example of this different French approach to transport and urban development. Here, the new high speed rail, the motorway system and proximity to airports are all seen as an opportunity for major development. The planning of both takes place simultaneously, and the Société d'Economie Mixte allows both public and private funding. The publicly funded infrastructure is in place prior to much of the privately funded building on the site. The development process is fully integrated, with both private and public sector being fully involved, and the length of the whole decision process also seems to be shortened.

The most celebrated urban public transport project in the US is the Bay Area Rapid Transit (BART), and Cervero and Landis present the findings from surveys carried out 20 years after BART was opened. Transit developments have not generated higher than expected land values or significant shifts in population and employment, particularly if changes elsewhere in the local and regional economy are considered. Greater growth has taken place in corridors with new road investments. The conclusions are informative as there are some capitalization benefits in the immediate vicinity of the rail station, but the impacts are not generalizable as they depend on many factors including the technology and the spatial extent of the rail system. The concept of value capture is important and it does seem to be possible to measure it, but it is much harder actually to recoup those costs from developers or to get them to co-fund schemes. In the US, which has a heavy level of car dependence, it is difficult to get modal transfer even if housing is built near to the rail system. The links between land development and transport in the US are tenuous, and often very specific in their impact and extent.

A key concept, much used in transport and planning analysis, has been accessibility, and this has been central to conventional land-use and transport modelling since Hansen's seminal paper (Hansen, 1959). But, as Wegener argues, the relationships between land use and transport may be much weaker than traditionally assumed. If this relationship is a weak one, it is then difficult to argue for higher density, mixed use developments near to rail stations on the basis that significant modal shifts might take place. His conclusion is that the land-use transport feedback cycle remains in effect only where accessibility is a scarce commodity, and this means that both incentives and restrictions are required. Incentives are needed for higher density, mixed use development and the promotion of environmentally friendly modes, and restrictions are required through land-use controls and other limitations on the use of the car.

It seems that much the same conclusions can be drawn from Townroe's presentation of the impact of the Supertram in Sheffield. A wide ranging approach to the measurement of the impact of the urban rail system has been devised to cover the image of the city with a new rail system, the land and property changes, the impact on business activity and the effect on labour market patterns. Even after the specification of the components of a comprehensive impact study, there are still methodological issues which relate to the use of a before and after survey technique and the question of attribution of change. The direct benefits to rail and road users may be easy to determine, but it is the secondary benefits which cause problems. These secondary benefits can be measured but are often small in scale and may only reflect a redistribution of benefits rather than a net increase in benefits.

The comments from Worsley reinforce these conclusions, but he argues that it is still important to measure the impacts as this is the only way to achieve a better understanding of the wider effects of transport investments. It is the achievement of unambiguous attributions which provides the greatest challenge to researchers, and if this can be obtained, new perspectives on the nature of the urban economy can be achieved.

The case of Manchester Airport is presented by Twomey and Tomkins as an example of one sector of transport which has had tremendous growth and substantial development impacts. Again, the difficulty of measuring the development impacts is illustrated as multiplier analysis only gives a crude indication of the wider effects. It is estimated that there are about 1,000 jobs created at the airport site for every additional 1 million passengers. Off site employment is about 50% more than on site employment. So the current employment of 10,000 people at the airport (10m passengers) results in the creation of 15,000 jobs off site. The basic problem here is not one of attribution but the specification of the counterfactual situation. These problems are apparent in the linkage analysis carried out by Twomey and Tomkins on the employment in the airport and the wider regional economy.

Barrett in his commentary takes up the question of the counterfactual, arguing that there is still much to be done, but perhaps not along the lines suggested in the chapter. There is such a range of values relating to the employment impacts of the airport. For example, a greatly enlarged Manchester Airport with a second runway may create over 100,000 new jobs. Perhaps the concern should not be so much over the associated airport development and employment generation potential as over the overall efficiency of Manchester Airport in the competitive airline market. The market-led model only allows the most efficient airports to survive and those with the highest levels of productivity will attract inward investment and employment.

Ports offer a contrasting picture. Van de Voorde concentrates on the development effects of the mainland European ports, arguing that the impacts of ports are concentrated within the port rather than the wider city or region. Port competitiveness relates to a range of factors, including levels of investment, standardization and containerization, productivity and meeting capacity (but having some flexibility). Again, as with all the detailed case studies, problems with methodology, techniques for analysis and data are all prominent. With the breakdown of national and international barriers, ports are no longer restricted in a narrow hinterland as there are opportunities for a much wider catchment area provided that competitiveness is maintained.

The changing nature of trade, movement and transactions has made the role of terminals and interchanges more critical to the overall efficiency of the transport network. Button, in typically robust style, summarizes the problems of the counterfactual, the use of spatial impact multipliers and the focus on the internal efficiency of transport investments. Questions of management must also be addressed as should the attribution of the full costs of the investment to the beneficiaries – these include the cost overrun, environmental costs and legacy effects. Again, further complexity is added.

The final major contribution relates to roads and the US experience on toll roads. Gomez-Ibanez and Meyer summarize the recent limited successes and come to the conclusion that there are few new opportunities for financially viable toll roads. Most possible candidates have already been built and the difficulties of exactions from landowners or developers severely complicate the situation. Even if a more detached view is taken, it seems that there is no inherent reason to suggest why the private sector would be able to make major savings in construction or operating costs over the public sector. The only possible exception here might be in the use of innovative methods of design and construction. This essentially pessimistic view still concludes that there is a (limited) role for the private sector.

Similar conclusions can be drawn from the European experience on private toll roads as the road network is even more dense than that in the US. In his complementary view, Banister argues for a partnership between the private and public sectors in road construction and the operation of toll roads which goes beyond the current customer-client relationship. Different procedures need to be adopted, with the appropriate planning, development and financial packages, in different situations. As stated at the beginning of this introduction, the issues have changed dramatically over the last 40 years, yet there is a huge backlog of investment in infrastructure of all kinds. The links between transport and urban development are crucial to decisions on the nature and type of investment which should be made and who should pay for it. This is particularly true if governments are to move towards strategies which involve sustainable development and the maintenance of cities with a high quality environment.

This book aims to present an international review of the arguments about the links between transport and urban development, both from the methodological and empirical perspectives. In their concluding chapter, Hall and Banister suggest that on both counts the jury has not yet come to a decision. The precise relationships between transport investment and urban development are not well known, even theoretically. There seems to be no single methodology available to test the relationships, the counterfactual situation is difficult to determine and the question of causality not addressed. Decisions have been based more on faith than understanding. Even where clear methodological approaches have been tried, problems arise concerning available data and the inherent complexity of many of the relationships. The links between land use, transport and development are much more profound than just an examination of the physical, social and economic relationships might produce. Institutional, organizational and financial concerns are equally important, as are the longer term changes which are taking place in cities and lifestyles in the late twentieth century. The links which need to be understood are based on a combination of relatively ancient transport technologies, each of them (electric transit, commuter rail, the internal combustion engine, the airplane) developed between 1879 and 1903, with very little subsequent advance. Even if the links between traditional forms of transport and urban development could be understood, the new technologies present a much more complex and rich challenge. How will the high speed rail network, the intelligent vehicle highway and the potentially enormous impact of the new technological revolution affect transport and urban development? A century after the first transport revolution, we are now facing the new transport and technological revolution.

References

Aschauer, D.A. (1989) Is public expenditure productive? *Journal of Monetary Economics*, **23**(2), pp. 177–200.

Banister, D. (1994) *Transport Planning*. London: E & FN Spon.

Banister, D., Andersen, B. and Barrett, S. (1993) Private Sector Investment in Transport Infrastructure in Europe. Paper presented at the European Conference on the Evolution of Transport and Communications Networks in Europe, Padua, Italy, December 14–18, and to be published in Banister, D., Capello, R. and Nijkamp, P. (eds.) *European Transport and Communications Networks: Policy Evolution and Change*. London: Belhaven, 1995.

Blonk, W.A.G. (ed.) (1979) *Transport and Regional Development: An International Handbook*. Farnborough: Teakfield.

Deakin, E. (1991) Jobs, housing and transportation: Theory and evidence on interactions between land use and transportation. Transportation Research Board and National Research Council *Transportation, Urban Form and the Environment*, Special Report 231, pp. 25–42.

Department of the Environment (1994) *Planning Policy Guidance 13: Transport*. London: HMSO.

Hansen, W.G. (1959) How accessibility shapes land use. *Journal of the American Planning Association*, **25**(1), pp. 73–76.

Lee, D.B. (1973) Requiem for large scale models. *Journal of the American Institute of Planners*, **39**(2), pp. 163–178.

Lee, D.B. (1994) Retrospective on large scale urban models. *Journal of the American Planning Association*, **60**(1), pp. 35–40.

Lichfield, N. (1988) *Economics in Urban Conservation*. Cambridge: Cambridge University Press.

Lichfield, N. (1994) *Community Impact Evaluation*. London: University College Press.

Mitchell, R.B. and Rapkin, C. (1954) *Urban Traffic – A Function of Land Use*. New York: Columbia University Press.

Munnell, A. (1993) An assessment of trends and economic impacts of infrastructure investment, in OECD, *Infrastructure Policies for the 1990s*. Paris: Organisation for Economic Cooperation and Development.

Nijkamp, P. and Blaas, E. (1994) *Impact Assessment and Evaluation in Transportation Planning*. Dordrecht: Kluwer Academic Publishers.

Wegener, M. (1994) Operational urban models: State of the art. *Journal of the American Planning Association*, **60**(4), pp. 17–29.

Chapter 2

Transport Infrastructure Investment and Economic Development

Joseph Berechman

2.1. Introduction

The observation that investments in transportation infrastructure (including highways, rail, mass transit, ports and airports) generate accessibility, economic, environmental and social impacts, is hardly news for transportation economists and planners. Numerous studies have documented these impacts and, in general, have classified them as being adverse ones (e.g. air pollution, community displacement) or positive ones (e.g. job creation and economic growth). While it is generally agreed that improved accessibility should be the prime objective of transportation investments (Mohring, 1993), in many cases the presumed capability of a project to generate other positive impacts is regarded as the main motivation for undertaking the investment. Presently, in many countries, the alleged ability of transport infrastructure investment to enhance employment and promote economic development constitutes a major driving force behind governments' propensity to allocate funds for such purposes.[1]

In this chapter I use the term 'urban and regional development' to imply increase in the level of regional economic activity, mainly regional employment, output and income, and examine the conjectured impact of transport infrastructure development on regional economic growth.[2] In particular, I focus on several fundamental questions that underlie the potential association between infrastructure investment and urban and regional development. These are first, what is the structural mechanism which transforms infrastructure investment into economic growth? Second, how can we model and measure effects from a public infrastructure investment at the urban and regional level? Third, for the purpose of carrying out a Cost Benefit Analysis (COBA) of a particular transportation investment, is it justifiable also to consider non-transport benefits, including local economic development? Review of the key issues pertinent to answering these questions, defines the scope of this chapter.

I begin the discussion, in Section 2.2, by succinctly examining the basic rationale for public investment in infrastructure. Subsequently, Section 2.3 distinguishes between macro- and micro-level analyses of capital investment. Sections 2.4 presents macro-level models and results. Section 2.5 focuses on micro-level analysis and provides empirical results from an analysis of the effect of accessibility changes on employment. Based on the discussion in previous sections, Section 2.6 examines key issues that need to be considered when evaluating the effects of transportation infrastructure investment on regional and urban economic growth. Concluding remarks, regarding conceptual issues pertaining to cost-benefit analysis of a transportation investment, are discussed in Section 2.7.

2.2.   THE RATIONALE FOR PUBLIC INVESTMENT
IN INFRASTRUCTURE

It is useful to begin a review such as this by briefly considering the theoretical basis for the provision of infrastructure capital by the public sector – the main reason being that a tenable analysis of a public investment should take into account public sector objectives, constraints and measures of costs and benefits. Moreover, the ability of the public sector to raise sufficient funds for capital investments is not independent of these objectives and constraints. However, it needs also to be recognized that the mere existence of such theoretical grounds is, in itself, insufficient to warrant public supply of infrastructure facilities since, in many cases, public production and funding can result in excess burden (deadweight loss), heavy administrative costs and intrinsic inefficiencies.

A standard textbook argument for the provision of transportation infrastructure by the public sector is that, left to the private sector, these facilities would be produced at a substantially sub-optimal social level. The generic name given to this phenomena in the economic literature is *market failure*. A key representative case of market failure is when an infrastructure facility is regarded as being a *public good* where exclusion of individuals from its consumption is not feasible while the long-run marginal costs of servicing an additional user are negligible. Inter-city and inter-state highways, local streets and feeder roads as well as forms of mass-transit, are typical examples. Under these conditions, individuals have an incentive not to reveal their true preferences regarding their desired level of consumption of these goods, thereby benefiting from their provision without having to bear the associated costs (the free rider phenomenon). Consequently, private enterprises would not be able to earn sufficient revenue to cover the capital and maintenance costs of building and maintaining these infrastructure facilities which, in turn, would not be produced at all or, if produced, at a level which is way below the optimal societal level. Indeed, historical records show that the provision of transport facilities like local roads, turnpikes, canals and bridges, in the long-run, could not be supported by the private sector mainly because of heavy losses induced by the inability to enforce excludability, recover capital costs and by competition from substitutable facilities and modes (Taylor, 1951, chapters 2 and 3).

Large *economies of scale* are another reason used to explain the public provision of infrastructure systems. These economies pertain to two major types: in facility construction and in travel time reduction when capacity is expanded. Regarding the first, I distinguish between: (*a*) scale economies that arise in the actual construction of road facilities; (*b*) scale economies embedded in the assembly of massive units of land necessary for the building and connecting large transport networks; and (*c*) scale economies in securing rights of way. While economies of facility construction have been discussed thoroughly in the literature (e.g. Mohring, 1976, pp. 140–143; Kraus, 1981), economies of land assembly and acquiring rights of way have not. In this regard I would argue that in well developed and highly populated urban areas the economies associated with the public sector's ability to secure rights of way, assemble land and ensure that various components of the transport network are properly connected, may significantly exceed those associated with facility construction. In general, under conditions of scale economies in the provision of transport systems, the levy of optimal user charges as a means of capital funding (and controlling traffic levels), will not generate sufficient revenues to cover capital costs. Consequently, a substantial portion of the infrastructure stock will need to be subsidized to pay for the ensuing deficit. Given its enormous size, this subsidy can only be provided by the public sector which can use dedicated or general tax revenues to that end.[3]

Another type of scale economies arises from the fact that providing additional units of capacity to the present stock of transport capital can induce more use (traffic), or reduce the costs of present users, by more than proportionally. For example, it has been observed that adding a second or third lane in each direction, can reduce highway travel time for existing traffic by more than proportionally (Meyer and Gomez-Ibanez, 1981, pp. 191–192).[4] In actuality, the magnitude of these economies critically depends on a number of technical factors such as the geometry of the highway, time of day and make-up of traffic and thus may be quite problematic to measure.

The generation of *externalities*, positive and negative, by the provision of transport facilities and by their use is another argument put forward to support public supply of such infrastructure facilities. Accordingly, the internalization of these externalities, which is necessary for the optimization of social welfare, can be achieved only if the public sector owns and controls the capacity and level of utilization of these infrastructure systems.

Lastly, there is the argument of *equity* which essentially implies that spatial mobility, provided by infrastructure facilities, is a merit that should be provided at a minimum level to all citizens, irrespective of their ability to pay for it. Furthermore, rural areas where population is sparse cannot pay for infrastructure facilities needed to make them accessible to activity centres. Hence the need for the government's involvement in the provision of transport infrastructure.

In evaluating these arguments, two key questions need to be addressed. First, to what degree does the government indeed attain the objectives, embedded in the rationale discussed above, when undertaking capital investments? Given the case, providing a satisfactory answer to this question is a formidable task which requires detailed information (in many caset, unattainable) and careful analysis. It is beyond the purpose of this chapter to elaborate further on this issue. However, it should be observed that, by and large, the above rationale is regarded by many as a 'maxim' that does not require analytical examination or empirical verification. The numerous documented cases of the so-called 'government failure' cast a doubt on this perspective. The second (and related) question is how should the government finance infrastructure projects. Again, an in-depth treatment of this issue is not within the scope of this analysis. Suffice it to say, that alternative methods (e.g. general taxation versus user charges) are not inconsequential with respect to social welfare and optimal use of resources.[5] Next I discuss approaches for modelling the effects of infrastructure investment on economic development.

2.3.   MACRO- VERSUS MICRO-LEVEL ANALYSIS

In analysing the relationships between infrastructure development and economic growth it is important to distinguish between two categories of analysis: macro- and micro-levels. At the macro-level, relationships between aggregate investment in infrastructure capital and macroeconomic indicators (e.g. GDP or income per capita) are derived and used to predict the rate of return to the economy from an additional investment in infrastructure facilities. A micro-level analysis, focuses on relatively small economic areas, such as cities and regions, and tries to associate infrastructure development with changes in local economic indicators such as regional employment and output. In other words, at the macro-level the subject of the analysis is the effect of the level of the capital stock on output and overall productivity within the economic sector (or state). In contrast, a micro-level analysis considers the reaction of economic units, like firms and households located in a given area, to specific transport infrastructure investment. This distinction is rather consequential not only from a modelling point of view but, more importantly, from a policy-analysis point of view. For example, assuming scale economies of aggregate output with respect to infrastructure development, a 1 per cent increase in the state's budget designated for infrastructure investment will raise GDP by more than 1 per cent. At the regional level, however, if firms relocate in response to accessibility changes, induced by infrastructure development, an investment of the same magnitude can disproportionally affect neighbouring regions by substantially raising output in one region while not changing or even lowering it in another. If economic growth in the latter region is the main objective for undertaking the particular investment, an alternative policy may be required.

From a modelling perspective, the spatial behaviour of firms and households relative to transport infrastructure investment is rather extraneous for a macro-level analysis whereas the opposite is true at the microlevel. A productive transport infrastructure investment always affects

Table 2.1.   Comparing macro- with micro-level analysis.

	Macro-Level	Micro-Level
Geographical unit of analysis	• State • Country	• Region • Metropolitan area
Type of public investment	• Total capital stock • Capital stock by type	• Transportation infrastructure by type
Modelling approach	• Economy production function • Sectorial production or cost function	• Land-use model • Accessibility model • LUT[1] equilibrium model
Measured effect	• GDP growth • Total factor productivity • Partial factor productivity • Social rate of return	• Change in location of firms and households • Use of inputs by firms • Output by firms
COBA	• Not applicable	• Transportation and non-transportation benefits and costs

Note
1. LUT = Land Use Transportation.

accessibility levels which, in turn, affect the long-run equilibrium locations of firms and households as well as their demand and supply of
input factors (e.g. labour and land) and level of output. It is for this reason
that micro-level models need to define in a formal way the spatial dimensions of the production decisions of economic activities and cast them
within an equilibrium framework.

The principal differences between the two types of analysis are de-
picted in table 2.1. It is obvious from this comparison that these categories
of analysis fundamentally differ relative to objectives, formal modelling
approach, type of data required and implications for policy analysis.
Nevertheless, while methods and results from the macro-level are, in
general, inapplicable for the micro-level, they do provide insight into the
mechanism which links public capital stock with economic growth and
job creation. Hence their usefulness for the modelling of the functional
relationships between specific transportation infrastructure investment
and regional development.

2.4. MACRO-LEVEL ANALYSIS OF PUBLIC INVESTMENT IN CAPITAL STOCK

As a prototype macro-model I consider the one used by Munnell (1990,
1993) to assess the contribution of public capital to economic growth. At
the outset it is important to point out that the use of macro-level models,
like the one presented below, has been criticized extensively relative to
their analytical and empirical foundations (Jorgenson 1991; Tatom, 1991).
While many of these arguments are quite valid, the fact remains that most
econometric studies, done on this issue, report positive and significant
relationships (albeit quite small, at times) between the level of public
capital and the rate of economic growth.

Given the above qualifications, Munnell's model is essentially a production function, adjusted for marginal factor productivity (MFP) with
public stock (of all types) as an input:[6]

$$Y = (MFP) * e^{\lambda t} * f(K, L, G) \qquad (1)$$

where Y is (aggregate) output, t is time (to capture technological
changes),[7] MFP is marginal factor productivity (level of technology), and
K, L, G are, respectively, private capital, labour and public capital. Estimating a log-linear form of this model for US data,[8] Munnell reports the
elasticity of labour productivity with respect to public capital to range
from 0.31 to 0.39 (i.e. 10 per cent increase in public capital would raise
labour productivity by 3.1 to 3.9 per cent). From additional calculations of
multi-factor productivity she concludes that much of the increase in MFP
during the early part of the period 1948–1987 is, in fact, due to the build-
up of public capital *vis-à-vis* its effect on output. Based on her 1993 esti-

mates (for the period 1970–1990), the effect of a 10 per cent increase in public capital was to increase aggregate output by 1.4 per cent.[9]

This model implicitly assumes that the effect of public capital on output takes place at the same period without a time lag and that constant elasticity of substitution exists between public capital and between private inputs (capital and labour). As an example of an empirical model which assumes time lags, consider the following model which consists of two simultaneous equations (2) and (3), and (2) and (4):

$$\log(Y_t) = a_0 + a_G \log(G_t) + a_K \log(K_t) + a_L \log(L_t) \tag{2}$$

$$\log(K_t) = b_0 + b_{G_{t-1}} \log(G_{t-1}) + b_L \log(L_t) \tag{3}$$

or

$$\log(L_t) = c_0 + c_{G_{t-1}} \log(G_{t-1}) + c_K \log(K_t) \tag{4}$$

In this model public capital at time t, G_t is assumed directly to affect output at time t while also affecting private capital and labour at time $t + 1$. A 2SLS estimation of the first set of equations using Israeli data[10] (for the years 1964–1989), shows that a 10 per cent increase in public capital in year t will increase output at this year by 3.5 per cent and private capital by 5 per cent at $t + 1$. Estimation of the second set of equations (2) and (4) shows a much smaller effect of public capital on output. Specifically, a 10 per cent increase in public capital at year t will increase labour at year $t + 1$ by 0.33 per cent and, as a result, total output by 0.73 per cent.[11]

The results presented above imply that investment in public capital affects total output both directly (by increasing total factor productivity) and indirectly *vis-à-vis* its effect on partial productivity of labour and private capital. The results from the estimation of equation (2) and (4) above further accentuate the question of the functional relationships between public capital and the demand for private inputs by non-public sectors. To investigate this issue Nadiri and Mamuneas (1991) estimated a cost function model of the following general structure:[12]

$$C = C(w, y, g, t) \tag{5}$$

where C is cost (of an industry), w is a vector of input factor prices, y is output quantity, g is a vector of public capital, and t is index of time (to capture technical change). The authors have used a translogarithmic form of this model with three private inputs: labour, intermediate and private capital and two public inputs: infrastructure and R&D capitals. The model was applied to USA data describing manufacturing industries at the two digit level.

Major results from this study indicate first, that the elasticity of costs with respect to public infrastructure capital expansion, ranges from -0.11

to −0.22 (which is lower than previous studies have determined). Second, with respect to the demand for private inputs, an increase in infrastructure capital leads to a *decline* in the demand for labour and private capital in each industry and to an increase in the demand for intermediate inputs. These results further indicate a non-constant degree of substitution between public infrastructure and private inputs. These conclusions are in accord with further results which indicate that the level and change in labour productivity, during the period of analysis, have been affected by the public sector's provision of capital. Thus, changes in the demand for labour are the result of two effects: (*a*) a downward shift of the sector's cost function (thus in average costs of industrial firms), induced by investment in public capital stock; and (*b*) the substitution of private inputs (e.g. labour) with public ones.

Focusing on the first effect, if indeed public infrastructure serves as an input factor in a private production process, additional public capital will enhance output (or will reduce the costs of producing a unit of output). Given declining marginal productivity of capital (including of the public one) this 'output effect', *ceteris paribus*, will abate as additional public capital is introduced. Hence, in terms of aggregate output, what matters is not only the size of the annual investment in public capital stock but, more importantly, the absolute size of this stock which is in place and, consequently, the annual *per cent* expansion of this stock.

Regarding the second effect, if public capital is a substitute for labour, additional infrastructure investment may have a counter effect on job creation and use. Since the output effect tends to foster greater aggregate demand for labour, while the substitution effect operates in the opposite direction, the overall impact of further investment in public infrastructure on labour is, *a priori*, not certain. The empirical results presented above seem to suggest that, on the average, outcomes from the output effect surpass those of the substitution effect. While at the macro-level this conclusion has primarily macroeconomic implications (e.g. in formulating the state's budget), at the micro-level it is of critical importance when assessing the contribution to employment of individual infrastructure projects in specific areas. This issue is examined next in the context of micro-level analysis.

2.5. MICRO-LEVEL ANALYSIS OF PUBLIC INVESTMENT IN TRANSPORTATION INFRASTRUCTURE

In the title of Section 2.4, which focused on macro-level analysis, I have used the phrase, 'Public Investment in Capital Stock' whereas the title of this section refers to 'Public Investment in Transportation Infrastructure'. The reason for this distinction is that at a macro-level the *specific type* of the capital investment including its location, by and large, does not enter the analysis mainly because at this aggregate level the distinct effects of specific capital investments are either undetectable or inconsequential. In contrast, at a micro-level, the type of the infrastructure facilities and nature of services they render are of primary importance.

Theoretically, when examining the effect of investment in public capital on economic growth, this capital is regarded as an unpaid input factor used in private production processes. However, whereas in macro-level models (like that of Nadiri and Mamuneas, 1991) the effect of changes in the economy, caused by changes in the level of this unpaid input, was confined to changes in aggregate output, in total costs of industrial sectors and in the aggregate demand for private inputs, in a micro-level analysis they also encompass changes in the location of economic activities in a well-defined area. Thus, in order to evaluate correctly the economic benefits from a given infrastructure investment in a given geographical area, it is necessary to consider its effect on spatial decisions of firms which use location as a major variable optimizing their output and use of inputs. Similarly, the location of households, their supply of labour inputs and consumption of final goods are also influenced by these infrastructure investments. (For reviews of spatial regional models which consider these factors see Berechman and Small, 1988; Giuliano, 1989.)

In a previous study (Berechman, 1994) I have proposed a spatial equilibrium model in which changes in accessibility, from transport capacity expansion, simultaneously affect the location of firms, their demand for labour and level of output, as well as the supply of labour by households. In a subsequent analysis (Berechman and Paaswell, 1994a) these equilibrium conditions were estimated empirically to assess the effect of changes in accessibility on various types of employment. Given the scope and objectives of this chapter I present and discuss some illustrative results, not presented before, derived from these analyses.

The theoretical model (Berechman, 1994) conjectured that agglomeration economies in production induce firms to locate in close proximity in order to maximize their level of output, given their production functions. On the other hand, given the level of infrastructure, increased congestion in home-to-work travel negatively affects the supply of labour by households and thus firms' output level. This in turn causes these firms to locate further away in order to reduce congestion. Based on this, the following equilibrium condition was derived:

$$\Delta L = -\Delta A + \Delta \pi \qquad (6)$$

where L denotes labour used by locating firms, A denotes accessibility (in units of travel time) and π denotes profits of these firms. This condition implies that firms achieve spatial equilibrium by locating at a site where a marginal increase in their use of input factors (labour) equals the sum of a marginal change in accessibility (i.e. decline in home-to-work travel time) and a marginal change in profits. Since such changes in accessibility also affect households' allocation of time between work and leisure activities, investment in transport capacity will affect both the households' supply of labour and the firms' profit levels *vis-à-vis* the effect of accessibility on firms' location, on their output level and demand for inputs.

On the basis of these conditions, and assuming long-run equilibrium land-use-transportation markets, Berechman and Paaswell (1994*a*) have

Table 2.2.   Effect of accessibility changes on retail employment by county.

Employment			*Retail*			
Borough	*Bronx*	*Manhattan*	*Queens*	*Staten*	*Brooklyn*	*NY*
Income (in $1,000)						
0–9.9		−0.036				
10–19.9		0.090				
20–29.9						
30–39.9						
40–49.9						
50–59.9						
60+	−0.104	−0.060				
Mode						
Car			−0.236			
Transit				−0.237		
Walk	−0.04					
Travel Time of Work Trips (in minutes)						
0–14	0.084	0.272	0.259	0.279	0.288	0.150
15–29	0.225	0.151	0.256	0.294	0.165	0.202
30–34	0.414	0.214	0.381	0.222	0.075	0.438
35–44	0.094	0.081	0.104		0.091	
45–59	0.106	0.126	0.208		0.085	
60–89		0.192	0.168	0.427	0.218	0.224
90+			−0.042	0.176	0.034	0.123
Constant		−0.073				
R^2 Adjusted	0.94	0.93	0.95	0.98	0.91	0.95

Notes:
All parameters shown are significant at 5%.
* Indicates level of significance between 5% and 10%.
Insignificant parameters are not shown i.e. boxes are empty.

estimated regression functions in which the optimal level of labour, of a given type, used by firms at a given location (i.e. a census tract), is explained by various accessibility variables and by income which is regarded as a surrogate variable (presumably unsatisfactory) for firms' profits for which data were unavailable. Data for this analysis were drawn from a detailed data-base pertaining to the Bronx borough in New York City (for details see Berechman and Paaswell 1994b). Some illustrative results from this analysis are provided in tables 2.2 and 2.3.

Table 2.3. Effect of accessibility changes on business services employment by county.

Employment			Business Services			
Borough	Bronx	Manhattan	Queens	Staten	Brooklyn	NY
Income (in $1,000)						
0–9.9						
10–19.9		−0.043	0.048*			
20–29.9						
30–39.9		0.033				
40–49.9		−0.056				
50–59.9		−0.033				
60+		0.124			−0.027*	
Mode						
Car	0.169		0.385		0.116	−0.090
Transit	0.520	0.523	0.494	0.411	0.392	0.608
Walk						
Travel Time of Work Trips (in minutes)						
0–14	0.171	0.139		0.414	0.043	0.360
15–29	0.155	0.244			0.211	0.128
30–34	0.141	0.095			0.115	
35–44			0.036		0.027*	
45–59	−0.130	−0.037		0.236	0.097	
60–89						−0.134
90+		0.027	0.034	−0.102	0.024	
Constant	0.178	0.245		0.196*	0.104*	
R^2 Adjusted	0.90	0.97	0.97	0.99	0.97	0.98

Notes:
All parameters shown are significant at 5%.
* Indicates level of significance between 5% and 10%.
Insignificant parameters are not shown i.e. boxes are empty.

While an in-depth discussion of these empirical results is not intended here, with regard to the main focus of this chapter, several important conclusions can be drawn from these tables. First, the (equilibrium) level of different types of employment responds differently to changes in the (equilibrium) level of accessibility. For example, whereas retail employment is quite sensitive to changes in travel time in the 30–34 minutes range and, to a lesser extent, in the 15–29 minutes range, business services,[13] in general, are not very responsive to travel time changes, especially not in the middle range (travel time of 30–34 minutes and above). On the other hand, while mode of use in home-to-work travel has no significant impact on retail employment, it has a profound impact on the level of employment in business services. Thus, a 10 per cent increase in accessibility (travel time reduction) by transit will, *ceteris paribus*, increase employment in business services by an average of 3.9 to 5.2 per cent.

A further conclusion is that the effect of accessibility on a given category of employment is not identical in all areas (in this case the five boroughs in New York city). For example, an accessibility improvement, which will reduce by 10 per cent the number of trips to work in the 30–34 minutes category, will result in a 4.1 per cent increase in retail employment in the Bronx. In Brooklyn, however, the same improvement will increase retail employment by 0.75 per cent only. A further conclusion is that households' income, by and large, has an insignificant effect on the level of employment regardless of the type of employment and location. This might indicate that indeed, in this model, income is a poor surrogate for firms' profits.

The main lesson from this discussion is that when carrying out a micro-level analysis it is incorrect to presume that a given change in accessibility, caused by infrastructure improvement, will have an identical effect on all employment types in all areas. Hence, in analysing the economic effects of a specific transportation infrastructure investment it is necessary to examine these effects distinctively, mainly with respect to the particular travel conditions and households' characteristics in each of the studied sub-areas. Attempts to aggregate these effects can produce false results and lead to wrong conclusions regarding optimal investments. A comparison of the estimated results for the individual boroughs with the results obtained using the entire metropolitan region as the unit of analysis (the column labelled 'New York', in tables 2.2 and 2.3) shows that the parameters derived for New York, at best, are averages of the five boroughs, mainly because the differences between the five boroughs are substantial.

2.6. TRANSPORTATION INFRASTRUCTURE INVESTMENT AND LOCAL ECONOMIC GROWTH

Given the above discussion it is pertinent to ask whether improved accessibility is the only (or even the major) cause for economic development from transport infrastructure investment. Generally, any large-scale infrastructure investment has a substantial regional income-multiplier effect caused by the sheer magnitude of the public capital outlay, henceforth labelled as the *investment effect*. The expenditures used to employ local workers, to purchase land and procure capital equipment, generate a sequence of local investment and consumption cycles whose combined effect is regarded as economic growth. Two points should be observed about growth from the investment effect. First, the income-multiplier effect is bound to endure mainly for the duration of the infrastructure investment and hence cannot be regarded as a *permanent* effect. Secondly, it is likely that the same degree of economic growth from the transportation project investment effect can be achieved by a different type of a project (e.g. investment in water and sewage facilities). These two qualifications raise a cardinal question: to what extent should the investment effect be regarded as a primary benefit when analysing the overall benefits from a transport infrastructure investment?

Adhering to the view that improved accessibility from transport infrastructure investment is indeed the primary promoter of economic growth, we further need to examine which transport investment contributes most to regional accessibility. Thus far we have treated transportation infrastructure investment as a ubiquity relative to the type of investment, its spatial location and impact on travel behaviour. Obviously, this is not the case so that a correct assessment of the effect of transport infrastructure investment on economic growth *vis-à-vis* its effect on accessibility needs to consider further the particular transportation attributes of this investment.

The *travel mode*, in which a particular capital expenditure is made, is probably the most significant characteristic of a transportation investment. The reason is that, when given the spatial structure of a metropolitan area, not all modes provide the same degree of accessibility. For example, a given capital outlay invested in a suburban highway link can generate less accessibility (in terms of total travel time reduction) than would an identical investment in a radial rail link. Moreover, some improvements of accessibility by alternative travel modes are not equivalent relative to their effect on location of firms and households, and thus regional output and employment. Hence the need to identify and measure *modal accessibility*.

The spatial layout and extent of the *network* of a given mode is another factor affecting the resultant level of accessibility. An investment in a well-developed highway network may yield a minute improvement in regional accessibility whereas a new rail line added to an under-developed rail network may improve overall accessibility quite significantly. Still, an investment which provides linkage between two disjointed parts of a network (e.g. a bridge or a tunnel linking two road or rail networks) can, accessibility-wise, be more effective than the addition of a new segment to each of these networks.[14] A corollary to this conclusion is that capital projects should also be ranked on the basis of their contribution to the level of *connectivity* of networks and not necessarily on the basis of their marginal contribution to accessibility of a given network.

In most metropolitan areas, even a large investment in a transportation facility, which is part of a well developed network, will have a small relative (and probably also an absolute) effect on the region's total accessibility. Accessibility is a function of the *level* of the existing physical capital stock as well as of its *quality* and *composition*, and overall *transportation policies* like the use of tolls, parking restrictions and exclusive bus lanes to affect traffic volumes. Thus, when considering the effect of transportation infrastructure facilities on urban and regional growth, it is the variety of travel modes in the studied area, their degree of complementarity and quality in terms of spatial availability, direct cost of use and degree of reliability which matters.

2.7. Concluding Remarks: Pertinent Issues for a COBA of Transportation Infrastructure Investment

In previous sections I have tried to highlight major issues associated with the modelling and measurement of the relationships between transportation infrastructure investment and economic development. In this section I raise some questions pertaining to the execution of a cost-benefit analysis (COBA) of a particular transport capital investment. Given the objectives and scope of this chapter, and given that the many facets and problems of COBA have been extensively explored in the germane literature, here I wish briefly to discuss four issues which are relevant to transportation investment policy-making, and which ensue from the preceding discussion. These are: (*a*) treatment of supply prices of input factors; (*b*) the appropriate criterion to measure the contribution of a public capital investment to the local economy; (*c*) the soundness of including economic growth as part of the benefits from an infrastructure investment; and (*d*) the effect of the time-period which is regarded as the life-span of a transport infrastructure investment.

In carrying out a cost-benefit analysis of a particular infrastructure investment such as the expansion of road capacity, a key question is how to treat the supply prices of input factors, mainly of land. A number of authors (e.g. Keeler and Small, 1977; Small *et al.*, 1989) have argued that the correct prices should be those which take into account input supply conditions such as the reduction in land availability following the investment. Others (e.g. Kraus, 1981) have argued the opposite, i.e. that factor prices should be kept constant. Berechman and Pines (1991) have shown that the latter view is the correct one if road capacity is regarded as an intermediate good together with time spent in travel in the production of highway services (measured in traffic volumes). Implicit in this conclusion is the assumption of a competitive land market. If, however, the public sector behaves as a monopolist in this market by extracting monopoly rents, other pricing rules become necessary.[15]

Turning to the question of the appropriate criterion for measuring the contribution of a public investment to the economy, it should be emphasized that in evaluating the benefits (and costs) from a public capital project it is necessary to regard them within a framework applicable for the public sector. In particular, such a framework should include measures of the overall contribution of the transportation project to social welfare like the social rate of return of the public investment. In their study, Nadiri and Mamuneas (1991) measured the marginal benefits from infrastructure investment in terms of the willingness of the private sector to pay for services rendered by additional public capital infrastructure.[16] Based on this measure they subsequently defined the social rate of return of a public investment as the sum of the marginal benefits of the public capital services in each industry divided by the cost of an additional unit of public capital. Given their sample of industries, they reported a social rate of return of about 7 per cent.[17]

I have already concluded that two main factors are responsible for economic development from transportation infrastructure investment: the investment effect (income-multiplier) and improved accessibility. Since any large scale public capital investment is liable to generate income at the region where it takes place, it is pertinent to ask whether this income should be included as part of the benefits attributed to this capital project. For if it is, the scope of the COBA needs to be broadened to consider other, non-transportation projects with a possible larger multiplier effect. However, considering the fragmented nature of decision-making in the public sector, this conclusion is largely impractical.

Regarding economic development effects from accessibility improvements, if we view changes in accessibility as the main benefits from the project and then combine them with economic growth effects as additional benefits, we may run the risk of *double counting* benefits. In other words, if the sole effect of enhanced accessibility is to improve the allocation of resources, thereby raising total produced output and demand for labour (the output and labour effects mentioned above), then measuring changes in the input side (improved travel times) jointly with changes in the output side (increased regional output and development), may produce an inflated estimate of benefits from the investment.

This conclusion, however, is subject to two important qualifications. First, as recently pointed out by Mohring (1993), if transportation facilities are priced inefficiently (e.g. highways are not priced to cover the full social costs of their use), then at least part of the double counting of benefits may be justifiable. A major source of such inefficiency is the case of scale economies in the provision and use of transportation infrastructure systems. In this case, the public investment will generate output levels, regarded as economic growth, which could not be obtained without this investment. Consequently, this growth represents *additional* benefits which need to be accounted for in the cost benefit analysis.

A second qualification stems from the fact that geographical regions tend to trade with each other. As a result, an investment in transportation facilities in one region may raise land rents and labour wages in this region which, in part, will be paid by inhabitants of neighbouring regions (Mohring, 1993). In such a case benefits from the investment, in the form of new jobs created in the first region, cannot be considered as double counting. This potential source of benefits needs to be balanced out with the phenomenon observed above namely that, following a transportation capital investment which improves accessibility, firms and households may decide to relocate to other regions to benefit from lower input factor prices like of land and labour. Accepting the view of scale economies, associated with public infrastructure development, as a source of economic benefits, raises an interesting question regarding the *time-span* of the investment. Typically, the economic development of cities and regions extends over very long time periods so that benefits from a public investment may be realized only at a faraway future. The dilemmas associated with such distant benefits (including the effect of the discount rate) are rather well known. Here I would like to highlight an additional problem related to the particular nature of investment in transportation infrastructure. I have already pointed out that due to the network aspect of transportation systems not all facility investments generate the same accessibility and economic benefits. An investment which connects two disjointed parts of a network or which provides better linkage between modes (e.g. between bus and rail) can be considerably more beneficial than an alternative investment. Yet, the implementation of such an investment crucially depends on all previous ones, thus implying that the relevant time-span cannot be confined to that of the incremental investment but needs to take into account the life-span of the transport network as a whole.

In summary, to measure correctly the overall benefits from a transportation infrastructure investment, avoiding double counting and use of inappropriate supply prices and biased measures of overall profitability of the investment, a careful analysis of the issues outlined above is essential. Too often transportation investment projects are implemented on the basis of *assumed* economic development benefits which either never materialize or merely reflect direct transportation benefits.

Notes

1. The USA 1991 Intermodal Surface Transportation Efficiency Act (ISTEA) requires the assessment of potential economic development from transportation infrastructure investment (see Chapter 3 in this volume).

2. Elsewhere (Berechman, 1994), I have defined 'economic growth' as increase in the variety of goods and services produced in the economy rather than general increase in total output.

3. This observation does not imply that actual construction could not be subcontracted to the private sector. However, if optimal user charges are levied, subsidy will have to be rendered to cover the difference between long-run average costs and the per unit revenue from these charges.

4. Many studies have utilized a Vickery type volume-capacity function which has the form: $t = \alpha(V/K)^\beta$, where t is travel time, V, K are traffic volume and road capacity, respectively; and α, β are parameters. In this function an increase in K, will produce a decline in travel time proportional to β/K. Hence, scale economies, in terms of travel time reduction, ensue from such volume-capacity relationships. For empirical estimation of α, β see Berechman (1984).

5. See Banister *et al.* (1993) and Chapter 19 in this volume for a discussion of private sector financing of transport infrastructure.

6. For a similar model see Aschauer (1989).

7. In her 1990 study Munnell has implicitly assumed $\lambda = 0$.

8. The data pertain to non-military federal, state and local public capital for selected years, 1948–1987.

9. From these estimates, most of the increase in aggregate output was due to increase in factor productivity.

10. The data are from publications of the National Bureau of Statistics. Y is the net value of total private and public consumption of all goods and services plus net export in real terms (1986 prices); K and G are gross investments in fixed facilities, equipment, structures and buildings of the private and public sectors, respectively, adjusted for depreciation (also in 1986 prices). L is the number of employees in the economy.

11. These conclusions are based on estimated parameters which were significantly different to 0 at less than 5 per cent level. A Durbin-Watson analysis, however, showed a positive serial correlation.

12. The estimation of a cost function model as a means to circumvent problems arising from the specification and estimation of a production function model is, by now, a well established practice. For a general discussion see, for example, Johnston (1984).

13.   Defined as business and repair, personal and entertainment.

14.   See, for example, a discussion by Kristiansen (1993), on the linking of two Scandinavian transport networks.

15.   This conclusion holds if the change in the supply of input factors, caused by the investment, is small relative to the local economy.

16.   Measured this way they found very small marginal net benefits ranging from 0.0015 (for the stone, clay and glass industry) to 0.0060 (in the petroleum and refining industry).

17.   This figure is quite sensitive to the measurement of the costs of an additional unit of publicly financed capital. Using alternative cost measures proposed by Jorgenson and Yun (1990) and by Ballarad et al. (1985), respectively, Nadiri and Mamuneas (1991) report social rate of return of 4.6 per cent and 5.8 per cent.

References

Aschauer, D.A. (1989) Is public expenditure productive? *Journal of Monetary Economics*, **23**(2), pp. 177–200.

Ballarad, C., Shoven, J. and Whalley, J. (1985) General equilibrium computations of the marginal welfare costs of taxes in the United States. *American Economic Review*, **75**, pp. 128–138.

Banister, D., Andersen, B. and Barrett, S. (1993) Private sector investment in transport infrastructure in Europe. Paper Presented at the European Conference on the Evolution of Transport and Communication Networks in Europe, Padua, Italy, December 14–18.

Berechman, J. (1984) Highway capacity utilization and investment in transportation corridors. *Environment and Planning* A, **16**, pp. 1475–1488.

Berechman, J. (1994) Urban and regional impacts of transportation investment: a critical assessment and proposed methodology. *Transportation Research*, **28A**(4), pp. 351–362.

Berechman, J. and Paaswell, R. (1994*a*) Assessment of local economic impacts of large scale transportation investment project. Working Paper, University Transportation Research Center, City College of New York.

Berechman, J. and Paaswell, R. (1994*b*) The Bronx-Center project: Travel behavior of the Bronx' population. Working Paper WP93-BC-3, University Transportation Research Center, City College of New York.

Berechman, J. and Pines, D. (1991) Financing road capacity and returns to scale under marginal cost pricing. *Journal of Transport Economics and Policy*, **25**(2), pp. 177–181.

Berechman, J. and Small, K. (1988) Modeling land use and transportation: an interpretive review for growth areas. *Environment and Planning A*, **20**(10), pp. 1285–1310.

Giuliano, G. (1989) New directions for understanding transportation and land use. *Environment and Planning* A, **21**, pp. 145–159.

Johnston, J. (1984) *Econometric Methods*. New York: McGraw Hill.

Jorgenson, D.W. and Yun, Kun-Young (1990) The excess burden of taxation in the U.S., Harvard University. Department of Economics, Discussion Paper 1528.

Jorgenson, D.W. (1991) Fragile statistical foundations: the macroeconomics of public infrastructure investment. Paper presented at the American Enterprize Institute Conference on: 'Infrastructure Needs and Policy Options for the 1990s', Washington, DC, February 4.

Keeler, T.E. and Small, K. (1977) Optimal peak-load pricing, investment and service level on urban expressways. *Journal of Political Economics*, **9**, pp. 1–22.

Kraus, M. (1981) Indivisibilities, economies of scale and optimal subsidy policy for freeways. *Land Economics*, **57**, pp. 115–121.

Kristiansen, J. (1993) Regional transport infrastructure policies, in Banister, D. and Berechman, J. (eds.) *Transport in A Unified Europe*. Amsterdam: North Holland, pp. 221–247.

Meyer, J.R. and Gomez-Ibanez, J.A. (1981) *Autos Transit and Cities*. Cambridge, Mass: Harvard University Press.

Mohring, H. (1976) *Transportation Economics*. Cambridge, Mass: Ballinger Publishing Company.

Mohring, H. (1993) Maximizing, measuring and not double counting transportation-improvement benefits: A primer on closed- and open-economy cost-benefit analysis. *Transportation Research B*, **27**(6), pp. 413–424.

Munnell, A. (1990) Why has productivity growth declined? productivity and public investment. *New England Economic Review*, January/February, pp. 4–22.

Munnell, A. (1993) An assessment of trends and economic impacts of infrastructure investment, in Organization for Economic Co-operation and Development (ed.) *Infrastructure Policies for the 1990s*. Paris: OECD.

Nadiri, I.M. and Mamuneas, T.P. (1991) The effect of public infrastructure and R&D capital on the cost structure and performance of U.S. manufacturing industries. National Bureau of Economic Research, Working Paper No. 3887.

Small, K., Winston, C. and Evans, C. (1989) *Road Work*. Washington DC: The Brookings Institution.

Tatom, J.A. (1991) Public capital and private sector performance. *Review* (Federal Reserve Bank of St. Louis), **73**, May/June, pp. 3–15.

Taylor, R.G. (1951) *The Transportation Revolution 1815–1860*. New York: M.E. Sharpe Inc. N.Y.

CHAPTER 3

ISTEA: INFRASTRUCTURE INVESTMENT AND LAND USE

Robert E. Paaswell

3.1. INTRODUCTION

After nearly two decades of neglect, the infrastructure supporting the surface transportation system in the United States is about to receive massive amounts of new investment. Had such infusion occurred a few years ago, the investment would have been primarily for highways and, primarily to support the seemingly insatiable demand for vehicle miles travelled, and total number of trips by single occupant vehicles (SOVs). But, that is not to be the case now. The legislation supporting this new infusion of resources, the 1991 Intermodal Surface Transportation Efficiency Act (ISTEA), is the result of great deliberation among not only legislators and the usual transportation proponents (e.g. motor vehicle representatives) but those concerned with environmental issues and air quality; those concerned with energy use; those concerned with suburban sprawl and high levels of suburban congestion – said to be the US transportation problem; those concerned with the ever increasing cost of moving goods; transit supporters and citizens who believe that deterioration of their transportation systems reflects a deterioration of their quality of life.

So significant and complex is ISTEA that, two years after its passage, government representatives are still crossing the country telling local governments how to apply it and how to make it work. ISTEA has great promise, for it provides a number of new programmes that planners have wished for. These include multi and many modal approaches, funding that can be used for transit or highways or innovative combinations, funding that can be used to enhance transportation projects, demonstration funds for Intelligent Vehicle Highway Systems, more control at the local levels for planning, and greater input from a broader array of the public. More than just a transportation construction act, ISTEA attempts to deal with urban and suburban land use problems, such as congestion and sprawl, through disincentives for single occupant vehicles, congestion mitigation strategies and strong incentives to improve the environment.

But ISTEA comes with restrictions. Environmentatlly sensitive, it demands less use of single occupant vehicles, compliance with the Clean Air Act (CAA) and Clean Air Act Amendments (CAAA), financial planning linked to long-term (20-year) corridor and major project identification, managing demand, using innovative financing and tolls, and sensitivity to land use. It even requires concern for personal, if not regional, equity. And to make sure that projects meet these constraints, ISTEA has established an exhaustive planning process at both the state and regional levels that must be met and certified. It gives substantial planning and implementation power to the Metropolitan Planning Organizations (MPO), regional bodies that previously served as project organizers and have now become the regional consciences and programme negotiators. The MPO becomes the strong administrator and manager of this revitalized planning process, but this, as we will see, is made complex by a variety of constraints and mandates which call for new approaches to planning and implementing transportation infrastructure.

This chapter provides an overview of ISTEA, starting with the fundamental changes in philosophy it has engendered. It will identify key programme elements and how they are to be used, with particular attention to both the new planning process and the requirement for management systems. The chapter then addresses how some of the features of ISTEA, primarily the environmental issues, will act as constraints on business as usual and force investors to rethink their approach to transportation system design. Such design will be seen to cause a rethinking of land uses, and traditional approaches to mobility and accessibility. The chapter concludes with examples of current investment analysis concerns.

3.2.   ISTEA, the Legislation and its Requirements

Figure 3.1 summarizes the broad categories of ISTEA. ISTEA, as legislation, replaces (and incorporates) long standing highway (referred to as Title 23) programmes and transit (referred to as UMT Act of 1964 as amended) programmes, and makes possible by incorporating the funding base of these programmes a new multi-modal initiative.

The intent of ISTEA is, of course, to provide federal aid for highway and transit infrastructure – whether new or improvements. The process by which that aid is put in place is a two-tier planning process, the output of which is a Long Range Plan (LRP) (defined as having a twenty year horizon), and a Transportation lmprovement Programme (TIP), having

---

Broad Categories

National Highway System (NHS)
Surface Transportation Programme (STP)
Congestion Mitigation Air Quality Programme (CMAQ)
State planning
Metropolitan planning
Intelligent Vehicle Highway Systems (IVHS)

Programme Initiatives

Flexible funding
Non-motorized vehicle mandates
Enhancement funds
Toll road support
Corridor preservation
Management systems
Metropolitan Planning Organizations and Transportation Management Areas
Conformity – Air Quality and CAAA
Financial planning, alternatives analysis and EIS

Figure 3.1   ISTEA programmes

a one to three year horizon. Simply, major initiatives (e.g., new transit additions or starts, or major highway additions) must be identified on the LRP. Annual projects that achieve, or comprise the long range initiatives, as well as normal transportation improvements must be identified[1] and be part of the TIP. Funding for the capital programmes and some of the operating programmes comes from two sources – federal grants and local matching. Since the federal grants for most capital programmes represent 80 per cent of the project budget, states and local areas choose to get such grants, with the attached regulations and guidelines rather than seeking alternative (non-federal) funding sources. In fact funding for many highway and transit programmes is allocated to the states on a formula basis (based on population, lane miles of highway and other indices), putting in play the regulations for planning as well as implementation. For local regions and for states, the annual objective is to get to a TIP that represents a consensus of projects agreed on by the variety of agencies that have access to and utilize public funds for transportation.

Prior to ISTEA, surface transportation funding came, primarily through two separate sources, highway programmes identified in US Code, Title 23, and transit programmes identified in the Urban Mass Transportation Act of 1964, as amended. The highway programmes had been funded annually at levels greater than ten times the amount of the transit programmes. In addition, there were often inequities between the programmes in matching fund requirements. Many highway programmes required only 10 per cent local match, while transit programmes required 20–33 per cent local match. It was the intent of pre-ISTEA planning guidelines that the states and the Metropolitan Planning Organizations (MPOs) monitor the TIPs and ensure they were consistent with regional planning objectives, and simultaneously look at broad transportation as opposed to modal needs. But the reality is that highway and transit projects were each brought to the table, often competing for the same limited matching funds that were available. While issues of environment, energy, equity and system access were considered, the prime determinant in any economic analysis was facility demand, and reduction of user costs. Figure 3.2 summarizes many of the changes that accompanied planning and implementation with the passage of ISTEA.

While transportation programmes have meant, previously, assembling projects based upon their highly localized significance, ISTEA now creates new constraints, or opportunities, for such assembly. ISTEA programmes are designed to stimulate multi-modal approaches, demand satisfaction of air quality mandates and congestion relief. They require an efficient approach to overall systems management, and demand that a very broad array of participants have a say in how all of these objectives can be achieved simultaneously.

The two broad programme categories of greatest concern to most municipal agencies, as noted in figure 3.1, are the National Highway System (NHS) and the Surface Transportation Program (STP). Taken together, these define the broad majority of projects eligible for funding. The Congestion Mitigation Air Quality Program (CMAQ) is a quick start programme for achieving mandated air quality objectives.

What must change in approaching planning and implementing transportation systems post-ISTEA?

- from many to multi-modal
- environmental concern becomes environmental mandate
- using SOV as main solution, and thinking of non-motorized approaches
- strong use of public transit
- from weak MPO to strong, multi partner MPO
- underlying objectives of planning: from increasing supply to environmentally sensitive, cost effective, yet sustaining personal mobility
- from adding capacity to managing demand, and considering land use
- who has a say – and when in the process
- how projects are paid for – and accounted for
- approaches to modelling and analysis
- from hierarchical to participatory decision making
- from end oriented BCA to start oriented use of management systems
- from technology oriented to customer oriented

Figure 3.2   ISTEA: Transportation initiatives for the future.

NHS defines those highways of national significance, by classification, that states must include in their programmes as eligible for specific categories of funding (mostly 80 per cent federal). There is a national limit to the NHS of 155,000 miles (248,000 km). The Surface Transportation Program makes available both highway and transit funds. STP allows regions to use these funds flexibly, so that highway funds become eligible for transit projects and transit funds for highway projects.

The concept of flexibility is one of the defining aspects of ISTEA. The intention is to allow urban areas to decide on what the best multi-modal or intermodal solutions are to their transportation problems, and no longer to approach those problems as being singularly highway or transit. If a city believes it had received insufficient transit capital funds through previous transportation programmes, it could now allocate funds from the highway portions of the STP, including the NHS, to transit. It should be noted, however, that increased emphasis on transit is manifested through transit capital programmes, (rolling stock replacements, modernization and a limited number of new starts), but not operating funds.

The STP provides one link of infrastructure to the environment through the Enhancement Program. Ten per cent of the highway funds allocated to the states through the STP must be spent on defined transportation enhancements. These enhancements include parks, historic preservation, beautification and bicycle paths and footpaths. ISTEA's emphasis on the latter non-motorized forms of transportation is reinforced by the requirements for states and local regions to have full time bicycle and pedestrian coordinators. Enhancements are to be linked to normally programmed projects or areas served by such projects and are to be considered as an integral part of the intermodal system. Because they are a part of the overall transportation programme, enhancement projects must be part of the LRP and TIP, and therefore become part of the overall planning process.

So important is relief from poor air quality and congestion, a programme, separate from the STP, with its own funding has been established. This programme, Congestion Mitigation Air Quality (CMAQ), supplemental to normal programme funds, cannot be used to fund projects considered part of the routine operational projects normally found in the TIP. CMAQ is to be used to initiate projects that help achieve the State Implementation Plan (SIP) designed to achieve National Ambient Air Quality Standards (NAAQS).

3.3. AIR QUALITY

It is important to divert from the thrust of ISTEA at this point to provide insights into the importance of air quality programmes. More than 100 US

Examples of actions to be taken to comply with CAAA

Transit capital programmes
Construction of HOV or bus lanes
Employer trip reduction (vehicle emission reduction) policies
Traffic signalization and other programmes to reduce vehicle emissions
Fringe, transportation corridor parking to serve HOV, transit operations
CBD vehicle restriction policies, including pricing, restricted zones
Incident management systems, vehicle information systems

Intention is to sustain access to activity, residential areas, while reducing vehicle emissions

---

Figure 3.3   Clean Air Act Amendments – transport control measures.

urban areas violate national standards for permissible levels of ozone, carbon monoxide and particulates. The Environmental Protection Agency (EPA), following the mandates of the Clean Air Act (1970) and Clean Air Act Amendments (1990), requires all states to file a State Implementation Plan (SIP), indicating what steps they are to take to achieve NAAQS by specific dates. In particular, the CAAA describes transportation actions that can be employed to achieve these standards. Figure 3.3 lists some categories of action that are considered responsive. In general the actions are transportation pricing, demand modification, mode switches away from SOVs – including non-motorized modes, and changes in land use and development patterns. If the state is unable to meet its SIP as filed through the application of control measures, it becomes eligible to lose its transportation funding authorized under ISTEA. It is important to note here that a law administered by a non-transportation federal agency has extremely strong jurisdiction over transportation programmes. This will be discussed in more detail in the following section.

3.4.   CONFORMING TO AIR QUALITY MANDATES

ISTEA demands, through a certification process, that there be conformity between the transportation programmes developed and the air quality mandates of the CAAA. The MPOs and states must both show and be certified for this conformity. A few aspects of how this is to be done are presented in figure 3.4.

Transportation Management Areas (TMA).   Urban areas of more than 200,000 population and not in compliance with NAAQS are designated TMAs. These areas are required to put into place and make operational Congestion Management Systems (CMS). Such systems establish operational objectives and benchmarks and develop programmes for mitigating congestion, believed to be a major contributor to poor air quality.

Congestion and Air Quality

- **Conformity**

  State Implementation Plan – reduction of air pollutants
  Trip reduction policies
  Mandated increase in Average Vehicle Occupancy (AVO) 1.25 rule
  Employee trip reduction
  Single Occupant Vehicle constraints on capital programmes

- **Transportation Management Areas (200,000)**

  Congestion management systems
  Intermodal management systems
  Public transit management systems

Figure 3.4   Conformity elements.

Employee Trip Reduction Programmes. In TMAs employers with more than 100 employees are required to establish programmes that will increase the average occupancy of vehicles arriving at the employment site in morning peak hours by 25 per cent. Quite simply, the employer is to select programmes appropriate to that locale and work force that will reduce single occupant vehicle journeys to work. This major programme, while generating environmental savings, may create added costs to the employer – costs that in the long run the employer may not choose to bear. These will be evaluated in the future.

SOV Constraints on Capital Programmes. One of the strongest measures of ISTEA is to require that no new highway capacity be built, new lanes or additional miles of new highway, that will generate new SOV travel in a given, non-attainment area. High Vehicle Occupancy (HOV) lanes are eligible if it can be demonstrated that adding HOV lanes does not simultaneously add SOV vehicle miles travelled at that site.

The CMAQ programme, noted above, can be used to fund specific projects and programmes, including parking reduction programmes, HOV incentive programmes, the establishment of congestion management systems and other projects or operational changes whose direct output is reduction in congestion at an identified site.

3.5.   ADDITIONAL FACTORS

Figure 3.1 illustrates that in addition to the traditional highway and transit programmes, as reformulated, and in addition to the air quality constraints, there are a number of other factors that ISTEA mandates. I will describe these as operational and procedural.

Operational.   ISTEA permits federal funding for toll roads to be used for both capital support and for traffic management. Such support on a matching basis is less than for the non-toll roadways under the National Highway System (NHS). In addition, ISTEA allows current toll facilities, originally funded under highway programmes to stay as toll facilities, even after capital repayment has taken place, if the tolls (pricing) serve to reduce SOV demand. In an unusual way, federal law has allowed and encouraged road pricing as a demand management tool. Intelligent Vehicle Highway Systems (IVHS) are to be explored both through demonstrations and through research and development. While there are only preliminary demonstrations underway, many in the highway community believe that the full integration of computers and communications into highway systems will create substantial relief to congested highways and improve bad air. ISTEA provides substantial funding for demonstration projects to test such a hypothesis.

Procedural.   Two substantial changes to transportation procedures, required under ISTEA will greatly change how we implement infrastructure changes, and through that, how we evaluate investments and their impacts, especially on land use. These changes are the requirements for management systems, and the procedures for planning at both the state and metropolitan levels.

After nearly two decades of under investment and budget constraints, it is now proposed that no new infrastructure can be implemented until we evaluate the efficiency and effectiveness of the existing inventory. To achieve this objective, six management systems are required (see Item 9, figure 3.5). The management systems will be used to monitor the performance of the existing transportation systems, to develop system inventories, and to develop performance indicators and benchmarks against which changes in system performance can be measured. In addition, the management systems will be used to suggest strategies to guide improvements from existing conditions to the desired objectives. The management systems are regarded as the primary sources of data[2] for existing system condition and performance, for the definition of variables against which system future performance can be judged, and for suggestions – indeed, strategies, for improving performance. As such the management system information is to be used as input to the planning process. Figure 3.6, which shows the investment planning process, indicates how management systems precede planning.

The second major change is in the procedures for planning. Before reviewing the actual items to be considered as a part of the planning process, it should be noted that the procedures, at the regional level, give much greater powers to the MPO, and, in fact, reduce reliance on federal

1. Preservation of existing facilities and more efficient use of existing facilities
2. Consistency of transportation planning with energy conservation programmes
3. Relief of congestion – now and in future
4. Effect of transportation on land use
5. Programming of enhancement activities
6. Effects of *all* transportation projects – even if not federally funded
7. International borders, intermodal facilities, parks, historic sites
8. Connectivity of metropolitan area roads with roads outside the metropolitan area
9. Transportation needs identified through management systems
    *   Highway pavement
    *   Bridge
    *   Highway safety
    *   Traffic congestion
    *   Public transportation facilities
    *   Intermodal transportation facilities
10. Preservation of rights of way for future projects; identification of corridors
11. Methods to enhance movements of freight
12. Use of life cycle costs – bridges, tunnels, pavement
13. Overall social, environmental, economic, and energy effects
14. Expansion, enhancement of transportation services
15. Capital investments for increased security in transit systems

Figure 3.5   Metropolitan planning requirements.

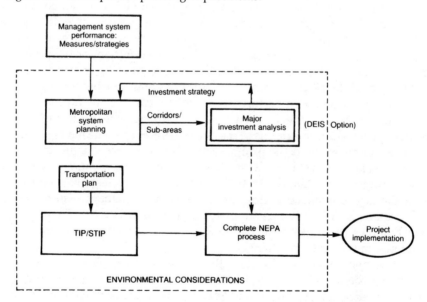

Figure 3.6   Major investment planning process. (*Source*: FHWA/FTA)

approvals – providing air quality conformity is met. In addition, in response to the more diverse issues of infrastructure investment raised by a highly heterogeneous, and often litigious population, ISTEA mandates that a much broader array of the population be brought into the planning process, at all steps of planning.[3] ISTEA mandates that MPOs and states design citizen and public participation processes that provide full access and hearing to the entire planning process. The planning regulations also specify that major projects, new highway additions or transit additions, that have significant impact on capacity, mode balance, or levels of service undergo a process of 'Major Investment Analysis'. This process, combining elements of Alternatives Analysis and Environmental Impact Analysis will be discussed below. To assure that project budgeting meets the needs of the long range and annual plans, ISTEA also requires that a Financial Plan be made. The financial plan must differentiate among projects that are targeted for existing sources of funds and those that will apply for new sources. It is assumed (and must be demonstrated) that applications for project support with new sources do not diminish the capacity to operate and maintain existing facilities. In fact, this is consistent with the overall intent of ISTEA, and the imposition of management systems whose purpose is to assure that the existing, multi-modal transportation systems are being operated at the most effective and efficient levels possible. When considering an economic analysis of a new facility, the analysis must incorporate the financial impacts of operating other elements of the system.

Since the mid-1970s, metropolitan regions have been required to carry on a planning process (3-C) that is continuing, comprehensive and coordinated. To these requirements have been added fifteen elements that define specific factors to, 'be explicitly considered, analyzed as appropriate, and reflected in the planning process products'.[4] These fifteen factors are summarized in figure 3.5. They deal with a broad array of planning issues, including the environment, land use, congestion mitigation, multi and intermodal issues, and finance and costing procedures. Through specific reference to the CAAA and National Environmental Policy Act (NEPA), and to management systems, the planning regulations make abundantly clear that implementation of the TIP or any projects that effect transportation system changes will take place only after specific environmental concerns have been addressed. Addressing such concerns has become a major task of the MPO. New approaches to evaluating air quality impacts of transportation actions, together with evaluating, as a normal part of the planning process, non-motorized modes of transport, travel demand measures, trip reduction strategies, and SOV constraints, must be developed. Further, they must be developed, not only to the satisfaction of the trans-

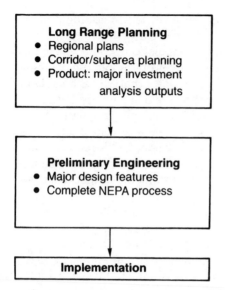

Long Range Planning
- Regional plans
- Corridor/subarea planning
- Product: major investment
  analysis outputs

Preliminary Engineering
- Major design features
- Complete NEPA process

Implementation

Figure 3.7 Combined FHWA/FTA process. (*Source*: FHWA/FTA)

portation providers, but, more importantly, the new customers of transportation – citizens groups, environmental groups and others. Nothing can state how significantly the planning business has changed as much as understanding the impacts of customer based, environmentally founded transportation issues. Understanding such issues lies at the heart of developing and using new tools to measure investment impacts and resultant changes in land use.[5]

Figures 3.6 and 3.7 illustrate the new planning process and its relationship to both the management systems and environmental review and control. While the traditional smaller projects, that often make up the majority of the TIP, will undergo a somewhat traditional review process provided that they do not stimulate SOV trips, large scale projects – those that must undergo investment analysis – will be subject to a more rigorous review than heretofore. Figures 3.8 and 3.9 show this new complexity. The proposed project must undergo multi-modal review and demonstrate that it is the most efficient and cost effective improvement. It must be negotiated among all of the interested and affected parties, and it must be environmentally sound.

3.6. A REVIEW OF ISTEA MANDATES

Before proceeding to a consideration of investment impacts of ISTEA, a review of the more salient points will be made.

• ISTEA demands compliance with the CAAA. This implies that trip reduction strategies must be an explicit part of the TIP.

Definition: High type highway or transit improvement . . . involving substantial cost . . . significant effect on capacity, traffic flow, level of service, or mode share

Cooperative process
MPO
State DOT
Appropriate local officials
Environmental, resource agencies
Transit operator(s)
Operators of other major modes of transportation
FHWA, FTA

Lead agency
MPO *or* state *or* transit operator: based on analytic capability and expertise

Alternatives
Do nothing – no build
Broad array: highway, transit, multi modal: presented early in the planning process
In air quality non-attainment areas, must deal with SOV restrictions through planning process *and* congestion management system

Necessary linkage
Planning process and environmental review (NEPA)

Result
Identification of preferred alternatives

Figure 3.8   Major metropolitan transportation investments. (*Source*: Federal Register, 28 October, 1993: *USDOT: Statewide Planning; Metropolitan Planning; Rule*)

Are the projected projects defined in the long term plan?

Are the projects in defined corridors or sub-areas?

Are all modes, highway and transit, and non-motorized vehicles considered?

Has current operational status of transportation system been evaluated using the management systems?

What is the impact of projected investment(s) on air quality?

What is the impact of the investments on regional operational performance?

What are the land use impacts?

What land use actions should be taken concurrently?

What are the impacts on equity, regional and personal?

Can these projects stimulate less SOV travel, fewer total trips, and fewer VMT?

How will the projects be paid for, what is the financial plan?

Figure 3.9   A check list for investment.

- In areas that do not comply with NAAQS, the SIP takes precedence in transportation planning. Employer trip reduction strategies and travel demand management, together with emissions controls, improved fuels and hardware fixes become the order of the day.

- In metropolitan regions, 15 factors must be studied as part of the ongoing planning process. State agencies must go through a similar process, but that process includes 23 factors.

- Non-motorized vehicle options must be developed and presented as serious alternatives to motorized vehicle travel

- Management systems must be developed and used as a fundamental input to the planning process. The planning process, that once started with goals and objectives and ended with a TIP, now starts with system performance as measured by management systems, and requires a broad set of environmental objectives be included[6] with the set of demographic and economic objectives, and ends with testing of the TIP against the promises of the SIP and air quality standards.

- Funding is flexible – almost fungible – encouraging a multi-modal approach to planning, and adding more weight to transit oriented solutions or non-motorized solutions to transportation problems.

3.7. THE MOMENTUM FOR MOBILITY

The discussion, so far, assumes that all is in the ready to change transportation planning and implementation. A review of recent data shows that this is far from true.[7] During the previous decade (1983–1990) there have been significant increases in personal mobility, coupled with sustained relocation to assure no decrease in accessibility to opportunities, work or non-work. In the US, total vehicle travel had increased 25 per cent, and VMT 40 per cent – more and longer trips per household or individual. The personal vehicle, long the prime means of travel, satisfied 87 per cent of trips in 1990, a 5 per cent increase over 1983. These trips were diverted from bicycles, walking and transit. Transit's share of trips in the US has dropped to 2 per cent. Work trips, once the majority of household trips, have declined to one-third of the household trips. The predominant work trip is suburb to suburb, no longer suburb and outer neighbourhoods to central cities. In the last decade in the NYC region, four housing starts were made in suburban areas for every one in the ten largest cities. Two jobs were added in suburban areas for every one in the ten biggest cities (Opurum, 1992). Further, this shifting of jobs and housing, while having obvious impacts on demand for autos and resultant inefficient land uses, sets the stage for long term regional inequities that might not be easily turned round through transportation solutions alone (Paaswell, 1993). With household car ownership continuing to grow, with VMT increasing at a rate far greater than the population, with discretionary travel growing, and creating its own congestion, and with intra-suburban travel the predominant trip, how then can ISTEA influence the next generation of investments?

3.8. ANALYSIS OF INFRASTRUCTURE INVESTMENT

In a letter to Commissioners of State Departments of Transportation (Replogle, 1993), the Environmental Defense Fund suggested a number of strategies that metropolitan areas and states should use to meet air quality standards – a major part of the conformity requirements of ISTEA/ CAAA. In particular they suggest, '...changes in pricing, ...public education, ...guiding community investments to favor efficiency, ... rethinking popular TDM strategies ...and expanding freedom to choose alternatives to the car.' That this letter is taken as fundamental to a new way to establish regional agenda setting shows how seriously agencies are taking the new environmental mandates.

At a time when we need new capacity in our highway systems, both through additional lane miles and through rehabilitation of now substandard rights of way, when new transit construction seems prohibitive in cost and when regional economics are paying great penalties for less than optimum transportation systems,[8] ISTEA is demanding limited construction for SOVs, more transit construction, better land use, travel demand reduction, and implementation of non motorized vehicle projects. What does the new investment picture look like and how do we assess it? Based on the discussion above, figure 3.9 presents a check list for investment.

The new investment analysis must take into account that there is a diverse set of groups attempting to set the transportation agenda. All will find a way to the MPO table, where the objectives are two-fold: (1) get major projects incorporated into the long term plan, and (2) influence project selection on the TIP. The post ISTEA difference in this agenda setting is that non-traditional players will be at the MPO table. It won't be just city versus suburb or highway versus transit. It will also be environmental agencies; non-transportation public agencies; other transportation providers, including private providers and non-traditional transit providers (taxis, etc.); citizens groups; unions and others. Goal setting, when accomplished, will have objective sets and criteria for project selection far different and more complicated than used previously. Savings in personal travel time may no longer be the major criterion for project evaluation. With complex objective sets and uncertain futures, risk analysis will play an important part in investment analysis.

Substitutes for traditional SOV only work trips

work at home
carpool and vanpool
guaranteed ride home
on-site day care, other important facilities
transit passes and employee subsidies

Substitutes for traditional SOV non-work trips

access to activities by bicycle, foot
more activities at work site
carpool and vanpool
shop by phone, mail and computer
medical care at work site
home gym or gym at work site
transit oriented land development

Figure 3.10   ISTEA and changing travel behaviour.

In fact, new investment strategies must be linked to the demographic and activity changes that have been evolving during the last two decades. In the 1960s and 1970s infrastructure investments were made primarily to accommodate the journey to work, using peak hour demand as a design variable. While the work trip, and peak hour travel can still be cited as the single largest trip generation category, solving this problem, alone, will not address the congestion problem – especially in suburban areas, nor will it alleviate air quality issues. Factors that planners must now address include (see figure 3.10):

• multi-worker households, both heads often working, travelling to separate work sites. Often these households have trips, by necessity linked to the work trip, including day care, school and other household business; because of trip chaining, optimal routeing through networks becomes much more complicated;

• an increasing proportion of non-work trips;

• an increasing number of activities satisfied at home, using computers and communications. These include working at home, a growing phenomenon in the US as the traditional structure of employment changes, and shopping at home – a multi billion dollar business – and rapidly growing; and

• continued growth of auto ownership and suburbanization of jobs and housing.

Because sustained increases in capacity of our highway systems will reinforce low density suburbanization, with its attendant lack of efficiencies, it becomes essential to examine land use changes that must occur in order to make new transportation investments successful. ISTEA implies that transportation goals will include:

- no loss of personal mobility;

- continued access to daily activities, although not necessarily by the same mode or in the same location;

- reduction in SOV travel, especially for the journey to work;

- more transit use;

- more attention to non motorized vehicle trips.

A growing body of planners and analysts concur that these objectives can only be reached through appropriate land use changes.[9] In his seminal work on suburban land use, Cervero (1990) notes that there will be significant institutional resistance in attempting to achieve requisite land use and zoning changes necessary to meet new planning objectives. But without such changes, the pressures to deal with transportation problems through capacity increases will again manifest themselves.

3.9. Infrastructure and Land Use: Investments Post ISTEA

There is growing agreement among transportation planners, urban and town planners, and development related public agencies, that new, transportation sensitive approaches to development must be encouraged in order to address the severity of current, primarily auto based, transportation problems. These solutions, under a variety of guises and names, essentially call for greater mixed use development, higher densities of development – both residential and non-residential, and an integration of footways, bicycle paths and transit into the land use structure. Such development approaches are assumed to allow individuals to sustain their mobility, but to do so with fewer vehicle trips. If development takes place as infill in older urban areas, the existing transportation and activity infrastructure should prove to be adequate, and a part of normal urban redevelopment. Figure 3.11 describes some of these land use strategies.

In suburban areas, mixed use development, i.e. integrating residential, commercial and retail together with other employment generators, is assumed to 'substantially reduce . . . reliance on the automobile', while shaping such development so that, 'transit oriented development is extremely effective in reducing vehicular travel demand', with the net result being a 'viable solution to the . . . area's near term and long range transportation problems'.[10]

Transportation problems in Oregon as noted above, or in Florida,

Infill – Urban	Increasing densities, primarily residential, in low density or vacated urban areas
Infill – Suburban	Increasing both residential densities, usually through multi-family housing, and increased commercial, retail, service activities and employment centres, at higher densities. See TOD below.
Pedestrian District	Retail and commercial areas designed to serve pedestrian traffic, and free from auto traffic. Can be in urban centres and in suburban, mixed use centres, within access of residences.
Transit Oriented Design TOD	Mixed use design, that has the densities and layout to make transit – either bus service, or a rail stop, practical. Such design provides for access from destinations of one quarter mile, and encourages access to adjacent residential areas by walking or bicycle.
Mixed Use Development	Integration of commercial, office, service, retail and entertainment areas, and some residential areas at the same community. Referred to as the Manhattanization of suburban areas.

Figure 3.11   Land-use approaches to minimize single occupant vehicle use.

where land use strategies have been introduced through growth management legislation, are designed to reduce personal VMT and, eventually, household auto ownership, with a resultant improvement in congestion and air quality, and a more pleasing quality of life. Another critical factor, is, of course, lessening the need for new lane miles of highways, either as additions to existing rights of way or development of new rights of way.

In long term planning, the resultant impact of this coordinated land use planning and transportation sensitive design implies that new capacity, when needed, can be programmed more into the future, and can be responsive to these new approaches of development.

For investment analysts, the bottom line, of course, is how much impact will these land use changes have on the demand for personal motor vehicle travel. Bookout (1992) suggests that with only a few built examples, much of the population (market) response to these initiatives is still speculative. Calthorpe Assoc. (1991) reinforces what data are available in a study of reported Transit Oriented Design (TOD) neighbourhoods or communities. They note that in TOD neighbourhoods there are 20 per cent fewer drive alone trips and 112 per cent more walk trips, and that annual VMT is substantially less than in new suburban neighbourhoods.[11]

3.10.   ISTEA AND INVESTMENT ANALYSIS

It should be clear now that few projects will be designed and built in the near future based primarily on travel time savings. While projects, in the past several decades have been evaluated on an individual basis, assessing their overall impact on regional objectives, such evaluations will now change. Investment analysis for the next decade, based on ISTEA mandates must include:

• dealing with multiple, perhaps conflicting objectives;

• dealing with rapidly changing demographics;

• addressing land use;

• an understanding of travel behavioural response to travel demand management and land use issues;

• understanding new approaches to financing; and

• understanding institutions and the roles of participants in decision making.

Multiple Objectives

The most obvious changes in investment analysis are those that address air quality and congestion. The cornerstones of ISTEA, these mandates demand that SOV constraint be adopted and multi-modal, transit sensitive approaches be taken. Variables that place greater weight on the achievement of air quality and congestion objectives, rather than those that simply support travel time savings through SOV capacity must be developed. In describing the NHS and STP programmes, ISTEA makes explicit that funds will not be available for SOV improvements. In evaluation, new models must be developed[12] that can look at specific air quality responses to transportation changes at a project and overall regional level, at traveller responses to travel demand management programmes, at traveller response to acceptance of non-motorized modes, and at trip generation responses to changing land use and to the ability to telecommute and teleshop. In summary, ISTEA demands the investment analysis consider,

• air quality, as a primary variable;

• congestion and relief of congestion;

• multi modal solutions, including non motorized vehicles; and

• land use changes.

Changing Demographics

There has been, as noted above, much discussion on changing demographics. While the major structural household changes of the last decades have been documented, changes in the last years of this decade still pose unknowns. As work, itself, changes in the US, there will be a change in the numbers of workers that travel to traditional 9 to 5 jobs. More workers, skilled and unskilled, are working part time, or non-traditional hours or at multiple job sites. In addition, there are growing numbers of workers that work at home or telecommute. Some large employers are providing remote office space to telecommuters who then travel to a new, closer to home job site. Some developers are building office complexes to serve such purposes for a number of workers. Finally, some employers are changing the nature of work at their job sites. IBM is going to experiment with the use of unassigned offices. At a central IBM facility a large number of offices will be available on a daily basis for their employees who are more mobile than fixed – a growing trend. All this suggests that new types of data must be collected to define the work trip patterns, and the reliance of those patterns on specific modes. Other demographics that define non-work trips, including patterns of an ageing population, child care, new approaches to shopping and other trip needs must begin to be transferred from the research of travel behaviour specialists, to active planning data input. Finally, new methods of collecting such data must be put in place to satisfy both the data needs of management systems and the data needs of the forecasting process.

Land Use

Land use remains complex, although much, as noted above, has been suggested that will make land uses more sensitive to the mandates of new transportation investments. ISTEA, through its strong planning and funding policies, encourages new development to include transit integration where possible, and non-motorized travel to satisfy the most immediate of household needs. Communities, to make best use of such programmes, must begin to develop new zoning and land use practices. Cervero (1990) presented a number of options, but noted that while such options are desirable for a number of reasons, existing institutions would mitigate against immediate zoning and other land use incentives. The initiatives in Oregon and Florida show that considered approaches can be turned into legislation. We must wait a short time more to see how the market responds. Replogle's suggestion that changes also be brought about through a process of education has great merit, for as recycling is now part of our environmental make up, he believes that institutions will adapt to new land use and transportation systems that decrease reliance on the SOV (Replogle, 1993). The analyst, incorporating the unknown rates of change of demographics, and the rate of institutional response to land use needs, would here apply uncertainty analysis to evaluate the likelihood of alternative futures and their expected values.

Travel Behaviour

The greatest unknown today is how the individual traveller will respond to all the initiatives suggested by ISTEA and CAAA. Car and van pooling have not in the past been effective. Transit use has declined, and with it an institutional ability to add significant amounts of capacity in the short run. And not every one will move tomorrow to a community that is transit sensitive and provides for walking and bicycling. Analysts have some sense of pricing as a travel constrainer or stimulator, but there are still many variables that must be measured to model work trips under TDM mandates or employer commute options, or telecommuting, as well as the use of modes for the work non work splits. Because of the learning that must take place among travellers (and analysts), new data collection efforts must be initiated. Panels are widely being discussed as one new source (Golob *et al.*, 1992), as are the collection of data sets for management systems and by employers for their trip reduction programmes. Finally, there is growing need to utilize geographic information systems to link land uses to transportation.

Financing

Great changes are taking place in financing, that will affect analysis. The first is that federal financing is flexible. Agencies have a chance to get not only funds mandated for their programmes, but funds available, traditionally, for other programmes. This is the effect, if not the intent, of flexibility. ISTEA means for transit providers and highway providers, and units of government to agree on the prior distribution of funds through federal programmes. Otherwise, each institution will plan for funds that might not be available when negotiation for the TIP takes place. But a greater source of problems will arise with matching funds. In conducting alternatives analysis, matching funds must be identified both to source and time stream. In the period of great project building, 1960–1985, most funds came from state and local treasuries, and were justified solely on the basis of their leverage. This rationale, during current periods of austere state treasuries and competing public interests, is no longer sufficient. General funds might have to be replaced, according to project, by bonds, tolls or pricing, taxes, tax increment financing, assessments or other methods. What is important to recognize, is that in a given corridor, or for a specific set of projects, different financing schemes will be dependent on the specific alternative posed. Thus analysing alternatives depends not only on the technical analysis, but the probability of success in meeting funding requirements. Finally, these funding strategies must be approved in a regional project financial plan.

Institutions and Participants

Analysts must cope with complex and potentially conflicting objectives set not only by ISTEA, but also by the interpretations of ISTEA made by public groups. An example, cited above, is the EDF letter to Commissioners, that lays out that groups expectation of (1) what compliance with ISTEA/CAAA means; (2) what programmes to initiate to comply; and (3) what modelling strategies to use in the analysis. ISTEA also incorporates social as well as environmental objectives. In the planning regulations equity – regional and social – is raised, and, in particular, the issue of reverse commuting by the lower income travellers is cited as an issue to be addressed. Regional and state agencies are utilizing many techniques so that they may define investment objectives in concert with all stakeholders in new investment, rather than in response after the plans have been drawn. For example, New Jersey will train their designers to have an environment first sensitivity. New York is having a variety of regional interest groups throughout the state respond and help define mission areas that are influential in making investment decisions. Oregon has had a major public involvement that has led to a new set of model regulations for transit design. While the 1980s may have been the era of litigation, the coming decade should be the era of true public involvement in transportation investments.

3.11. CONCLUSIONS

It is clear that at this point in time the rules for investment analysis are changing and evolving. Regions are just learning about the mandates of ISTEA, management systems and the data they will generate are not yet in place, reponse to travel demand management and trip reduction strategies is just being measured, and new analytic models to evaluate traveller choices under the new and permissible alternatives are in their development stages. The MPOs, the regional managers of these new approaches dictated by ISTEA, must gain new skills in all aspects of planning: management, modelling, finance and participation. Training of a new generation of professionals is today's top priority. The opportunities of ISTEA and the need to upgrade our transportation systems are great. Innovations in cities such as Seattle, Washington, Portland, Oregon, San Francisco,

California and Orlando, Florida are setting the stage for the next generation of environmentally sensitive investment. ISTEA has changed the rules, but our demand for mobility will be met.

Notes

1.   Identification means specifying the lead agency for implementation, and the source for all funds, federal and non-federal to complete the projects.

2.   The complexity of the requirements for management systems, planning requirements and air quality mitigation have led to the issuance of substantial regulations by USDOT, and EPA. Planning (USDOT) is found in Federal Register (FR) 28 Oct 93; Air Quality, issued by EPA, is in FR 24 Nov 93: Management Systems (USDOT) is in FR 1 Dec 93.

3.   In a paper presented at the annual ITE meeting, Orlando, Florida, 1993, 'New Voices in the Planning Process', I indicated that the diverse subsets of population would emerge only as their particular interests came up. Thus developers would try to influence the process at conception stage, environmentalists throughout the entire process, citizens when property interests were clear. While these groups were heard in the past, it was usually at project selection phase, and they had little opportunity to be heard during the initial, formative steps.

4.   FR 28 Oct 93, p. 58072, *op. cit.*

5.   The Environmental Defense Fund has taken a leadership role in assuring that the intent of ISTEA, as they see it, is manifest in the TIP, the output of the MPO planning process. To assure this, they have taken a number of steps, ranging from filing notice of intent to litigate to the issuance of letters to State DOT Commissioners indicating planning steps necessary for compliance. One difficulty MPOs currently have is in applying analytic techniques capable of addressing the new range of transportation options and preferences. The National Association of Regional Councils has issued a procedures manual as a first step in this new modelling process, see Harvey *et al.*, 1993.

6.   There is a subtle, but important difference between old and new approaches. In the old process, goals and objectives would be used to set alternatives that would then be subject to environmental impact analysis. ISTEA/CAAA mandate environmental objectives up front, which change the nature of the alternatives presented. Ten years ago, alternatives would not have included bikeways, or pedestrian zones or assume that planning officials would respond to denser development, infill and transit oriented suburban malls.

7.   Much of the data cited here is from, Pisarski (1992). The data is based primarily on the 1990 Nationwide Personal Transportation Survey.

8.   The 85,000 daily truck movements in and out of the New York City (Manhattan) Central Area have the highest hourly cost of truck movements in the US. Source: Regional Plan Association.

9.   Two groups, 1,000 Friends of Oregon, through their Land Use, Transportation Air Quality (LUTRAQ) project, and the Surface Transportation Policy Project (STPP), have been leaders in addressing requisite land use changes necessary for more efficient and environmentally friendly urban and suburban communities. They cite ISTEA/CAAA as the accommodating transportation link to achieve these goals.

10. 1,000 Friends of Oregon, 'The LUTRAQ Alternative/Analysis of Alternatives', Oct 1992. LUTRAQ spells out not only alternative approaches, but goes through a careful and analytic analysis of why such alternatives are proposed to replace traditional highway investments that have been suggested.

11. While it is stating the obvious, if people live in interesting neighbourhoods, they will get out and walk. If there is nothing to do or see, or if is too far to walk to some place interesting people will drive. Perhaps a great ironic inverse to this situation was told to the author by Dr. Ing. Harmut Topp. He noted that in many of the 'quaint' towns in Germany that tourists believe typify the best of town design, the centres are becoming museums and restaurants, while the resident population is flocking to the suburbs with their cars for more space and to be near the hypermarkets.

12. Such models are now being developed at various locations around the US. They address the current frustration faced by planners and citizens' groups alike that the array of models developed in the period 1960–1985 are not able now to examine, simultaneously, travel demand, demand management strategies, air quality impacts and land use changes. One example of new model development is the effort by the New York Metropolitan Transportation Council (NYMTC). NYMTC will spend $3 million over the next two years to develop those models for the NY region.

References

Bookout, L. (1992) Neotraditional town planning. *Urban Land*, February.

Calthorpe Assoc. (1991) *TOD Impacts on Travel Behavior*. August.

Cervero, R. (1990) Congestion relief: the land use alternative. *Journal of Planning Education and Research*, **10**(2).

Golob, T. *et al.* (eds.) (1992) *Proceedings of the First US Conference on Use of Panels for Transportation Planning*. Irvine, Ca.

Harvey, G. *et al.* (1993) *A Manual of Regional Transportation Modeling Practice for Air Quality Analysis*, Vers. 1.0. NARC.

Opurum, C. (1992) *Regional Transportation Status 1990*. PT1252801. New York: New York Metropolitan Transportation Council.

Paaswell, R. (1993) Transportation and Regional Economic Equity. Paper presented at the Port Authority of New York & New Jersey Regional Policy Roundtable, December.

Pisarski, A. (1992) *Travel Behavior Issues in the 90s*. Washington: US Department of Transportation.

Replogle, M. (1993) Letter to Commissioners of the State Departments of Transportation, 21 September.

Chapter 4

The Economic Debate: Theory and Practice

Ronald McQuaid

4.1. Introduction

In their chapters Robert Paaswell and Joseph Berechman raise many significant issues concerning both the development and the implementation of transportation infrastructure policies, and they provide useful empirical evidence. Paaswell analyses policy development and implementation issues, specifically related to the 1991 Intermodal Surface Transportation Efficiency Act (ISTEA) in the United States, and it can be argued that this Act marks a fundamental change in US policy, which may have important policy lessons for other countries. Berechman reviews a number of critical issues concerned with modelling or empirically measuring the impact of transportation infrastructure on economic growth – often an important policy objective. Here I propose to explore some of the issues and questions that arise from the analysis in these two chapters.

4.2. ISTEA: Infrastructure Investment and Land Use

Robert Paaswell considers the fundamental change by the US Federal government in its approach to funding transportation infrastructure, which led to the 1991 Intermodal Surface Transportation Efficiency Act (ISTEA). ISTEA is still in the early stages of implementation but lessons from its successes, or failures, will be of great interest to policy makers, academics and others in the US and elsewhere.

Before considering specific issues raised in Paaswell's chapter it is worth briefly considering the relevance of such US legislation for other countries, particularly in western Europe, and hence how important it is to those in other countries. Although heterogenous, the economies of western Europe and also of the US have great similarities in being private, market orientated, democratic countries with similar standards of living and high demand for fast, convenient and dependable transportation services (see for example Pucher, Ioannides and Hirschman, 1993). The US and western European countries, have experienced considerable increases in demand for transportation infrastructure, while facing financial constraints which limit investment and subsidies. Increasingly environmental limitations on transportation policies have also attained greater importance. These factors have arguably made governments more amenable to new ways of financing and operating transportation infrastructure, as illustrated by ISTEA in the US and other examples elsewhere.

Financially, the governments on both sides of the Atlantic have intervened heavily in transportation, particularly through large public subsidies, although the focus of subsidy has varied between countries and over time. For example, Pucher, Ioannides and Hirschman (1993) show that US Federal capital and operating subsidies to public transportation in the US have fallen between 1980 and 1991 in both absolute and relative terms. As a percentage of total public subsidy, the Federal share fell from 54 per cent in 1980 to 24 per cent in 1991 for capital and operating subsidy combined, with the remainder being taken up particularly by local and to a lesser extent by state authorities. They also point out some differences between the US and Europe, for instance there is much longer history of private ownership of public transport in the US and a stronger bias towards roads (with only 60 per cent of direct economic costs of roadway provision being covered by user taxes), while in Europe there has been a greater balance between modes. However, transportation investment policies may be converging due to the greatly increasing use of auto transportation and the increase in privatization in Europe on the one hand and the shifts towards a greater balance between modes in the US through ISTEA.

The responses to the growing and changing demand for transportation infrastructure, together with the increasing limitations on public finances, can generate a number of responses (see for instance Stevens and Michalski, 1993). Three main response are, first, shifting more resources from other areas of expenditure towards infrastructure, although here the opportunity cost of investing in infrastructure can be extremely high (an important issue brought out by Berechman); second, increasing resources available through greater private-sector participation in funding infrastructure; third, using the existing infrastructure more efficiently so as to reduce the need for additional capacity, through policies such as privatization, deregulation, wider application of efficient pricing, and managerial and organizational incentives. ISTEA has implications for each of these policy solutions, but in particular it has strong applications for the last one of increasing efficiency both within and between travel modes.

There are several of interesting aspects of ISTEA in terms of both the policy objectives and the processes for policy development many of which are covered by Paaswell. First, he brings out the attempt of ISTEA to consider transport from a multi-modal perspective rather than segmenting plans and funding by highway and transit modes. Alas, it is too early to analyse fully the distinctions between the theoretical outcomes and those in practice, although this will no doubt be subject to much future research.

Second, the environmental objectives (compliance with the Clean Air Act and Amendments) appear to be largely driving the transportation policy. The transportation policy is one of the means of achieving the environmental objectives. This, however, raises a number of possible conflicts, such as between supporters of stationary versus non-stationary pollution sources or, within transport, between different modes of transport. Issues that need to be resolved include: how choices between which groups should bear responsibility and cost for reducing pollution are made; the legitimacy and accountability of those making the choices; and the possibility of sub-optimal choices in terms of efficiency and equity. It is likely that new ways of achieving the goals will result and resolve these issues, and that these ways may vary according to location.

In a wider context this setting of objectives and leaving the local actors to determine ways of achieving a government's broad set of objectives is perhaps an example of what can be termed, in the European Union context, a form of subsidiarity (where the means of achieving objectives are determined at the lowest appropriate level). However, this raises the question of to what degree are the US Federal authorities willing to give up their power and how much will they interfere with decisions. Again there seem to be parallels with the way European Union policies are set and implemented, particularly in the case of regional development, where considerable decision-making authority is passed down to local level.

The third main issue concerns the process of policy development under ISTEA. There is to be a broadening of the contribution of different groups, including a greater involvement of the community in the decision-making process. Hence the political science literature on community involvement in transportation issues (such as subway extensions and new roads, see for instance Howitt, 1982) may provide useful insights on how well policies develop and are influenced, and on the skills and training needed by the various groups to participate effectively in the process.

The fourth point concerns how much ISTEA actually alters the amount and uses of resources, through taking a more comprehensive approach and relating the use of resources to improvements in the efficiency of the existing infrastruture. It will be interesting to see to what degree the allocation of resources does actually change over time. It is probably too early to answer the questions concerning most impacts of the policy and how conflicts between modes of travel and between different groups have been resolved. Will ISTEA lead to a fundamental change in transportation infrastructure investment, will it speed up the process of approving and building new infrastructure where necessary (will it reduce delays due to litigation etc), or will it in the end be watered down during implementation and have only limited effect on these issues? Paaswell provides an extremely useful basis upon which much future research into ISTEA and its wider lessons for other countries can be built.

4.3. TRANSPORT INFRASTRUCTURE INVESTMENT AND ECONOMIC DEVELOPMENT: A REVIEW OF KEY ANALYTICAL AND EMPIRICAL ISSUES

There is much conflicting evidence on the relationship between new transportation infrastructure investment and economic development (see for example: Gwilliam, 1979; Eagle and Stephanedes, 1987; and the debate on Aschauer's, 1989 and 1990, findings of a strong positive link between infrastructure and private sector total factor productivity, discussed by writers such as Munnell, 1993, Ford and Poret, 1991 and others). Berechman reviews a number of critical issues concerned with modelling or empirically measuring the impact of such infrastructure on economic growth. In discussing the choice and treatment of these issues, four main areas are looked at: the scale of perspective taken; the key variables linking transport and economic activity; the different impacts of different types of investment or industry; and the time period considered.

Firstly, Berechman considers the differences between the micro- and macro-perspectives (i.e. regional or metropolitan versus the state/country perspectives). From a micro-perspective economic growth may include both indigenous development, and also inter-regional moves into (or out of) the area. However, from the macro-perspective such inter-regional moves would form part of a zero sum game with no, *ceteris paribus*, effect on macro-economic growth. This does raise a number of questions concerning definitions and approaches to the analysis such as: the basis of the definition (e.g. administrative or functional); what are the implications of different definitions of the 'micro-level' for the analysis (e.g. the differences between focusing upon firms or local labour markets or interconnected systems of urban areas); which type of analysis should be used and in what circumstances; and how is the analysis affected by taking different definitions of economic growth? Also interesting is the question of the implications of different micro-foci of attention such as different actors (firms, labour etc.) within the local labour market, and the different implications for each of these?

Also, when considering different perspectives, there is a need to consider the differences between the policy and the modelling perspective, and the ways in which these may differ, when seeking to carry out economic analysis for policy development purposes (see Berechman and Small, 1988).

The second set of issues concerning Berechman's chapter is his use of accessibility as a link between transport infrastructure and investment and economic development. This usefully brings out a number of aspects of investment, such as: the differences between relative and absolute accessibility; the need for deeper analysis of access by different modes, travel time, etc; and the relative importance of accessibility compared to other factors. As transportation infrastructure investment may improve intra- and/or inter-regional accessibility, important policy issues revolve around differences between relative and absolute accessibility. Such investment may influence the accessibility of the region containing the infrastructure and of other regions, both relatively and absolutely. For example an investment made in a corridor region improves access in absolute terms (e.g. in travel times) of, say, the two regions on either side. However, an investment in one region will alter the relative accessibility of all other regions, for example large improvements in the airport of one region will affect the accessibility of other regions to, say, the core economic region relative to the region where investment has taken place. Hence the relative competitive advantage of all the regions will have changed.

Berechman shows that an investment will have considerably different impacts upon accessibility according to mode, travel time and industry, which raises the questions of which types of improved access are likely to have the biggest economic impacts (in given circumstances), and the equity implications of the impacts. In addition to infrastructure investments improving the potential physical accessibility, other factors will have a profound effect on actual usage such as costs and pricing mechanisms, including time costs, gasoline costs etc, and the pricing policies for the infrastructure and other transportation infrastructure.

Berechman considers the variables influencing the impact of infrastructure investments. The impacts of a given investment will be a function of: existing stock of infrastructure; the existing management policies; and the industries or households influenced. In particular the existing management policies such as bus lanes, quality of service, prices etc, highlight the need for a comprehensive analysis when evaluating the impact of investment. This need for a comprehensive approach is taken forward to some degree through the US Intermodal Surface Transportation Efficiency Act in the US.

In terms of time, the question arises as to whether the various issues raised by Berechman are equally applicable in the short-term and the long-term. In the short-term economic variables such as output and employment are usually measured; however, in the long-term the competitiveness and the growth capacity of a region, together with the standard of living, are other possible measures that can be linked with the more short-term measures. This raises the question as to whether the outcome and the issues raised are identical from a short-term and a long-term perspective or whether and how they are likely to differ.

Berechman shows the need for a deeper analysis of the impacts of new investment and how they vary according to: the nature of the investments; the local economy in which they are situated; and their effect upon other economies. In so doing, he also argues persuasively for the vital importance of *ex-post* impact analysis of transport infrastructure investment after implementation so as to improve future policy making and modelling.

In conclusion, both Berechmen and Paaswell raise important points for both the development of transportation infrastructure policies and for their implementaion. Their evidence shows the complexity of some of the issues and the importance of clear, explicit analysis.

References

Aschauer, D. (1989) Is public expenditure productive? *Journal of Monetary Economics*, **23**, pp. 177–200.

Aschauer, D.(1990) Why is infrastructure important? in Munnell, A.H. (ed.) *Is There a Shortfall in Public Capital Investment?* Boston: Federal Reserve Bank of Boston, Conference Series **34**, pp. 21–50.

Berechman, J. and Small, K.A. (1988) Research Policy and Review 25, Modelling land use and transportation: an interpretative review for growth areas. *Environment and Planning A*, **20**, pp. 1285–1309.

Eagle, D. and Stephanedes, Y.J. (1987) Dynamic highway impacts on economic development. *Transport Research Record*, No. 1116, pp. 56–62.

Ford, R. and Poret, P. (1991) Infrastructure and private-sector productivity. *OECD Economic Studies*, No. 17, Autumn, pp. 63–89.

Gwilliam, K.M. (1979) Transport infrastructure investments and regional investments, in Bowers, J.K. (ed.) *Inflation, Development and Integration – Essays in Honour of A.J. Brown*. Leeds: Leeds University Press.

Howitt, A.M. (1982) *Managing Federalism – Studies in Intergovernmental Relations*. Washington, DC: CQ Press.

Munnell, A.H. (1993) An assessment of trends in and economic impacts of infrastructure investment, in *Infrastructure Policies for the 1990s*. Paris: OECD, pp. 21–54.

Pucher, J., Ioannides, D. and Hirschman, I. (1993) Passenger transport in the United States and Europe: A comparative analysis of public-sector involvement, in Banister, D. and Berechman, J. (eds.) *Transport in a Unified Europe: Policies and Challenges*. Amsterdam: North-Holland, pp. 369–416.

Stevens, B. and Michalski, W. (1993) Infrastructure in the 1990's: an overview of trends and policy issues, in *Infrastructure Policies for the 1990s*. Paris: OECD, pp. 7–19.

CHAPTER 5

A EUROPEAN PERSPECTIVE ON THE SPATIAL LINKS BETWEEN LAND USE, DEVELOPMENT AND TRANSPORT

Peter Hall

5.1 INTRODUCTION

If there is a specifically European perspective on the links between transport, land use and development, it would have the following characteristics:

1. Europe, especially Western Europe, is densely populated and highly urbanized. Four out of ten people within the European Community live in major urban agglomerations; 50% in metropolitan areas with populations of 330,000 or more (Kunzmann and Wegener, 1991; Cheshire and Hay, 1989) (figure 5.1). These agglomerations are exceptionally concentrated in what could be called the Eurocore or Golden Rectangle, the boundaries of which are approximately Birmingham, Paris, Frankfurt and Dortmund (figure 5.2). This, one of the most highly urbanized regions of the world, includes South East England, three regions in France (Nord-Pas de Calais, the Paris Basin and Ile-de-France), all three in Belgium (the Walloon Region, Flanders and the Brussels Region) three in the Netherlands (South, West and East), one in Germany (North Rhine Westphalia), plus Luxembourg: twelve regions, essentially the Region of Central Capitals in the Europe 2000 study, occupies only 13 per cent of the land area of the EC (post-1990), but accounts for more than 25 per cent of the population, including 12 million people in the London metropolitan area, 11 million in Ile-de-France, between 4 and 5 million in the Randstad and 10 million in Rhine-Ruhr, not to mention the fact that these are among the major centres of global service activity in the entire world.

2. The position is complicated, of course, by the fact that the distribution of the population is very different from one European country to another.

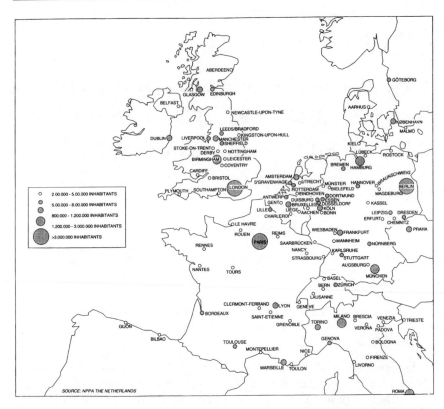

Figure 5.1   Europe: Urban agglomerations. (*Source*: Rijksplanologische Dienst)

France is like Britain in having a very high population concentration in its capital city. Other countries, like Germany, the Netherlands and Italy, have a more even distribution of the urban population in which a number of major provincial cities share, without one dominant conurbation. This is significant because very large cities tend to have a very much greater dependence on public transport, especially rail-based transport, than their medium-sized equivalents. London, Paris and now again Berlin have very elaborate rail systems which have no equivalents elsewhere. The other major European cities really compare much more closely with major provincial cities in Britain and France, like Birmingham, Manchester and Glasgow, Lille, Lyon and Marseille.

3.   These agglomerations, with rare exceptions, are based on old-established and traditionally structured cities with strong central business districts. Even though manufacturing and goods-handling activities may have registered sharp declines in some central cities, tertiary activities remain strongly concentrated there.

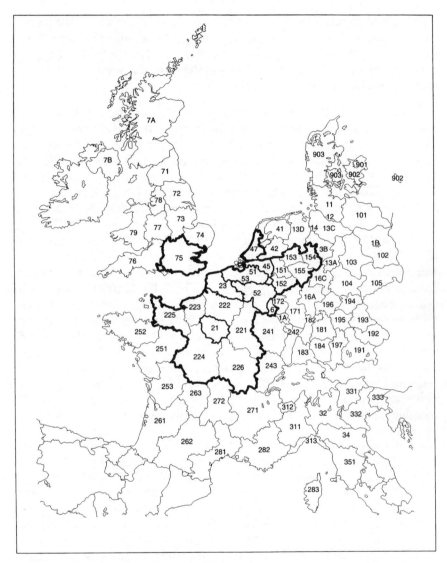

Figure 5.2   The 'Eurocore'. (*Source*: Eurostat)

4.   Traditionally all European cities were dense and compact, and depended almost exclusively on public transport. It is a common myth that British cities are less dense than continental European ones. Though inner Paris has roughly three times the population density of inner London, this is somewhat exceptional. If we compare the densities, ring by ring, of typical German and typical British provincial cities there is not much

significant difference; both have thinned out considerably over the last 60 years because of wartime destruction and postwar redevelopment. And, outside the city limits, cities in both countries have experienced low-density spread into the surrounding countryside, albeit reconcentrated in and around existing urban nuclei.

5. But, since World War II, at varying speeds and from varying starting points, cities in all Western European countries have decentralized: the process began in Britain and the Benelux countries in the 1950s, spread to Germany and Scandinavia in the 1960s and then finally affected the countries formerly thought immune – France, Italy, Spain and Portugal – in the 1970s and 1980s. The evidence is now overwhelming that both population and, behind it, employment are decentralizing, and that this process is most marked in the largest metropolitan areas, that is the ones with populations of one million and more (Hall and Hay, 1980; van den Berg *et al.*, 1982; Cheshire and Hay, 1989). With this process, especially the decentralization of employment, more and more journeys have transferred from public transport to the private car. And this has been associated with what researchers at MIT have called the Europeanization of the world-wide automobile revolution during the 1960s and 1970s, which caused Europe to enter the age of mass car ownership. Thus, though there is still a tendency for economic activity to centre on older central business districts, people and some activities have shown decentralization trends (Hall and Hay, 1980; Hall, 1988; Cheshire and Hay, 1989; Cheshire, 1994), and there has been a marked growth in suburban activity and in suburb-to-suburb commuting in recent years (Hall, Sands and Streeter, 1993).

6. With differences in detail from country to country, the pattern of urban decentralization has been contained by strong land-use planning systems, either into medium-density contiguous suburban extensions, or into outgrowths of freestanding smaller towns separated from their parent conurbations by green belts. In a few countries, planned new towns and satellite towns have played a major role in this pattern. Sometimes (as in the United Kingdom) these were planned as freestanding self-contained communities, though their self-containment seems to have weakened somewhat since 1970. In others (the Paris, Amsterdam and Stockholm areas) they were planned as part-commuter satellites from the start.

7. Planners have had a degree of control over this process because, especially in the early post-war years, public agencies directly provided a significant part of the total new housing stock. This, however, has greatly weakened in recent years with the movement towards a largely private supply of new housing.

8.   As elsewhere, personal and goods travel is dominated by the car and truck. But rail commands a significant share for commuting into the centres of the larger agglomerations, and for inter-city business and leisure travel. The development of high-speed rail during the 1980s has fortified the competitive position of rail *vis-à-vis* air.

In these respects, Europe resembles Japan and departs somewhat from American patterns of development.

5.2.   POLICY RESPONSES

Investing in Public Transport

In an effort to reduce the dependence on the private car, especially for commuting, European cities have invested extensively in new public transportation systems. It is perhaps significant that in most European countries during the 1980s, public transport shared in the general upward trend of passenger-kilometres travelled; Britain was an exception (Mackett, 1993). These investments have taken five main forms:

1.   Extensions of existing heavy rail systems in the largest cities; e.g. the Paris métro extensions beyond the gates of the traditional city, into the inner suburbs (the so-called *petite couronne*).

2.   New heavy rail systems (metros); generally, these have been built in cities of the second rank, including a number of capital cities or leading commercial centres that were growing rapidly, such as Stockholm (which actually started in the 1950s), Oslo, Brussels, Amsterdam, Rotterdam, Munich, Vienna, Lyon, Marseille, Madrid, Barcelona and Milan.

3.   Transformation of old tram systems into fully-fledged light rail systems, generally in third-order major provincial capital cities like Hannover, Frankfurt, Stuttgart, Nantes, Toulouse and Grenoble; Munich and Vienna have both heavy and light rail systems. In several of the German cities the systems have been undergrounded in the centres and the inner suburbs and relabelled (rather confusingly) U-Bahn, an appellation they share with the heavy rail systems. In general these systems do not extend very much farther than their old tramway equivalents, because they use the same tracks in the outer suburbs. Fully automated light rail systems, such as the VAL systems in Lille and Toulouse or the Docklands Light Rail in London, form a subset here, as do guided or unguided busway systems (Essen, Paris Sud-Est).

4.   New express rail systems (the RER in Paris, the S-Bahn systems in German cities) which are heavy commuter rail operations, usually run by the national rail networks, to connect city centres with major urban exten-

sions and with freestanding settlements within the extended commuter area. They have been built by connecting formerly separate commuter lines under the centres of the cities. Examples include Paris, Frankfurt, Stuttgart and Munich; in all these cities, they co-exist with heavy or light rail underground systems serving the shorter journeys, and are coordinated with them through well-designed interchanges and common ticketing systems. Merseyrail in Liverpool and the Blue Trains in Glasgow are British examples of this kind of operation; so is Thameslink in London; so, eventually (dependent on funding) would be Crossrail.

5.   High-speed inter-city rail systems, with sustained maximum speeds of 200 km/h and over, have been developed in Britain, France, Germany, Sweden, Italy and Spain. Though not intended as commuter routes, and even structured to discourage them (as in France), in at least one case (Britain) they have carried increasing numbers of long-distance commuters over the 70–130 km range (Reading and Didcot Parkway-London; Peterborough-London).

These new systems have been supported, indeed made necessary in some cases, by the growth of the major European cities to levels at which major new systems became viable. However, with the exception of the express systems and some limited light rail extensions along old rights of way, in general they have been restricted to the historic densely-built urban envelope. There is a good reason for this: the characteristics of the journey, including average speed and seating capacity, do not make them really suitable for longer-distance operations.

Restraints on the Car

Simultaneously, during the last two decades European cities have developed three striking innovations in curbing the use of the private car:

1.   Pedestrianization of central business cores, associated with special preferential access for surface public transport, or the undergrounding of surface transport, so as to make car access relatively less attractive, and access by public transport more attractive; to the extent that in the most spectacular cases, such as Munich, public transport becomes the preferred means of access (Hall and Hass-Klau, 1985). A variant, developed in Italian cities (such as Florence and Milan) during the late 1980s, consists in the complete barring of the central business district to the private car during daytime business hours.

2.   The use of traffic calming techniques, generally area-wide in networks of residential streets, but in a few cases – such as the Lister Meile in Hannover, a main radial street – to main traffic arteries with the aim of reducing speed and flow.

3. The major innovation of the 1990s: urban road pricing in major Norwegian cities – Bergen, Oslo and Trondheim – which charge for central access. The official justification of the Oslo scheme is not to restrain traffic but to pay for major road investments (in particular, a very expensive city-centre tunnel). But the next major Scandinavian scheme to come into operation, Stockholm in 1996, will have a double objective: the so-called Dennis plan, as well as helping to finance an expensive inner-ring road and an outer tangential highway, will restrain traffic in the entire inner city, with a predicted decrease in car traffic of no less than 34 per cent (Söderström, 1992; Tegnér, 1994) (figures 5.3(a) and 5.3(b)). A full road-pricing system is also under consideration for London.

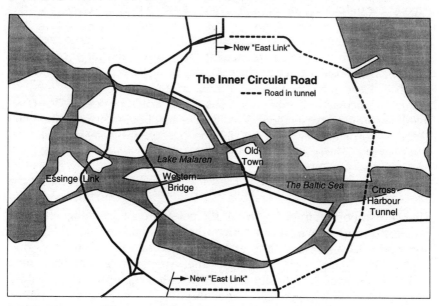

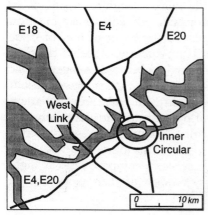

Figure 5.3(a)   Stockholm: The Dennis package: Inner ring. (*Source*: Söderström, 1992)

Figure 5.3(b)   Stockholm: The Dennis package: Western link. (*Source*: Söderström, 1992)

All these three kinds of scheme have been specifically urban, even inner-urban; conceptually, they assume that the problems of cities can be dealt with in isolation from the wider urban context. There is a resulting problem, as can be observed now in any German city: it has its S-Bahn, its U-Bahn, its pedestrian core, its traffic-calmed areas, its well-designed transport interchanges, its bike lanes. But, at the edge of the city, there are great flows of long-distance commuter cars, which extend far beyond S-Bahn range, into the villages which are the city's new outer suburbs – 60, 70, 80 kilometres distant – and as completely car-dependent as the outer suburbs of American cities. Similar effects may well occur with road pricing, which may well lead some kinds of activities, at least, to jump out beyond the outermost toll ring, to create a kind of polycentric spread-city urban form.

This is interesting because the countries that have experienced the most rapid long-term rises in car ownership have also been those that have invested the most in public transport, partly at least in reaction. These countries happen to have invested more in transport generally; there is nothing particularly virtuous about this, and it would be possible to argue that one country invests too little or that its neighbours invest too much. The question could be resolved only by a very elaborate international cost-benefit analysis, which has not been made.

5.3.   SIZE, DENSITY AND PUBLIC TRANSPORT STRATEGIES

There are important implications for the possibility of providing effective public transport. Newman and Kenworthy's well-known study (Newman and Kenworthy, 1989a,b, 1992) argues that overall, European cities (including British ones) are denser than either Australian or American ones, and that this is systematically associated with a higher usage of public transport and with lower energy consumption per capita: average petrol consumption in American cities is nearly twice as high as in Australian cities and four times higher than in European cities. Differences in petrol prices, income and vehicle efficiency explain only about half of these variations. What is significant is the urban structure: cities with strong concentrations of central jobs, and accordingly a better-developed public transport system, have much lower energy use than cities where the jobs were scattered. Overall, Newman and Kenworthy found a strong relationship between energy use and the use of public transport, especially rail, and provision for the car. In European cities, 25% of all passenger travel is by public transport and only 44% use a car for the journey to work. The importance of walking or biking in these more compact cities is highlighted by the fact that 21% use these modes for their work trip. In Amsterdam the proportion rises to 28% and in Copenhagen to 32%.

Newman and Kenworthy's work has been criticized methodologically (Schipper and Meyers, 1992) and ideologically (Gordon and Richardson, 1989; Gordon, Richardson and Jun, 1991). Gordon and Richardson argue that Newman and Kenworthy's analysis is faulty, that the problems are wrongly diagnosed, and that their policy and planning prescriptions are inappropriate and infeasible. Newman and Kenworthy, they say, neglect the considerable suburbanization of employment that has occurred in American cities. This co-location of decentralized firms and households has reduced, not lengthened, commuting times and distances.

The problem is that Gordon and Richardson's conclusion relates only to the United States. Even if we rework Newman and Kenworthy's figures (and a number of people are doing just that), the overall conclusion probably remains good. The point here is that, even though settlement structures may appear superficially similar, densities (of single-family homes for instance) tend to be higher in Europe than in Australia or America; this is fairly obvious from even a cursory comparison of, say, Paris new towns or the suburbs of the Hague with the outskirts of Sydney or Atlanta. If to this we join the fact that in general European settlements tend to be more compact, there is a better basis for viable public transport including rail-based transport.

But there does remain a question as to where these European cities are going. By trying hard to keep their major city centres strong in all respects – as centres for offices, for shopping, for entertainment – the policy-makers may be contributing to the very problem they are trying to solve. European strategic planners would deny this, arguing that it is possible to have the best of both worlds by encouraging central concentration, subsidizing public transport and restraining traffic. But Gordon and Richardson may also be right in arguing that we should encourage outward movement of employment closer to where the people actually live, thus reducing journey to work lengths – a process the British have been encouraging in the London region ever since the original Mark One new towns begun in 1946-50. And urban road pricing could actually act as an agent of this process, strengthening market trends.

5.4. THE RELATIONSHIP TO URBAN SUSTAINABILITY

Planning researchers have only just begun to think about these questions within the framework of urban sustainability. Much of the work is still quite theoretical (Banister, 1992; Banister and Banister, 1995; Banister and Button, 1993; Breheny, 1991, 1992; Breheny and Rookwood, 1993; Owens, 1984, 1986, 1990, 1992a,b; Owens and Cope, 1992; Rickaby, 1987, 1991; Rickaby et al., 1992). Owens concludes that the 'ideal' energy-efficient urban form would combine clusters of relatively small settlements at the regional scale, with compact settlements, probably linear or rectangular in form, at the sub-regional scale, and medium-high residential density, with well-dispersed employment, at the local scale. Energy efficiency, she stresses, does not imply very high densities, and a pedestrian scale cluster of 20–30,000 people will provide a sufficient threshold for many activities without resort to high densities. Breheny (1992) also criticizes the conventional wisdom that higher densities represent sustainability, questioning the EC's Green Paper on the Urban Environment on this ground. At the neighbourhood scale, an architect-planner like the Californian designer Peter Calthorpe has won a great deal of acclaim for his ideas for pedestrian pockets, which encourage people to walk to shops or public transport stops.

The problem is that more empirical work is needed. Some definitive work is now twenty years or more old (Stone, 1973). Most recently, research on energy use in transport (Banister, 1993; Banister and Button, 1993) has established that some robust empirical relationships have been developed; yet too little is known about the key parameters which make up an 'efficient' city in transport and energy terms. Especially this is true at the larger scale of the metropolitan region, where *strategic* decisions need to be made: for instance, whether to concentrate development at higher densities within the existing urban envelope – for instance, by redeveloping older lower-density housing by more dense forms of development, including apartments – or whether to encourage decentralization to new towns or satellite communities at some distance from the existing agglomeration. In terms of energy consumption and production of pollutants, it is not at all clear which is the better of these two courses of action. On the one hand, by concentrating development in higher-density, more compact cities, we would reduce the average length of trips; we would also allow more of them to be made by public transport. But this would depend very much on where the jobs were located. For instance, if jobs moved out to the edge of the city or beyond, while homes remained crowded in the cities, we might get the worst of both worlds: poor living conditions *and* long commuter journeys by car on congested roads. In that case, the result might be worse in environmental terms than if people, jobs and journeys were located in a relatively uncongested, properly planned new town.

What is critical here is first whether people will move in the ways the planners expect them to do, and secondly whether and when they also change the location of their jobs. As the experience of the British new towns suggested after World War II, satellite communities that provide housing and employment close to each other, at a sufficient distance from the parent metropolis, can prove highly self-contained and so highly sustainable in travel terms. True, that was forty years ago; it may be impossible to achieve a similar outcome today, with two-earner house-holds and much greater specialization and sophistication in the employment market, which means that people leave the same house each morning in quite different directions; but the fact is that we do not know.

Research might start by re-examining the work of Newman and Kenworthy, since only by addressing the criticisms directly can we hope to settle the debate about urban form and energy use. The importance of physical factors such as density would be supplemented by demographic, economic, social and spatial factors so that the complexity of city structure can be assessed against energy consumption. This empirical research would establish which are the key parameters in determining energy efficient urban form in terms of transport characteristics. At a later stage of research, the energy consumption of other types of land uses could be assessed to give a total picture of energy use in urban areas in terms of different kinds of land use – housing, commercial and industrial. As usual, it would be both necessary and desirable to alternate between the generation of idealized models of urban structure and function, and empirical validation. There will doubtless never be total agreement, but it ought to be possible to generate research findings that would serve as a robust basis for policy at different spatial scales and in different urban-geographical contexts.

This underlines the point that planners should consider land use and transport as one seamless web, and handle the two in some very delicate combination. The trouble is that this combination is so subtle, no one anywhere seems to have completely understood how to make it work at a fine-tuned level. Ever since Peter Daniels' pioneering work (Daniels and Warnes, 1990), we have known that if we decentralize activities two contradictory things happen: commuter journeys are shortened, but there is a huge transfer from public transport to the private car. Overwhelming evidence worldwide now shows that exactly this was happening in major metropolitan areas – in Europe, in America, in Australia – during the 1980s. Further, a recent study shows that typical metropolitan areas in Europe and in America – Paris, Frankfurt and San Francisco – have all decentralized homes and jobs, leading to a huge growth in suburb-to-suburb commuting and a corresponding shift from public transport to car. In the Frankfurt region, for instance, public transport had a respectable share of nearly 41% of all trips within and between cities, it captured just under 27% of suburb-to-city trips, and 15% of suburb-to-suburb trips. But the car dominated everywhere: it had more than 57% share of city commuting trips, 83% of those in inner suburbs and 86% of those in outer suburbs (Hall, Sands and Streeter, 1993).

The dominance of the car was particularly evident for local trips to work within the outer suburbs, which absolutely dominate the trip matrix in these zones: for the San Francisco Bay Area in 1980, the share was 98%; for Frankfurt in 1987, 86%; for Paris in 1982, 87%. The conclusion is hard to resist: though both the Paris and Frankfurt regions have invested massively in new public transport, and the Parisian planners have been extremely successful in integrating land-use and transportation planning for radial journeys, including reverse commuting, they have failed to do any better than other major metropolitan areas in adapting transit to the pure suburb-to-suburb commute. Reducing car dependence in these outer suburbs, then, can be regarded as the key element of a future metropolitan transportation strategy.

There are however some interesting details. In Paris, the inner suburbs are developed at a very high density, more resembling inner London than outer London. They go on supporting a dense use of public transport even for trips within and between the suburbs, as well as for journeys into Paris. The outer suburbs, including the new towns, are very different; there, everyone uses the car to get from one suburb to another.

5.5.   RECENT URBAN POLICY INITIATIVES

It thus appears that everywhere – in Britain, in Europe, in America – cities are actually moving away from sustainable patterns rather than towards them. It is not clear to anyone how, or even whether, we can reverse this trend. But there are one or two pointers.

Paris

Planners in Paris have developed a strategy to take care of the suburb-to-suburb commute problem that has resulted from suburbanization. ORBITALE (*Organisation Régionale dans le Bassin Intérieur des Transports Annulaires Libérés d'Encombrements*) is a new 175-km transit system to serve the higher-density inner suburbs, running mainly on grade-separated rights-of-way, but with some street stretches, and with 50 transfer points to the existing radial transit system, to be built at an estimated cost of 40 billion francs; 236 million francs per km exclusive of rolling stock, garages, or maintenance facilities. Four sections are open or under construction: a conventional tramway in the north; a dedicated exclusive busway in the south-east; an automated light rail (VAL) line in the south-west, serving Orly airport; and conversion to light rail of an existing rail line in the south-west. The first three are open; the last will be completed in 1996 (Direction Régionale, 1990, pp. 22–23) (figure 5.4(a)).

Completion of ORBITALE will, however, still leave the problem of connecting the outer suburbs and in particular the five new towns, which are located at an average distance of about 15 miles (25 kilometres) from the centre of Paris, with correspondingly long circumferential distances between them. Here, there is a longer-term plan: LUTECE (*Liaisons à Utilisation Tangentielle En Couronne Extérieure*), an extension of the RER (Regional Express Rail) system to link the new towns and strategic sectors with one another (Institut d'Aménagement, 1990, pp. 82–83) (figure 5.4(*b*)).

ORBITALE and LUTECE are integrated into the 1991 regional plan for the Ile-de-France, and form a central part of the transport element of the plan; they address some deficiencies of the primarily radial system developed as part of the earlier 1965 plan, and they link the principal activity nodes that are identified in the new plan (Anon, 1991*a,b*). But they are not consciously designed as part of an integrated land-use-transportation strategy; that would be impossible, given that the land uses are mainly in place and that the major emphasis over the next 20 years is on consolidation.

The Netherlands

So we must look elsewhere to find such an integrated plan. We find it in the Netherlands, where the government has taken some kind of a world-wide lead in trying to integrate land use and transport planning, within an environmental strategy, at a national level. Between 1990 and 2015, the Dutch planners predict another million and a half people to be added to the 15 million today; per capita income is expected to rise by more than 40%; there will be a need for two million extra dwellings; with more than five million cars today, they predict an increase to about eight million. All these pressures will be concentrated very heavily in and around the four great urban areas of Randstad Holland; of the two million extra houses, for instance, no less than one million will be built here.

The fourth report (EXTRA) on Physical Planning in the Netherlands, published by the Dutch Ministry of Housing, Physical Planning and the Environment in 1991 under the title *On the Road to 2015*, outlines a policy to cope with these pressures and to improve the quality of urban life and reduce car traffic in cities and urban regions, through an integrated approach integrating traffic and transport policy, environmental policy and physical planning policy. It has three bases. First, a location policy that keeps distances and trips to a minimum. Second, superior amenities for slower traffic and public transport. Third, promotion of public transport through stricter parking policy, and perhaps other measures.

The key is to concentrate residences, work areas and amenities so as to produce the shortest possible trip distances, most being possible by bicycle and public transport. So housing sites are being sought first in the inner cities, next on the urban periphery and only in the third place at

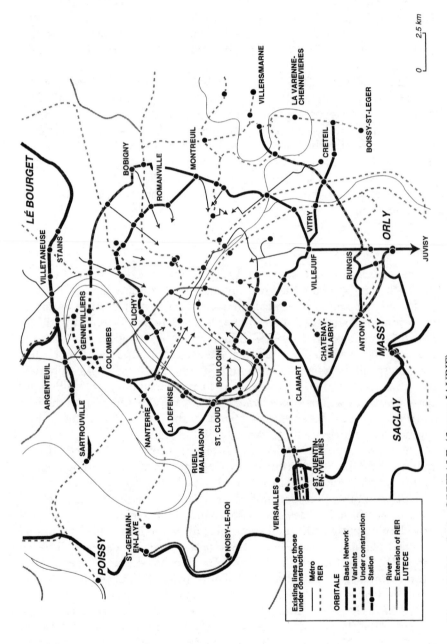

Figure 5.4(a) Paris: ORBITALE. (Source: IAURIF)

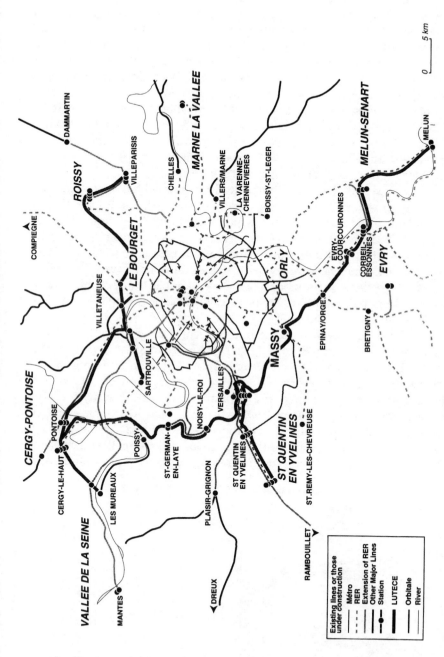

Figure 5.4(*b*) Paris: LUTECE. (*Source:* IAURIF)

more distant locations; wherever the sites are found, transport will be a key factor. Businesses and amenities are planned by relating their user requirements to location features. Those activities involving a large number of workers or visitors per hectare, such as offices oriented to the general public, theatres and museums, are rated A-profile, that is they should be located close to city-centre stations. B locations are those with both good station access and good access to motorways, making them suitable for access by both car and public transport; activities suitable for location here include hospitals, research and development, and white collar industry. C-locations, close to motorways, are suitable only for activities with relatively few workers and visitors per hectare and with a need for high accessibility by car or truck (figure 5.5).

Associated with this, the Report calls for integrated transport/land-use planning so as to enhance the role of public transport. Three spatial levels are linked to the three public transport networks: the national level to inter-city (including European inter-city) and inter-regional rail traffic; the urban level to commuter trains, underground, fast tram services and express buses, and the local level for regular trams and buses. Related to this is a third element: promotion of the use of public transport by restricting long-term parking places, associated with the provision of good public transport (Netherlands, 1991).

The Dutch approach is stimulating a great deal of interest and even imitation elsewhere in Europe (e.g. London Planning Advisory Committee, 1994). But there is a problem: trends all over Europe suggest that people and activities are continuing to disperse into ever-more-car-dependent forms of living and working. Michael Breheny's recent analysis shows that in Britain (1993), dispersion has led to more energy use than if the population distribution had remained constant in the patterns of 1961. However, and this is perhaps surprising, the effect is not nearly as large as might be expected, of the order of 2–3 per cent. Recent

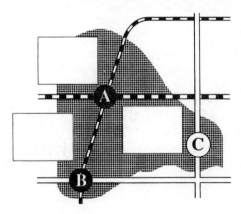

Figure 5.5   Netherlands: The A-B-C strategy. (*Source*: Netherlands, 1991)

work from the United States and Australia reveals no agreement: but perhaps near-consensus could be reached on one point, that, because jobs were moving out to the suburbs where the people were, commuter journey lengths were not lengthening very much and were actually shortening in some cases. However, they were transferring from energy-efficient public transport to private cars, which was anti-sustainable. That suggested one solution: develop a public transport system that could cope with dispersed suburban journeys. It might be something like the French ORBITALE and LUTECE, but the American approach, used recently in a number of cities, was both less ambitious and perhaps more radical: it was fleets of deregulated minibuses running in all directions, using specially-designated motorway lanes wherever congestion threatened to delay them.

From this standpoint, the Dutch 2015 Report could be criticized on the grounds of fundamentalism: it is not evident as to how the Dutch derive their policies, or indeed whether there is any firm research justification at all. One can argue that it must be correct to encourage activities close to public transport access. Where it does become complicated, and perhaps tendentious, is in assuming that town-cramming is axiomatically justified, quite apart from the question of feasibility. In the Dutch context, it might make equal or more sense to relieve pressure on the Randstad by promoting moderately-sized, moderate-density cities elsewhere in the Netherlands – a policy the Dutch supported in the 1960s, but then abandoned.

5.6. HIGH-SPEED RAIL IMPACTS

The new high-speed rail systems present an additional complication here, since they are relatively new in Europe and their impacts are by no means yet clear. Studies in Japan and in France seem to show that they will revolutionize the pattern of business travel, seizing from the airlines the great majority of all trips – between 80% and 90% – in the distance range between approximately 100 miles (160 km) and 300 miles (500 km) and about 50% of the traffic up to 500 miles (800 km) (Berlioz and Leboeuf, 1986; Bonnafous, 1987; Houee, 1986; Journet, 1989; Kamada, 1980; Pommelet, 1989; Potter, 1987; Sanuki, 1980; Straszak and Tuch, 1980). That is evident from the well-documented cases of the original Tokaido Shinkansen, which has now been in operation for 30 years and is operating at capacity, and the original TGV Sud-Est opened in 1986 (Bonnafous, 1987). Since the key urban agglomerations of the Eurocore region – London, Ile-de-France, Brussels, Randstad-Holland and Rhine-Ruhr – are large and are within the magic 300-mile radius, we should assume a quite radical reorientation of travel in this region; the impacts will surely be similar to those of the original railways 150 years ago, or jet air service 40 years ago.

The impacts will be particularly profound in South East England. Heathrow was located as the result of a secret decision in 1943; at the last count it had a direct employment of 53,000 people and an indirect employment that no one can accurately estimate but must be at least twice, and perhaps three times, that figure. The total effect on the subsequent development of South East England can never be accurately estimated; we do know that, for instance, American and other multinational electronics manufacturers were critically attracted to locate in the M4 Corridor by the airport's existence, and by the opportunities it offered for rapid movement of key personnel (service engineers, for instance) and high-value air freight (Hall, Breheny, McQuaid and Hart, 1987).

Effects like these suggest that the location of the new high-speed links will be equally important. But there is only fragmentary evidence of what might happen: there are relatively few high-speed railways, the oldest is less than 30 years old, and most are much newer than that. It is also because in each case the effects are very difficult to disentangle from the effects of other phenomena. Just as on the M4 it is difficult to unpick the Heathrow effect from the impact of the Government Defence Research Establishments that were clustered here, or from the generally high quality ambience of the corridor, so it is difficult to unpick the impact of the Shinkansen from the fact that the Tokaido Corridor west of Tokyo, through which it runs, is the Japanese equivalent of the M4 Corridor, the crucible of Japan's high-tech revolution.

We must therefore speculate from anecdotal evidence. British Rail's first high-speed line, the InterCity 125 from London to Bristol, opened in 1976. The area around Reading Station is now the third office centre in southern England after Central London and Croydon. However, office development was occurring even before 1976, associated with Reading's favourable position west of Heathrow, in the high-technology manufacturing belt that has come to be known as the M4 Corridor (even though the motorway was completed only in 1971, just five years before the train service opened). Similarly, at Bristol Parkway station 111 miles from London, there has been extensive recent campus-type office development; but again, Bristol has been a successful high-technology industrial centre and a favoured location for decentralized offices because of its location on the M4 Corridor, and the site is close to the major interchange between two national motorways, the M4 and M5.

An early example of the impact of high-speed line was the development of the new commercial quarter around the new station at Lyon Part-Dieu, now the most favoured office location in the city, where total office space rose by 43 per cent between 1983 and 1990. On the other hand, the new station at Le Creusot, standing in a greenfield site, conspicuously failed to attract development (Sands, 1993a, p. 25).

In Nantes, a major regional centre in Brittany, located 230 miles (380 km) from Paris, the city and private developers have collaborated to develop a mixed-use development incorporating a major conference centre and office park with about 592,000 ft² (55,000 m²) on the 6.7 acre (2.7 ha) site of an old biscuit factory (the Quartier Lu, officially the Quartier Champ-de-Mars-Madeleine), next to the new TGV-Atlantique station, which opened in 1990. Rents are running at about 20 per cent above the city centre average (Sands, 1993a, pp. 31–36). However, like Reading and Bristol, Nantes was already a high-tech centre in its own right, and was proving attractive as a regional office location. At Massy in the south-west suburbs of Paris the local authority plans a huge European business centre around the TGV station which opened in 1993, serving the new Interconnection around Paris which was opened in 1994; but, once again, this will exploit the fact that the site is gateway to the *Cité Scientifique Ile-de-France Sud*, the French equivalent of the M4 Corridor. Similarly, there is very extensive office and other commercial development at the other end of the Paris Interconnection, at Roissy-CDG Airport; but this is attracted to the airport location at least as much as to the TGV. In Lille a public-private partnership is building the Euralille Centre around the new TGV station, which opened to coincide with the start of through Eurostar services via the Channel Tunnel.

In Sweden the 1991 Mälardalen Regional Plan specifically proposes the use of new high-speed train services as a way of linking Stockholm with cities in this distance range such as Ensköping, Västerås, Eskilstuna and Örebrö. This appears to be the first case in which a regional development plan has been deliberately structured around the existence of high-speed links.

But the most important case, because the best-documented, is a Japanese example: Shin Yokohama, some 15 miles south-west of Tokyo. Shin Yokohama, New Yokohama, was a station in a green field, when it opened on the New Trunk Line in 1964. Ten years later it had achieved a ridership of 15,000 a day, but the figures fell to an average of 10,000 a day for the next decade. But then an underground station opened, cutting the journey to central Yokohama, four miles away, to 12 minutes. Then the Japanese Railways improved the service: as well as the ordinary Kodama express trains, which make stops about every 50 miles (80 km) or so, rather like the British 125s, they added the Hikari super-expresses which now run at 170 mph (270 km/h) stopping only at Nagoya, Kyoto and Osaka. Now, nearly half of all the super-expresses, 48 out of 105 each day in 1990, stop here. In a mere five years ridership nearly trebled, to 27,000 a day in 1989, the fastest growth of any station on the entire system. The physical result is quite anomalous: half the site, on one side of the railway, is still a rather derelict green field defiled by scrapyards and similar uses, because local

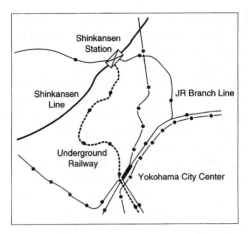

Figure 5.6   Shin-Yokohama.
(*Source*: Sands, 1993*b*)

citizens have resisted development. The other is an Edge City of concentrated new office development, which is evidently the creation of the railway: about one kilometre long and one third of a kilometre deep (Sands, 1993*b*) (figure 5.6).

Shin Yokohama makes quite clear the development potential of high-speed trains. The only question is how many such development nodes it is realistic to create. In Britain, the government in 1993 confirmed the route of the Channel Tunnel High Speed link to London through the East Thames Corridor, and has confirmed that three sites within the Corridor are being retained as possible candidates for intermediate stations (G.B. Department of Transport, 1994). It is a fair assumption that not less than one and not more than two will be taken forward. Promoter groups have already suggested possible developments, but so far without firm commitments. At Stratford they propose offices, an hotel, retailing, and a science park around parking for 5,000 cars, relying on the fact that St Pancras will not be and could never be a park-and-ride station, and that by the year 2000 the North Circular improvements and the Hackney-M11 link will have created a new northern expressway through the north London suburbs from Ealing to the river, passing within half a mile of Stratford. They are also, of course, relying on the synergistic effects in helping to trigger the revival of London Dockland Development Corporation based redevelopment both on the Isle of Dogs and in the Royal Docks, a few minutes away. At Havering Riverside (also known as Rainham) there are ambitious ideas for an international trade mart, a university campus, a technology park and international offices, as well as an hotel, benefiting the big tracts of developable land at that point, and from the location close to the M25 via the new A13, due to start construction next month. At Ebbsfleet, Blue Circle are proposing a huge European-oriented office business park, again benefiting from the location close to the M25 Dartford toll plaza.

Whatever the outcome of the negotiations, which should be completed sometime in 1995, the long-term outcomes will remain uncertain until the line is opened, probably about 2002. Even then, as the limited previous experience indicates, it is extremely difficult to distinguish the effect of high-speed trains from a multiplicity of other effects that in effect made the high-speed investment viable: the general regional dynamism of a corridor, the industrial mix and changes in it, the relationship to major population and employment centres, and the accessibility arising from previous investments in conventional rail, highways and airports. As with previous waves of transport and urban development, new transport technologies reinforce the importance of old-established axes of communication, but also powerfully transform the relative positions of different centres along them; and this new technology will be no exception.

Because of this uncertainty, it is unsurprising that expert estimates of the development potential of high-speed rail stations should differ quite profoundly. This is particularly the case at Stratford in east London, close to the London Docklands redevelopment, where the independent assessments of development potential, in terms of developable floorspace – by PIEDA for Union Railways, and by Victor Hausner Associates and Llewelyn Davies Planning – appear to vary by a factor of between 2.5 to 3.8 or even more (PIEDA, 1993). These discrepancies partly arise from different evaluation frameworks, in both geographical and time terms; they also reflect the huge uncertainty of predicting demand for new office, retail and commercial facilities at a time when the property market is very depressed and there is a large overhang of unlet office space in central London and Docklands.

There is however an even more basic factor: the difficulty of predicting long-term parametric shifts in the pattern of development potential and resulting land values, arising from fundamental transport investments and/or major redevelopment schemes involving public-private partnership. The same would undoubtedly have been true for consultants attempting to assess the development potential of Heathrow in 1943, had such a step even been contemplated. It would equally have been true of London Docklands in 1980: the original expectations of the Development Corporation appear to have been quite modest, and the Canary Wharf proposal consequently came as a surprise. Since future developments around high-speed stations involve both a new technology and public-private partnership, any forecasting exercise is likely to approach the limits of the possible.

References

Anon (1989a) Roissy et le Bocage de France, Porte d'Entrée française en Europe. *Cahiers de l'Institut de l'Aménagement et d'Urbanisme de la Région d'Ile-de-France*, **89**, pp. 8–26.

Anon (1989b) Un Pôle Européen à Massy. *Cahiers de l'Institut de l'Aménagement et d'Urbanisme de la Région d'Ile-de-France*, **89**, pp. 32–48.

Anon (1991) *La Charte de L'Ile-de-France: Une Ambition à l'Heure de l'Ouverture de l'Europe.* (*Cahiers de l'Institut d'Aménagement et d'Urbanisme de la Région d'Ile-de-France, 97/98*). Paris: Conseil Régional Ile-de-France.

Anon (1991) *The Ile-de-France Planning Strategy: Our Ambition as Europe Opens Up.* (*Summary of the Project presented by the Regional Executive*). Paris: Conseil Régional Ile-de-France.

Banister, D. (1992) Energy use, transportation and settlement patterns, in Breheny, M.J. (ed.) *Sustainable Development and Urban Form* (European Research in Regional Science, 2). London: Pion, pp. 160–181.

Banister, D. (1993) Policy Responses in the U.K. In: Banister, D. and Button, K. (eds.) *Transport, the Environment and Sustainable Development.* London: E. & F. Spon, pp. 53–78.

Banister, D. and. Banister, C. (1995) A macro level analysis of energy consumption in transport in Great Britain. *Transportation Research*, **29A**, pp. 21–32.

Banister, D. and Button, K. (1993) Environmental policy and transport: An overview, in Banister, D. and Button, K. (eds.) *Transport, the Environment and Sustainable Development.* London: E and FN Spon, pp. 1–15.

Berlioz, C. and Leboeuf, M. (1986) Les résultats du TGV Paris – Sud-Est. Bilan *a posteriori* du TGV Sud-Est. *Révue Générale des Chemins de Fer*, **196**, pp. 759–768.

Bonnafous, A. (1987) The regional impact of the TGV. *Transportation*, **14**, pp. 127–138.

Breheny, M. (1991) Contradictions of the compact city. *Town and Country Planning*, **60**, p. 21.

Breheny, M.J. (ed.) (1992) *Sustainable Development and Urban Form* (European Research in Regional Science, 2). London: Pion.

Breheny, M. (1993) *Counterurbanisation and Sustainable Urban Forms.* Paper presented at the Fourth International Workshop on Technological Change and Urban Form: Productive and Sustainable Cities, Berkeley, California, 14–16 April.

Breheny, M. and Rookwood, R. (1993) Planning the sustainable city region, in Blowers, A. (ed.) *Planning for a Sustainable Environment*, London: Earthscan, pp. 150–189.

Cheshire, P.C. (1994) A New Phase of Urban Development in Western Europe?: An Analysis of 1990/1 Census Data for EU Countries. University of Reading, Discussion Papers in Urban & Regional Economics, No. 91. Reading: University, Department of Economics.

Cheshire, P.C. and Hay, D.G. (1989) *Urban Problems in Western Europe: An Economic Analysis.* London: Unwin Hyman.

Daniels, P.W. and Warnes, A.M. (1980) *Movement in Cities: Spatial Perspectives in Urban Transport and Travel.* London: Methuen.

Direction Régionale de l'Equipement d'Ile-de-France (1990) *Les transports de voyageurs en Ile-de-France, 1989.* Paris: DREIF.

G.B. Department of Transport (1994) *Channel Tunnel Rail Link: Report of the Interdepartmental Working Group of Officials.* London: Department of Transport.

Gordon, P. and Richardson, H.W. (1989) Gasoline consumption and cities – A reply. *Journal of the American Planning Association*, **55**, pp. 342–346.

Gordon, P., Richardson, H.W. and Jun, M. (1991) The commuting paradox – Evidence from the top twenty. *Journal of the American Planning Association*, **57**, pp. 416–420.

Hall, P. (1988) Urban growth and decline in Western Europe, in Dogan, M. and Kasarda, J.D. (eds.) *The Metropolis Era*. Vol. 1: *A World of Giant Cities*. Beverly Hills and London: Sage, pp. 111–127.

Hall, P., Breheny, M., McQuaid, R. and Hart, D. (1987) *Western Sunrise: The Genesis and Growth of Britain's Major High-Tech Corridor*. London: Allen and Unwin.

Hall, P. and Hass-Klau, C. (1985) *Can Rail save the City? The Impacts of Rail Rapid Transit and Pedestrianisation on British and German Cities*. Aldershot: Gower.

Hall, P. and Hay, D. (1980) *Growth Centres in the European Urban System*. London: Heinemann Education.

Hall, P., Sands, B. and Streeter, W. (1993) Managing the Suburban Commute: A Cross-National Comparison of Three Metropolitan Areas. University of California at Berkeley, Institute of Urban and Regional Development, Working Paper 596.

Houee, M. (1986) The relations between high speed trains and the organization of regional transport services. *Journal of Advanced Transportation*, **20**, pp. 107–132.

Institut d'Aménagement et d'Urbanisme de la Région d'Ile-de-France, and Consiel Régional Ile-de-France (1990) *ORBITALE: Un Réseau de Transports en Commun de Rocade en Zone Centrale*, Paris: IAURIF.

Journet, M. (1989) Link round Paris forges TGV network. *Railway Gazette International*, **145**, pp. 471–473.

Kamada, M. (1980) Achievements and future problems of the Shinkansen, in Straszak, A. and Tuch, R. (eds.) *The Shinkansen High-Speed Rail Network of Japan: Proceedings of an IIASA Conference, June 27–30, 1977*. Oxford: Pergamon, pp. 41–56.

Kunzmann, K.R. and Wegener, M. (1991) The pattern of urbanization in Western Europe. *Ekistics*, No. 350, pp. 282–291.

London Planning Advisory Committee (1994) *1994 Advice on Strategic Planning Guidance for London*. Romford: LPAC.

Mackett, R. (1993) Why are Continental Cities more Civilised than British Ones? Paper presented at the 25th Universities Study Group Annual Conference, Southampton.

Netherlands, Ministry of Housing, Physical Planning and the Environment (1991) *Fourth Report (EXTRA) on Physical Planning in the Netherlands: Comprehensive Summary: On the Road to 2015*. The Hague: Ministry of Housing, Physical Planning and the Environment, Department for Information and International Relations.

Newman, P.W.G. and Kenworthy, J.R. (1989a) *Cities and Automobile Dependence: A Sourcebook*. Aldershot: Gower.

Newman, P.W.G. and Kenworthy, J.R. (1989b) Gasoline consumption and cities: A comparison of U.S. cities with a global survey. *Journal of the American Planning Association*, **55**, pp. 24–37.

Newman, P.W.G. and Kenworthy, J.R. (1992) Is there a role for physical planners? *Journal of the American Planning Association*, **58**, pp. 353–362.

Owens, S.E. (1984) Spatial structure and energy demand, in Cope, D.R., Hills, P.R. and James, P. (eds.) *Energy Policy and Land Use Planning*. Oxford: Pergamon, pp. 215–240.

Owens, S.E. (1986) *Energy, Planning and Urban Form*. London: Pion.

Owens, S.E. (1990) Land-use planning for energy efficiency, in Cullingworth, J.B. (ed.) *Energy, Land and Public Policy*. Newark, Del.: Transactions Publishers, Center for Energy and Urban Policy Research, pp. 53–98.

Owens, S.E. (1992a) Energy, environmental sustainability and land-use planning, in Breheny, M.J. (ed.), *Sustainable Development and Urban Form* (European Research in Regional Science, 2). London: Pion.

Owens, S.E. (1992b) Land-use planning for energy efficiency. *Applied Energy*, **43**, pp. 81–114.

Owens, S.E. and Cope, D. (1992) *Land Use Planning Policy and Climate Change*. London: HMSO.

PIEDA (1993) *Intermediate Station Options: Socio-Economic and Development Aspects. Final Report*. Reading: PIEDA.

Pommelet, P. (1989) Roissy et Massy dans le Project Régional d'Aménagement. *Cahiers de l'Institut de l'Aménagement et d'Urbanisme de la Région d'Ile-de-France*, **89**, pp. 27–31.

Potter, S. (1987) *On the Right Lines? The Limits of Technological Innovation*. London: Frances Pinter.

Rickaby, P.A. (1987) Six settlement patterns compared. *Environment and Planning B*, **14**, pp. 193–223.

Rickaby, P.A. (1991) Energy and urban development in an archetypal English town. *Environment and Planning B*, **18**, pp. 153–176.

Rickaby, P.A., Steadman, J.B. and Barrett, M.(1992) Patterns of land use in English towns: Implications for energy use and carbon monoxide emissions, in Breheny, M.J. (ed.) *Sustainable Development and Urban Form* (European Research in Regional Science, 2). London: Pion, pp. 182–196.

Sands, B.D. (1993a) The Development Effects of High-Speed Rail Stations and Implications for California. University of California, Institute of Urban and Regional Development, Working Paper 566.

Sands, B.D. (1993b) The development effects of high-speed rail stations and implications for California. *Built Environment*, **19**, pp. 257–284.

Sanuki, T. (1980) The Shinkansen and the future image of Japan, in Straszak, A. and Tuch, R. (eds.), *The Shinkansen High-Speed Rail Network of Japan: Proceedings of an IIASA Conference, June 27–30, 1977*. Oxford: Pergamon, pp. 227–251.

Schipper, L. and Meyers, S. (1992) *Energy Efficiency and Human Activity: Past Trends, Future Prospects* (Cambridge Studies in Energy and the Environment). Cambridge: Cambridge University Press.

Söderström, J. (1992) The Dennis Agreement: A 15-Year Program for Construction and Financing of Roads and Public Transportation in Stockholm. Paper presented at the Conference 'Mobility and Territory in Major Cities: The Role of a Road Network', Madrid.

Stone, P.A. (1973) *The Structure, Size and Costs of Urban Settlements* (National Institute of Economic and Social Research, *Economic and Social Studies*, Vol. XXVIII). Cambridge: Cambridge University Press.

Straszak, A. and Tuch, R. (eds.) (1980) *The Shinkansen High-Speed Rail Network of Japan: Proceedings of an IIASA Conference, June 27–30, 1977*. Oxford: Pergamon.

Tegnér, G. (1994) The 'Dennis Traffic Agreement' – a Coherent Transport Strategy for a Better Environment in the Stockholm Metropolitan Region. Paper presented at the STOA International Workshop, Brussels.

Van den Berg, L., Drewett, R., Klaassen, L.H., Rossi, A. and Vijverberg, C.H.T. (1982) *Urban Europe: A Study of Growth and Decline* (Urban Europe, Volume 1). Oxford: Pergamon.

CHAPTER 6

TRANSPORT PLANNING, ENERGY AND DEVELOPMENT: IMPROVING OUR UNDERSTANDING OF THE BASIC RELATIONSHIPS

Michael Breheny

6.1. THE WEAKNESS OF THE RESEARCH BASE

In his chapter, Peter Hall reveals that he is uniquely equipped to reflect on the relationships between transport, land-use change and environmental impact across western Europe. However, the overall result of his detailed and knowledgeable reflection is ultimately depressing, for he shows just how ignorant we remain about the way that some of these relationships work, and hence how weak is the basis for any policy intervention. This is particularly bad news at this time, because issues of environmental protection – often under the label of 'sustainable development' – transport investment, and the promotion of economic development, are high on political agendas across much of Europe. Just when we need certainty, Hall reminds us of our ignorance.

Another interpretation might be that Hall's chapter is actually rather timely. Because of the high priority given to transport and environmental issues at present, and the desire of national and local governments to appear to be doing something – particularly on the sustainable development front – policies are being hastily assembled and implemented with little regard for their likely efficacy. Half-formed, but attractive, research findings are being hastily adopted by practitioners and politicians as the basis for policy. A prime example is the package of 'compact city' policies currently being promoted by the British government, and hungrily accepted by local planners. While some of these policies may have merit, a firm reminder is required that the intellectual basis for such policies is as yet rather weak.

Hall's chapter reflects on the research base underlying two specific issues: firstly, the role of planning, and in particular changes to urban form, in promoting lower energy consumption; and secondly the role that transport investment, and particularly rail investment, plays in promoting local economic development. The two are related in many ways, of course; but most obviously because transport investment has a direct bearing on energy consumption and also on changes to urban form. They are also related at present because the concern with sustainable development has also produced, in the UK at least, powerful protests over the continuing programme of road-building.

The two issues can now be considered a little further.

6.2.   TRANSPORT, PLANNING AND URBAN ENERGY CONSUMPTION

Relative ignorance in this particular field may be understandable. It has only become a fashionable area of academic research in recent years, driven by the mania for 'sustainable development'. There has, however, been considerable pressure from politicians for usable research findings because of the demands of international agreements for action. Interestingly, a number of national governments have looked primarily to their land-use planning systems as the means by which progress towards sustainable development can be achieved. One feature of the debate has been a lack of reflection on the potential of the planning system – which can manipulate land-use change only very slowly – relative to other means of effective action. Perhaps much too much is expected of planning. This focus on the planning system has led in turn to a focus on the possibilities of changing urban form and transport systems as a way of reducing energy consumption and hence pollution. As Hall demonstrates, the general drift of the resulting academic debate has been in favour of greater urban containment, higher density cities, promotion of public transport, and a reduced dependence on the motor car. A general set of policies along these lines – in shorthand, the 'compact city' – has gained favour, at least in the European Commission, the UK, the Netherlands, Australia, Germany and the USA.

Yet, as a small number of dissenting voices have claimed, the merits of the compact city are not at all clear. Hall reviews some of the contradictory concerns. These concerns can be summarised under three tests of the compaction proposal: its *veracity*; its *feasibility*; and its *acceptability*. The test of *veracity* asks the fundamental question of whether significant transport energy savings can actually be achieved through greater urban compaction. Although some researchers might still dispute the fact (Gordon and Richardson, 1990), there is a general consensus that savings can be made if cities can function at higher densities, with commensurate improvements in public transport. Most of the empirical evidence suggests that this is the case. The question rarely asked, however, is whether these savings are likely to be significant? Breheny (1994) has suggested that the policies required to halt urban decentralization imply such major social and economic upheavals that 'they had better be worth it'. He then demonstrates that they may not be worth it. Crude calculations suggest that had urban decentralization been halted in Britain 30 years ago (a proxy for halting it in the next 30 years) the resultant savings in petroleum consumption would have been in the region of 2–3% per year. This level of savings, achieved through planning only over very lengthy timescales, might be achieved readily – indeed, almost overnight – by other means. For example, recent research in the Netherlands has suggested that a 10% increase in petroleum prices will reduce car-kilometres by about 2% (MuConsult, 1992). The implication of this is that before introducing possibly draconian urban containment policies, we need to be sure that commensurate environmental gains will ensue.

The test of *feasibility* requires that, regardless of the veracity issue, the practicability of actually halting urban decentralization is investigated. As Hall explains, decentralization has been a consistent and powerful force in western Europe since 1945 at least. Although there is now evidence that the power of this force is diminished in some countries, it remains a major determinant of urban structure. In the UK, for example – a country with longstanding policies of urban containment – throughout the 1980s the largest cities continued to lose population and jobs, while rural areas and small towns were the major recipients of migrants. Behind these movements lie powerful economic and social forces that may prove impossible to stop. Some slowing down may be feasible, but the idea, promoted by the European Commission (1990) for example, that all future growth take place within existing urban areas, would require much more than this. The simple point to be made here is that during the lengthy and intense debate on the compact city, this question of feasibility has rarely been addressed.

The test of *acceptability* is one that has also been largely ignored. This test is closely related to that of veracity, because what is acceptable in terms of the social and economic implications of greater containment will depend to some degree on the extent of environmental gains that result from urban compaction. If such gains are likely to be low, as suggested above in the case of energy consumption, then city dwellers are unlikely to be happy about living in higher density cities and being denied the benefits, afforded to past generations, of suburban or ex-urban living. Perceptions of these issues will depend on cultural backgrounds. Perhaps the British obsession with suburban lifestyles – the 'every man must have his shed' view, as Colin Buchanan put it – is the exception in Europe. But large scale decentralization across western Europe suggests that it is not that exceptional. Certainly, the European Commission's (1990) promotion of the merits of a high density, creative urban milieu, and its disdain for suburbs, seem to be out of tune with realities across much of Europe.

Although the question of the acceptability of the compact city has been addressed only on the margins of the debate, three specific responses can be identified in the UK. The first, with an obvious urban focus, is a concern over 'town-cramming'. As Hall suggests by way of example, even the Dutch – who have given most thought to all of these issues – seem to have sidestepped the town cramming problem. The concern over town cramming in the UK can be seen to some degree as an urban backlash against the hegemony of the rural protectionist lobby, which has found a new and welcome tool in the compact city notion. The second, and only barely articulated, response has been a concern over the effects of the halting of decentralization on already weak rural economies. Such economies have been sustained in recent years by a steady in-flow of new businesses and new people. The third, and potentially most powerful, response has been from business, and particularly property, interests. In the UK, for example, these interests have opposed the introduction of the government's PPG13[1] guidance note, which encourages local planners to introduce compact city policies. Constraints on locational choice are seen as direct constraints on business activity. A very high proportion of property investment in the UK has been into decentralized locations – reflecting demand – over the last twenty years or so. The prospect of being forced to develop only urban sites is viewed with dread. An interesting twist to this particular issue is evident in The Netherlands, where high environmental standards, for example on the required soil quality of sites, make urban sites still less attractive to an aggrieved property market.

6.3. TRANSPORT INVESTMENT AND ECONOMIC DEVELOPMENT

If researchers can be forgiven for their uncertainties over the newly-fashionable area of transport, land-use and energy consumption, this cannot be so in the area of transport investment and local economic development. The question of the degree to which such investment does or does not promote economic growth is a longstanding one. Nevertheless, as Peter Hall explains, the logic is still not clear. The problem that has bedevilled attempts to clarify the logic is that of separating out the effects of transport investment from all the other local determinants of economic change. Hall quotes numerous examples of where an apparent link between transport investment and economic development is clouded by other factors that would have promoted economic development without transport investment.

Breheny, Hart and Robson (1993) have suggested that the longstanding assumption that road investment will boost weak local or regional economies – still an official view in the UK – is no longer significant. They develop a simple typology in which the localized economic effects of major road investment might be considered. They ask in what circumstances might road investment appear to have been a necessary and sufficient condition for economic development, and where has it been necessary but not sufficient? They add a further possible case: where road investment appears to have been not necessary (and hence where sufficiency is not an issue) for economic growth. They provide UK examples as follows:

Case:	Examples:
Necessary and Sufficient	Cambridge (M11), South Hampshire (M27), Warwickshire (M40)
Necessary but Not Sufficient	Merseyside (M57, M62), Tyneside (A1M), Kent (M2, M20)
Not Necessary	Aberdeen, Norwich

According to this view, road investment will only make a significant difference where it is the only missing feature of a strong economy. Thus, in the cases of Cambridge, South Hampshire and Warwickshire, new motorway investment appears to have completed the economic jigsaw. On the other hand, there are depressed economies where major road investment appears to have made no, or little, difference to economic prospects. Finally, there are instances where the lack of superior road infrastructure does not hinder economic performance. The only two towns in the UK with populations of over 60,000 not within 16 km of a motorway are Aberdeen and Norwich; two of the UK's strongest local economies.

This framework might also be useful in considering the case of rail, rather than road, investment, which is the main focus of Peter Hall's review. The study of the link between rail investment and economic development is much less familiar than the case of road investment. However, in the cases reviewed Hall identifies the same difficulties in pinning down the specific effects of rail investment that occur with roads. One problem in drawing conclusions about the effects of rail investment is that it is a much more heterogeneous mode of transport than roads. Hall reviews a wide variety of systems, from international high-speed rail through to local, light rail networks. These have different purposes and different effects. The chances of prediction are confused still further, as Hall concludes, because many cases of rail investment arise in conjunction with public-private development schemes, which themselves are unpredictable.

6.4. Conclusion

The two issues reviewed in Peter Hall's chapter – transport/environment and transport/economy links – are inevitably bound together. Indeed, we should really be considering a transport/environment/economy triangle, rather than these two pairs. Transport will be at the core of the economy/ environment debate whenever – despite our lack of confidence about cause and effect – transport investment is intended to promote or maintain economic competitiveness. This is now obvious from localized wrangles over minor road schemes through to debates over major proposals such as the expansion of Heathrow and Schiphol airports. Ironically, given the new mood of protest, some of the public transport investments that might generally be regarded as environmentally sound, such as new urban rail systems, will be seen by some people as environmentally intrusive.

Despite the complexity of the issues, it is difficult not to agree with Peter Hall that for each of the two issues reviewed above the Dutch and French governments, respectively, probably come closest to a sound approach; the Dutch in promoting packages of urban containment policies, and the French in promoting large-scale integrated public transport systems.

This leads to a final point, and one that might usefully have been reviewed in Peter Hall's chapter. There are important political, institutional, and even cultural factors across Europe which determine popular attitudes and political judgements about the importance of transport, the environment and the economy. Why is it, for example, that the Dutch appear to adopt enlightened policies ahead of everyone else? Why do French governments, of whatever persuasion, believe in public intervention in general and rail investment in particular? Why is policy discontinuity so inevitable in Britain? Answers to these questions might help to explain what is happening and the limits to what can happen.

Note

1. PPG13 (Planning Policy Guidance 13) (Departments of Environment and Transport, 1994) is on transport. The intentions of PPGs are to interpret government policy and to give guidance to local authorities about how it should be implemented. The aim of PPG13 is to reduce the growth in the length and number of motorized trips, to encourage alternative means of travel which have less environmental impact, and to reduce the reliance on the private car. One interpretation of PPG13 has been to introduce compact cities policies.

References

Breheny, M. (1994) Urban Decentralisation and Sustainable Development, Discussion Paper 20, Department of Geography, University of Reading.

Breheny, M., Hart, D. and Robson, B. (1993) *Current Regional Planning Issues*, Report to Department of the Environment, London: DoE.

Commission of the European Communities (1990) *Green Paper on the Urban Environment*. Brussels: Commission of the European Communities.

Departments of Environment and Transport (1994) PPG13 – Transport. London: HMSO.

Gordon, P. and Richardson, H. (1990) Gasoline consumption and cities – A reply. *Journal of the American Planning Association*, **55**, pp. 342–345.

MuConsult (1992) *Evaluatie Tussenbalans: Effecten van de Verandering in Vervoerskosten op de Mobiliteit* (Evaluation of the Mid-Term Review: Effects of the Change in Transport Costs on Mobility). Utrecht: MuConsult.

Chapter 7

The Channel Tunnel: The Case for Private Sector Provision of Public Infrastructure

Roger Vickerman

7.1. Introduction

The Channel Tunnel finally opened for service during 1994. Even at the last minute the actual date posed problems and served to vindicate the views of sceptics and opponents in the Press and City. On the other hand to deliver a working transport system of such complexity within about a year of a date originally fixed eight years previously and after 200 years of dreams and aborted attempts compares favourably with other infrastructure schemes (the Humber Bridge, the Thames Barrier) and rail based transport systems (Manchester Metrolink and Sheffield Supertram both faced last minute delays; more inauspiciously BR's Advanced Passenger Train never achieved full scheduled revenue service).

The object of this chapter is therefore to assess, at the point of its entering service:

1. whether the decision to make the Tunnel a private sector project can be evaluated as a success, and the lessons to be learned from it as a model for future major investments; and

2. how far predictions of the Tunnel as an instrument of the generation or relocation of economic activity can be validated.

These are not separate issues, since one of the major arguments for private sector involvement in the provision of public infrastructure is that private sector development gains need to be included in evaluations such that the private sector contributes to the public infrastructure from which it gains.

There are four main sections to this chapter, the first and second review the key questions of the location and the historical development of the project which are argued to be vital as precursors to understanding the central issues of the financial and legal structure and the economic impact, dealt with in the third and fourth sections.

7.2. THE TUNNEL IN ITS LOCATIONAL CONTEXT

The Tunnel consists of three 50 km tunnels, two running tunnels and a service tunnel, just over 30 km of which are under the sea. These join two large terminals, at Cheriton, near Folkestone, in Kent, and Coquelles, near Calais, in the French region of Nord-Pas de Calais (figure 7.1). The Tunnel provides four distinct types of service on its standard gauge, 25 kV electrified railway track, running in 7.6 metre diameter tunnels:

1.   Le Shuttle tourist shuttles for cars and coaches, linking the M20 Motorway and A16/A26 Autoroutes. Terminal to terminal travel time is 35 minutes, motorway to motorway time 1 hour. Passengers travel in their vehicles. Minimal facilities are provided on Le Shuttle, though substantial terminal facilities are provided, partly to meet the short-term continuing availability of duty-free concessions for travellers to and from the UK which Eurotunnel has demanded to avoid its being placed at a disadvantage relative to its competitors who will continue to be able to sell duty-free goods on board until 1999.

2.   Le Shuttle freight shuttles for accompanied lorries. Lorries travel in open-sided wagons with drivers catered for in a special club coach, with on board meal facilities.

3.   BR/SNCF through freight trains for intermodal traffic (containers and swapbodies), automotive traffic (new cars), and ultimately classic wagon load (siding to siding) traffic, linking major centres in the UK with those in Germany, France, Switzerland and Italy. An inspection facility has been constructed at Dollands Moor adjacent to the Eurotunnel terminal at Cheriton. Although through haulage of trains by new multi-voltage locomotives will be possible, late delivery of these will see SNCF locomotives operating to Dollands Moor from the start of operations (these cannot proceed further due to the smaller loading gauge and absence of 25 kV overhead on the BR tracks). The development of 'freight villages' to serve as regional hubs for this traffic was the subject of major discussions by British Rail, as required under Section 40 of the Channel Tunnel Act (Gibb et al., 1992). Several of these are now ready for operation and have involved considerable private sector activity. A number of combined traffic operators have invested heavily in new wagons for these services which pose problems because of the differences in loading gauge between UK and continental minimum standards.

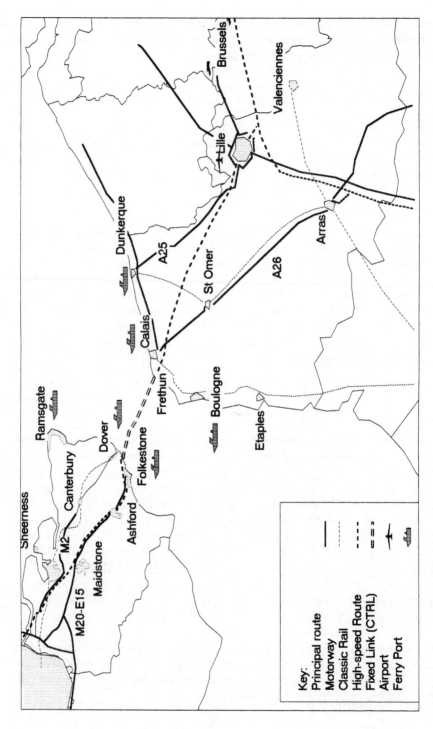

Figure 7.1. The Channel Tunnel and approaches.

4. BR/SNCF/SNCB through Eurostar services for passenger traffic between London and Paris (3 hours) and Brussels (3 hours 10 minutes until completion of Belgian high speed link in 1996 then 2 hours 40 minutes). Completion of a Channel Tunnel Rail Link in the UK could reduce these times by a further 30 minutes. New trains, essentially a development of SNCF TGV trains, built to the smaller UK loading gauge and with additional safety and other features to meet Eurotunnel specifications, are being provided for these services. The delivery of these was also delayed, due in part to major difficulties with operating highly complex multivoltage trains on the third-rail electrical system in the UK. Eurostar, which is the passenger only train from London to Paris, Lille and Brussels, will provide a premium service with basic fares being pitched to compete with airline rates for business travellers, although deep discounting for discretionary travellers on off-peak services is expected, even when a full service is in operation. Provisional timetables for 1995 indicate a basic hourly service to each of Paris and Brussels, with a train stopping at Lille every 2 hours and four trains a day at Calais-Fréthun. A further intermediate stop will be made by some trains at Ashford International when this is ready for service, probably in early 1996. On these services immigration formalities will take place on-train, but customs and security will be undertaken off-train. In addition to the inter-capital services, limited through north of London day services will operate from 1995, to and from the West and East Coast Main Lines. Night services will also operate on these routes to the north of London and to the West Country on the Great Western Main Line. More distant continental destinations such as Amsterdam and Basle will be included as part of these night services. Due to lack of secure facilities at the stations, both immigration and customs checks will take place on-train for these services.

The Tunnel system owned by Eurotunnel simply provides a connection between the British and French coasts, between Folkestone and Calais. However, it will already be clear from the descriptions of the through rail services that successful operation of the Tunnel depends critically on investment by rail operators in both infrastructure and rolling stock, much of the former at substantial distances from the Tunnel. The purpose of the Tunnel is not to provide simply a link between the two towns, nor, indeed, between the County of Kent and the French region of Nord-Pas de Calais. The strategic significance of the Tunnel is that it links the road and rail networks of the UK and the whole of continental Europe. Direct connections from the motorway networks on to Eurotunnel's shuttle trains for road vehicles, and direct links between the rail networks, including from the newly constructed French TGV Nord high speed rail line, make it part of much wider networks. These networks provide the key links between the major conurbation areas within the central European

Capitals region, which stretches from London to Amsterdam, to Frankfurt and to Paris, with Brussels roughly situated at its centre. This is a major region of the European Community, with over 25% of the EC population and over 30% of the Community's GDP (Vickerman, 1994*a*).

Good and improving communications are seen as vital to the continuing economic performance of this wider region. Cross-Channel passenger traffic grew from 9.6 million in 1962 to 71.4 million in 1993, and is forecast to continue to grow to 101 million by 2003, and 136 million by 2013. Meanwhile, freight traffic is growing, if anything even faster, from 29 million tonnes in 1971 to 89 million tonnes in 1992, with forecast levels of 147 million tonnes in 2003 and 215 million tonnes by 2013. Actual traffic levels have continued to outstrip forecast levels with great regularity over the past 30 years. It is this incessant growth in traffic which makes the Channel Tunnel project viable (Holliday *et al.*, 1991*b*; Le Maire and Pevsner, 1992).

Such a situation has to be considered within the overall development of transport in the region. In this the PBKAL (Paris-Brussels-Köln-Amsterdam-London) high-speed rail network is the key element. Growing congestion, both on roads and in air links, has placed a new emphasis on the development of high-speed rail links, which are optimal for distances of up to around 500 to 600 kilometres, roughly the distance between London and Paris. Linking London into the system validates the rest of the network by ensuring viable levels of flow on other links. Most of this traffic will divert from overcrowded airways and airports. The Tunnel is a vital link in this network, but the Tunnel depends on the rest of the network if it is to achieve its full potential.

The first section of this high-speed network, from the Tunnel via Lille to Paris, came into service in 1993. From 1994 this is linked to the existing two TGV lines to the south-east and south-west of Paris via the new La Jonction route around the east of the French capital. This also provides an interchange with Paris-Charles de Gaulle Airport. The link from Lille to Brussels is now under construction for completion in 1996. The final authorization for the mixture of upgrading and new line planned for the sections between Brussels and Amsterdam and Köln is awaited with completion expected for 1996–98. The new line between Köln and Frankfurt am Main is due for completion around the same time. This leaves the final link from the Tunnel to London, which awaits private finance and a lengthy period of authorization following the final route announcement in January 1994. Completion is not currently expected before 2002 at the earliest.

Given that Eurotunnel provides a multi-modal service, its position within wider European road links is also of importance. From a position where access roads to the ports of Calais and Dover were relatively poor, the Tunnel has acted as a catalyst to the completion of the main motorway routes, the M20 motorway in Britain and the A26 and A16 Autoroutes in France. The coastal A16 route is seen as particularly important in reducing the isolation of places such as Boulogne and also improving the location of Amiens. There is no such coastal route in the UK, although there is some interest in the development of a Kent-Hampshire route on the grounds of opening up an otherwise neglected part of the South East (East Sussex) and providing an alternative route to the major growth points of South Hampshire and the M4 corridor avoiding the most congested sections of the M25, M3 and M4.

The essential impact of the Tunnel is, however, to act as a catalyst to the completion of key inter-metropolitan transport links, to remove a key bottleneck, but also to expose other weak links in the network. In this it fits into the emergent trans-European networks for both rail and road, but also that for multi-modal transport (Vickerman, 1994b, 1995).

7.3. A Short History of the Channel Tunnel

The first proposal to restore the fixed link between the British Isles and continental Europe broken in the last Ice Age was made by Nicolas Desmaret in 1751, but most sources date the first serious proposal from 1802 (see Bonavia, 1987; Holliday et al., 1991b, for more detailed discussions of the history). This scheme was for twin bored tunnels, though designed for horse drawn carriages with a mid-Channel staging post on the Varne Bank, and followed a route fairly close to the present Eurotunnel project. This was the first of a long line of proposals, at least 26 according to some sources, prior to the present scheme. There is a great similarity between these various proposals – most involved a bored tunnel between a point to the east of Cap Gris Nez and a point between Folkestone and Dover (i.e. the shortest undersea distance), and from 1830 onwards were principally rail based. All of these schemes failed principally because of British objections, and from 1883 to 1955 as a principle of defence policy.

In the 1870s, the heyday of Victorian railway activity, rival schemes were started from either side of Dover, one of which, on almost the identical line of the Eurotunnel project, reached over a mile from each side before the 1883 abandonment. These projects instituted the essential framework of bi-national agreement. An Anglo-French Commission of the early 1870s had recommended a tunnel scheme and a draft Treaty had been drawn up. The promoters were bi-national in origin, although this disguised the strong British financial investment in the development of railways in Northern France. The nineteenth-century schemes also bred and fostered the mistrust and often misplaced strategic reasoning later to be mustered against renewed fixed link schemes in the 1970s and 1980s. Palmerston's 1857 view opposing the tunnel, 'a work the object of which is to shorten a distance we find already too short' contrasts with that of Marshal Foch in 1918 that a tunnel would have shortened the First World War by two years. This highlights two issues we need to address later, that a tunnel runs in two directions and that its role in total logistic systems is of great significance.

When the defence objections were lifted in 1955, not only were the traditional tunnel schemes resurrected (in fact the original tunnel companies established in the 1870s had merged in 1883 and remained in existence), but new proposals were brought forward, especially for a bridge. The major change was the growth of road traffic for which a completely tunnel-based system was technically impractical. Consistently, however, government and parliamentary enquiries in 1963 (Ministry of Transport, 1963), 1973 (Department of the Environment, 1973) and 1982 (Department of Transport, 1982) rejected alternatives to a rail-based bored tunnel as the core of the system, now with increasing emphasis on the carriage of road vehicles in addition to through rail services. In 1973 work was begun on a pilot phase of a government guaranteed project (albeit with some private sector involvement), but failure to ratify the Treaty brought the project to a halt in January 1975. A major reason for failure to ratify was the escalating cost of the project, especially that of the connecting high speed rail link to London (considered to be an essential element of the 1970s scheme) – a pointer to future problems. Further analysis of the collapse of the 1970s project also suggests that the lack of a 'champion' for the project, independent of both governments, able to exercise both political and financial muscle, was a major factor – after the abandonment the independent Channel Tunnel Advisory Group, in a wide ranging Report (Department of the Environment, 1975) confirmed the viability of the project (although with reservations about the financial viability of a rail link).

Although the project was officially abandoned in 1975, it never really died. Pressure for a link came from three main sources. One was private sector interests seeking major new projects both for financial and construction firms. The second was the European Commission developing a growing interest in the completion of obvious missing links in the European transport networks. These two came together in a Report for the Commission by Coopers and Lybrand (Commission of the European Communities, 1980). The third was from the national railway companies, who themselves put forward their own scheme for a single small bore tunnel in 1979. In 1980 the UK Government, responding in part to construction interests identifying the BR/SNCF proposal as a missed opportunity and in part to Conservative Party concern that such a scheme was too much a typical public sector scheme, invited the private sector to submit alternatives. These were examined by the House of Commons Transport Committee (1981), but real progress only came after the first Thatcher-Mitterrand summit in September 1981 when it was agreed to set up an Anglo-French Study Group (Department of Transport, 1982).

It is interesting to note that much of the running came from the British side at this time, but, not surprisingly following the earlier British history of the project, the French remained sceptical of British commitment. However, although the British response to the Study Group's recommendation in favour of the familiar twin bored rail tunnels (also supported by the Transport Committee's Report) was mainly to concern itself with the feasibility of private finance, the French started to conduct the necessary consultations at the regional level to ensure support and prepare for a rapid conclusion of the public inquiries necessary under the French planning system prior to a project being declared a public utility. The financial feasibility was examined by a group of banks which also concluded in favour of the rail tunnel scheme, but significantly reported that government financial guarantees were imperative for a successful financing.

To some extent the British moves could be seen as largely going through the motions. There was no real driving force at a political level pushing the project. The successive studies had failed to come up with a good reason for rejecting the project, but it was clearly no priority. Despite the convenient view that Thatcher saw the Tunnel as the culmination of the private sector's ability to take over even a project of this magnitude ('the ultimate privatization'), in reality her support was both opportunistic and ephemeral. In 1984, following the success of the budgetary negotiations at the Fontainebleau Summit it seems that Thatcher took the view that it was opportune to do 'something exciting' to underline the European commitment (Young, 1990). The Tunnel project just happened to be there and ready to go, if it coincided with other political objectives then so much the better. The one major disadvantage with the rail-based scheme was that it conflicted with the more general policy preference for road transport schemes. This bias against rail investment also reflected a broader antagonism against the symbolism of a nationalized rail industry with a strong and militant union. The arguments were used to promote a road based solution to the Channel link. Perhaps the most significant indication of the unimportance of the Tunnel to the Thatcher view is the complete absence of even passing reference to it in the Thatcher memoirs (Thatcher, 1993) except for a rather oblique mention of a meeting with Ian Macgregor, then Chairman of British Steel, during the coal strike of 1984.

In France there was a driving political force, principally in the person of Pierre Mauroy, Mitterrand's first Prime Minister, 1981–83, but a man who remained First Secretary of the Socialist Party for the rest of the decade and, most significantly, the Mayor of Lille. The main feature of this was the close involvement of national and local political interests. Such interests were not consulted in the UK until after the decision had been taken. The local authorities in Kent had to make their representations through petitions to the Hybrid Bill as it passed through Parliament, and although it can be argued that this provides better safeguards in terms of gaining binding agreements on negotiated changes to plans than would a Public Inquiry, such confrontation rarely brings about better plans for supporting policies than the 'concertation' followed in France (Vickerman, 1994c).

This would be re-enacted with even greater disadvantage during the rail link saga which followed. The government, advised by many of the same officials who had presided over the 1970s scheme's eventual demise, successfully decoupled the Tunnel project chosen in 1986 from any new rail line through Kent. The environmental opposition to the Tunnel was thus largely neutralized since this was local to the Tunnel terminal and to the main construction site. Away from this it could be argued that attraction of increased traffic from road to rail had environmental advantages. BR argued that the loss of commuter traffic since the early 1970s provided more than sufficient spare capacity for running international trains. Whilst this secured an easier (though far from straightforward) passage of the Channel Tunnel Bill in 1986–87, it sowed the seeds of much greater problems when it became clear, almost as soon as the legislation had been enacted, that capacity would not be adequate from soon after the Tunnel's opening. Moreover, enormous potential advantages to capitalize on the Tunnel would also be lost if rail were not to be used to the fullest possible extent.

The development of the Channel Tunnel Rail Link (CTRL) has a complex history. The main problem has been the lack of a clear promoter, one lesson from earlier Tunnel schemes. The government argued that promotion was British Rail's responsibility, but used Section 42 of the Channel Tunnel Act (which prohibits any subsidy to international rail services), in addition to BR's usual financial constraint to obstruct progress. It also appeared to be more sensitive to environmental matters than in parallel road schemes. The government relaxed its initial position when it became clear that the line was not capable of wholly private sector financing, but the first attempt at introducing a private sector partner, in 1990, proved incapable of reaching an agreed position on the amount of public money to be made available. The use of the line for improved regional and commuting services from Kent to London could lead to a case for some government finance. The next move, in 1991, was to couple the rail link with the new East Thames Corridor as an instrument of economic regeneration. This involved a completely new route for the western end of CTRL and another delay in planning. Following detailed examination of the route, the government approved the final route details in Spring 1994 and began a new competition for a private sector partner to invest in Union Railways, the new BR subsidiary set up to develop the route. This new private sector partner will be allowed to share in revenue from the Eurostar services started in 1994 operated by European Passenger Services, which was transferred from BR to direct government ownership in anticipation.

We see here, therefore, that the British attitude to the Tunnel was always responsive and pragmatic and rarely to do with transport. The economic and geographic significance of the Tunnel was always ignored or misunderstood. Increasingly it has become clear that this failure had potentially led to considerable missed opportunities. Although the Tunnel itself has been completed this time it is still a candidate for inclusion in the list of 'Great Planning Disasters' (Hall, 1980) because of the failure to resolve the planning problems it poses.

7.4.   FINANCIAL AND LEGAL FRAMEWORKS – THE CONTRACT DRIVEN PROJECT

The Channel Tunnel project can be described as a series of four sets of contractual agreements (figure 7.2) between Eurotunnel – the concessionaire company – and, respectively:

1.   the national governments of Britain and France through a Concession Agreement;

2.   Transmanche Link (TML) – the contractors – through a construction contract;

3.   a consortium of some 200 banks worldwide – through a loan agreement;

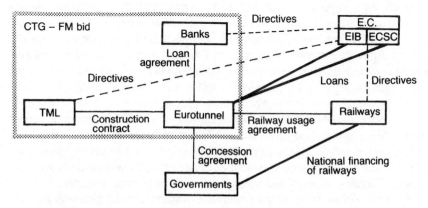

Figure 7.2   Channel Tunnel contractural arrangements. (*Source*: Vickerman, 1994*c*)

4.   the state railway companies, BR and SNCF – through a railway usage agreement.

In addition, it should be noted that Eurotunnel is itself a partnership, between the English and French concessionary companies – the Channel Tunnel Group Ltd and France Manche SA. Furthermore, the construction consortium TML involves a joint venture between British and French joint venture companies, themselves representing groups of English and French major construction companies.

Each of the four sets of contracts is fully inter-dependent. The Concession Agreement confers certain rights and responsibilities on both Eurotunnel and the governments. Principally, Eurotunnel has to construct the Tunnel to certain standards approved by the governments; the governments have to ensure the provision of adequate linking infrastructure. Since only some 20% of the Tunnel's total cost (currently estimated at around £10.5 billion in 1985 prices) is equity financed, the loan agreement is critical to the continued viability of the project. Variations in design, some occasioned by changing governmental requirements, lead to variations in the construction contract, which raise costs and thus require approval of the banks as chief financiers. As 50% of the Tunnel's capacity has been let through the Railway Usage Agreement for the use of the railway companies on through rail services, the governments' roles as providers of railway finance also place them in a crucial role.

There has been an increasingly important role of the European Community, which has both provided finance through European Investment Bank (£1.3 billion) and European Coal and Steel Community (£200 million) loans, whilst, more problematically, insisting on the full implementation of rules on competitive tendering for equipment to be used in the Tunnel.

Such a large number of separate contractual arrangements clearly makes for a project which is, on the one hand, problematic to manage, and, on the other, involves large numbers of interests remote from the primary purpose of providing a fixed link across the Channel. It will also be clear from this, that the represented interests are remote from both the users and the most directly affected local communities, or their democratically elected governmental agencies.

The government's White Paper of January 1986 (Department of Transport, 1986a) and the Anglo-French (Canterbury) Treaty of February 1986 eulogize the benefits of the Tunnel to the UK and to the greater purpose of European integration. However, nowhere in these documents is any real concern expressed for the development of transport as a whole.

All the contracts were put in place immediately following the announcement of January 1986, and this speed has itself been at the source of many of the ensuing problems over their detailed provisions. Speed was necessary since all the elements are interdependent. The Concession requires that the Tunnel should be financed and built within a given timescale, the construction contract depends on finance being available, the financial case depends on guaranteed revenue from the railways and each depends on the Tunnel being ready at a specified time which requires a minimum of delay during the necessary legislative processes. The Concession Agreement of April 1986 (Department of Transport, 1986b) is the key document since it defines the critical relationships between Eurotunnel, as Concessionaire, and the two governments. This Agreement commits the governments to facilitating the construction of the Tunnel, but public funding and financial guarantees were ruled out, including public subsidy to rail services using the Tunnel.

The Concession Agreement required initial terms for the other three contracts to be in place, but also defined many of the conditions which would affect both construction costs and potential revenues and hence the financial return. For example, without the approval of the arrangement where passengers remain in their vehicles on the passenger shuttles, the time advantages of the Tunnel would be lost. This was incorporated in the Concession Agreement, subject to approval by a Safety Authority. Changes to initial designs insisted on by the Safety Authority have added to costs, caused delays in rolling stock procurement and hence affected the rate of return. The Concession Agreement makes the reference to the provision of necessary infrastructure by public authorities, who must 'use reasonable endeavours to carry out the infrastructure necessary for a satisfactory flow of traffic, subject to statutory procedures'. The assumption of this provision was built into financial estimates, but no provision was made for compensation if this was not achieved.

Fast-track design and construct contracts, where final design detail is only determined after commencement, are common in the case of private sector involvement in major infrastructure. The risk to private capital of long delays during the planning and design phase typically requires their use. Furthermore, even though largely existing technology was to be used during construction, the size and complexity of the project raised new problems of logistics both during construction and commissioning. In this case, however, the original promoters, the banks and construction companies who were granted the concession, distanced themselves from the financing and ultimate operation of the Tunnel by setting up Eurotunnel. The TML consortium of construction companies was granted an exclusive contract to build the project by Eurotunnel, and Eurotunnel became responsible for the costs of redesign. Where such changes were imposed on it by the governments, including any changes during the passage of the Bill which became the Channel Tunnel Act 1987,

Eurotunnel had no redress (except through normal legal process). It still required nearly two years from the announcement to put the finance in place since the loan depended on a successful equity flotation, which in turn depended on the project having received a formal Parliamentary approval enabling ratification of the Treaty (see discussion in Holliday *et al.*, 1991*b*).

A particular concern is the right of the government to change its mind and impose costs on a private sector concessionaire. In many cases this is not arbitrary; few would challenge the right of governments to insist on the highest standards of safety and it is a difficult question to determine how far such standards should be paid for by the users who benefit directly, or society which benefits indirectly. In other cases, changes in the financial position of the railways as a major user, changes in policy towards the provision of duty-free goods or the level of customs inspection facilities required, all have major financial implications where there is a clearer case for redress. Governments are supposed to have longer and clearer planning horizons than the private sector, which is why the public sector has traditionally had to undertake public infrastructure projects (Helm and Thompson, 1991; Szymanski, 1991). If the private sector is to be involved in public infrastructure provision in a major way, it too has some right to expect at least this level of public sector guarantee.

The translation of the initial decision into a workable project thus involved a set of legal contractual issues which it appears had not been sufficiently thought through. It would also appear that one of the major problems, which has continued to cause problems for the project, has been the lack of a coherent policy framework into which the Tunnel could be seen to fit. Such a framework would have reduced the risks faced by transport operators, such as the railways, and potential investors. Although the UK government has rejected this view on the grounds that it would amount to a public guarantee implying public expenditure, this might have enabled Eurotunnel to concentrate more on managing the contract. This was the area from which many of the efficiency gains from a private sector scheme were expected (see Vickerman, 1994*c*, for a more detailed discussion).

We have concentrated so far on the role of government in the contractual framework. We turn now to a brief review of the other contractual areas. Much of the publicity surrounding the project has naturally focused on the very public disagreements between Eurotunnel and TML. We have already suggested that the fast track approach carries with it problems of apportioning cost increases between contractor and client. In public infrastructure the client is usually also banker and regulator in the form of the government (or a government agency). Here Eurotunnel suffered the problem of being squeezed between the contractor and both the regulator (in terms of the Intergovernmental Commission and its Safety Authority and also the Maitre d'Oeuvre, who ensures compliance with the terms of the Concession Agreement) and its bankers (the loan syndicate). In the early days Eurotunnel was weak in all of these dealings, the contractors could delay work on the tunnel, shifting risks to the shareholders and banks; the governments would have had some problems in a collapse of the project, but could have made some political profit by pointing out how public money had not been lost; the banks could simply foreclose or put in new management to protect their investment (Holliday, Marcou and Vickerman, 1991).

It could be argued that one of the lessons of the project is the need to create a more powerful concessionaire. Later concessions in the UK (Dartford Bridge, Second Severn Crossing) have transferred a revenue earning asset (the existing crossing) to a consortium of established companies. These include the main contractors as did the original concession companies in the case of the Channel Tunnel. A similar arrangement is envisaged for the CTRL. In the case of the Tunnel, however, the contractors rapidly distanced themselves from the concession, overtly to establish a proper client-contractor relationship, but also shedding as much risk as possible. That the ultimate settlement of outstanding claims by the contractors involves a payment in new shares, plus a requirement to exercise founder warrants, shows the importance of sharing risks in such a project.

Nevertheless, the project did receive some indirect government support at various times. In October 1986, Eurotunnel was rescued from difficulty in the private placing of Equity II by the exercise of pressure on reluctant UK institutions by the Bank of England. The Bank was again involved in early 1987 in securing Alastair (now Sir Alastair) Morton as co-Chairman of Eurotunnel when the project appeared to be losing momentum. In France the decision on TGV Nord was taken in October 1987 just days before the critical phase of Equity III. The Bank of England was again involved as the broker of the agreement between Eurotunnel and TML in 1993.

Alternative indirect governmental financial assistance came through the involvement of European institutions. The European Investment Bank (EIB) participated in the initial financing with a loan of £1 billion, unusually secured against letters of credit from the private sector loan syndicate rather than via the more usual government guarantees which were not possible here. The EIB increased its interest in the refinancing of 1990 by a further £300 million, this time secured against the assets of the tunnel itself rather than against further bank guarantees. The European Coal and Steel Community (ECSC) also made available a loan of £200 million on favourable terms as a subsidy for the use of European steel in the project, under one of its normal financing deals.

The major financing of the Tunnel was that of Equity III in November 1987, which raised some £5.8 billion despite the inauspicious timing following the October 1987 Stock Market crash. As at each stage a complex balancing of equity and loan finance was required. Equity investors needed to know that the core of loan funding (it is a very highly geared project for obvious reasons) was agreed, but the lenders needed to be convinced that the full equity would be underwritten. By far the major share of the loan debt comes from outside the UK and France which had a total of only 12% and 20% respectively by November 1990. The loan syndicate has kept a close eye on the project. Eurotunnel's forecasts made by independent Traffic and Revenue Consultants are vetted by the Banks' own independent forecasts; the cost control audited by the Maitre d'Oeuvre is also vetted by the Banks. Thus the project has had at least two sets of revenue forecasts and at least four sets of cost estimates (TML's, Eurotunnel's and those of the MdO and Banks). For much of the construction period Eurotunnel was technically in breach of the loan agreements and had to seek waivers to continue to draw down finance to keep the project going. This maintained the powerful position of the banks over the project.

At the time of the refinancing at the end of 1990, which aimed to raise a further £2.7 billion of equity and loan finance, the project entered a somewhat different phase. The refinancing coincided with the breakthrough of the service tunnel, making it finally clear that the Tunnel could be completed, but it also coincided with the UK government's rejection of a request by the Eurorail consortium for public funding and guarantees for the rail link. In the vital Japanese financial markets (Japanese banks held 23% of the debt after the November 1987 financing), such a lack of support threatened Eurotunnel's attempt to raise the additional finance it needed. It was reported that Mrs Thatcher had to write to the Japanese Prime Minister to confirm the government's continuing commitment to the Channel Tunnel Project (*The Independent*, 1 September 1990).

The further refinancing in 1994 had to take into account the continuing delay in commissioning such that only skeleton services had begun. Rather as with the original 1987 flotation it also coincided with a degree of nervousness in the stock market such that the value of Eurotunnel shares slumped from just less than 600p in early 1994 to around the highly discounted price of the rights issue shares of 265p. Although the issue was fully underwritten and although Eurotunnel was able to make consistently good long-term revenue forecasts, borne out by the buoyant market for cross-Channel traffic even through the recession, investors were growing impatient with circumstances largely beyond Eurotunnel's control. The take up by investors in the UK was around 68%, but only about 25% of Eurotunnel equity is held in the UK. French take-up has been much higher. This reflects the continuing greater enthusiasm for the project by financial markets outside the UK where long-term, high-risk projects have never been favoured by fund managers and private investors have tended to seek the immediate returns obtainable form investing in highly discounted privatizations. The banks too only agreed to their share in the refinancing at the last moment. It remains to be seen whether this will be the last major call for new finance as the poorer short-term revenue forecasts with delays to both tourist shuttle and through rail passenger services lead to an increase in the debt overhang, despite resolution of the major cost disputes with TML largely in Eurotunnel's favour.

The final contractual area in that of the Railway Usage Agreement. Under this Eurotunnel let 50% of the Tunnel's capacity to the railway operators for the provision of the through passenger and freight rail services. This guarantees to Eurotunnel an important source of revenue and thus the terms of the agreement are critical. The initial terms, again signed with great speed at the start of the project, were thought to be unfavourable to Eurotunnel and were renegotiated in 1987. More recently, the delays in both procurement and commissioning of railway traction equipment, which will delay the provision of full passenger and freight rail services after the expected opening date, have become a matter of contention. The loss of potential revenue to Eurotunnel led to a claim being made against the railway operators, but not surprisingly the delay to the start of services necessitated by Eurotunnel has led to a counter claim from the railways for their inability to run at least through freight services. Successful operation of through rail services is vital to the commercial success of the Tunnel, but this has become more critical with the proposed reorganization of rail services in the UK (international passenger and freight services are likely to be amongst the earliest real privatizations). Here also the imbalance of the British and French rail operators leads to potential difficulties.

The problem with CTRL also relates to this. Rail revenue predictions depend heavily on the overall speed of through journeys; the division of revenue between the three railways (British, French and Belgian) depends on their relative contributions to that overall speed. The question here is not so much one of the contribution of CTRL to the growth of this revenue, but the continuing uncertainty which prevents potential users planning both their overall logistics and any relocations these may involve. This is not just a question of potential passenger users, but also affects freight users of existing tracks which will become less congested with the development of CTRL. That private finance is to be a key component of CTRL, even with its adoption as part of the trans-European rail network with associated preferential EU funding, adds financial uncertainty to the existing planning uncertainty.

The overall conclusion from this section is that the complexity of the inter-relationships between the contracts has hindered the achievement of wider policy aims, but at the same time this complexity may have helped to ensure the project's completion since it has become difficult to disentangle any one contract from the others, whilst through time Eurotunnel itself has gained more power.

7.5.   THE ECONOMIC IMPACT

The economic impact of the Tunnel can be considered at three different main levels:

1.   On the directly affected regions of Kent and Nord-Pas de Calais, where the emphasis is on capitalizing on proximity and securing local access to the Tunnel related networks, whilst minimizing the initial clear negative effects.

2.   On the UK as a whole, where the effect is likely to be relatively neutral on different regions (and possibly marginal in terms of direct aggregate impact), but highlights the need for supporting infrastructure in networks to capitalize on opportunities, especially with regard to the potential bottleneck posed by London.

3.   On Europe, where the Tunnel can be seen as part of the development of high-speed transport between major cities, reinforcing the role of the major metropolitan areas over both peripheral areas and non-metropolitan areas in geographically central regions, but increasing the competition likely to be felt between the major metropolitan areas.

Kent and Nord-Pas de Calais

The usual, though rather misleading, contrast which is drawn is between Kent as a relatively rich and environmentally attractive region and Nord-Pas de Calais as an inherently poor, old industrial region in urgent need of restructuring. This picture was helped until 1993 by Nord-Pas de Calais being in receipt of substantial national and European regional aid whilst Kent received virtually nothing (exceptions being an Enterprise Zone in North Kent and some Rural Development Aid to parts of Romney Marsh).

Nord-Pas de Calais' entitlement to such assistance is not questioned. The former dominant industries of coal and textiles have dwindled to the extent that the last coal mine closed in 1990. Employment in coal had been over 200,000 in the 1940s and over 100,000 in 1968. Textiles and clothing employed 160,000 in 1962, less than 70,000 by 1988, although textiles still accounted for nearly 20% of regional employment (15% of French textile sector employment). A total loss of some 200,000 industrial jobs (one-third of the total) in the 20 years from the mid-1960s had led to a regional unemployment rate of over 13% by the time the Tunnel was announced in 1986, with some areas, including Calais and Boulogne, facing rates of 16 to 18% (Holliday *et al.*, 1991a; Bruyelle and Thomas, 1994).

Although Kent is part of the relatively rich South East region, it can lay claim to be one of the poorest parts of that region, along with Essex and East Sussex, the other counties which lie to the east and south of London. Kent does not have the extensive heavy industry of Nord-Pas de Calais, but nevertheless did have coal, shipbuilding and steel, the former two having been lost since 1980 and the proportion of employment in manufacturing was higher than that for both the South East and the UK as a whole. East Kent in particular has suffered from the decline of its traditional industries, coal mining, traditional seaside tourism and light manufacturing in such industries as toys. It is particularly noticeable that Kent had not shared in the growth of new sectors which characterized the South East economy in the 1970s and 1980s. North Kent has many features in common with southern Essex and East London, leading to its later inclusion in the East Thames Corridor. At the announcement of the Channel Tunnel project in 1985 unemployment in this part of Kent was not dissimilar to that in the coastal part of Nord-Pas de Calais, it was also substantially higher than the South East regional average, whilst both earnings and GDP/per capita were well below average (Channel Tunnel Joint Consultative Committee, 1987).

Construction of the Tunnel had a major impact on the unemployment situation, coming at the same time as the rest of the UK economy was experiencing an economic boom. This reduced unemployment rates of 9.7% in Ashford, 11.4% in Dover and 18.1% in Thanet in 1986 to 3.3%, 5.1% and 8.3% respectively, by 1990. However, the end of the main construction phase also coincided with the move into recession and unemployment quickly rose again to high levels which have proved remarkably resistant to the end of the recession in 1993. In December 1993 unemployment stood at 8.1% in Ashford, 10.4% in Dover and as high as 16.4% in Thanet, one of the worst ten local labour markets for unemployment in Britain. This shows that the long-term structural problems had not been resolved during the construction phase and that any induced response to the Tunnel remained to be experienced. In France the employment situation was helped by the requirement to take 80% of labour employed on Tunnel construction from the local region, a target more than met.

One of the features relevant to the performance of both regions is their relative inaccessibility within national contexts, both to other regions and to major airports, and this is particularly relevant for Kent. International links are less of a problem and have handled enormous increases in traffic.

Dover, the largest ferry port by a long way, handled 18.47 million passengers and 1.06 million freight vehicles in 1993. Most of the traffic is now concentrated on the Dover-Calais route which sees up to 50 conventional ferry sailings a day. The growth in traffic has had an important impact on the local economy with employment both on ferries and in the ports. However, it has also allowed attention to be drawn away from the severe structural problems in the rest of the economy.

Both regions have seen a concerted attempt to harness potential opportunities from the Tunnel as a means of restructuring the local economies, mainly through designation of business parks. The Calais region had as much land designated for development as the whole of Kent in 1987. What is also notable is that very little of this proposed development has been achieved in advance of the Tunnel's opening. Both regions face an internal problem of a natural focus of business activity away from the areas near to the Tunnel termini which are in most need of new economic activities. In Nord-Pas de Calais this competition is from Lille where a major commercial development based on the new TGV station is in progress. In Kent the competition comes from the attractiveness of sites closer to the M25, including developments in Docklands, reinforced by the creation of the East Thames Corridor which has the effect of dividing Kent's focus of development between the two ends of the county.

A key development has been that of the INTERREG (cross-border cooperation) programme which has enabled the non-assisted coastal regions to participate in some European funding for joint projects with assisted areas in Nord-Pas de Calais. This has enabled a cross-border regional focus to be started which has the advantage of increasing the scope for coordinated responses to the Tunnel. More importantly, the continuing problems of the local economy were recognized in 1993 by the grant of Intermediate Area status to most of the coastal Districts of East Kent (the exception being Canterbury). Thanet has also since been designated an Objective 2 region for European Regional Development Fund assistance. This redressed, albeit eight years after the announcement of the Tunnel, the explicit position of the UK government that regional assistance not only was not necessary to capitalize on the opportunities of new infrastructure, but would be a breach of its commitment to the private sector status of the project. This again demonstrated the failure to understand both how and where infrastructure has direct impacts.

Important contrasts between the UK and France can be drawn between, not just the role of government, but also critically between the degree of inter-governmental cooperation and coordination between different levels of government. In France the planning system required the planning response to be concerted into a series of planning contracts which assigned a specific role to each level of government. As we have already noted the regional authorities had been heavily involved in the pre-decision process. In the UK, the decision to construct the Tunnel was exclusively a central government decision. The local government authorities in the areas directly affected were not formally consulted. This meant that local interests were only able to influence detailed aspects of the planning through petitions against specific aspects of the Bill.

One of the main developments, however, was the creation of the Channel Tunnel Joint Consultative Committee (JCC) (Vickerman, 1994c). This established a new model for central-local government consultation in major projects, together with provision for private sector involvement which has been used in a slightly different form in later projects such as the East Thames Corridor. The JCC brought together relevant central government departments (Transport, Environment, Trade and Industry, Employment), local government (Kent County Council and the six District Councils of East Kent), Eurotunnel, TML and British Rail. The JCC was chaired by the Public Transport Minister and thus although not a statutory body with executive powers did have a direct route to government. The initial objective was to provide a forum through which problems with the passage of the enabling legislation, the Channel Tunnel Bill, could be resolved.

However, the JCC became more important than this and the local interest pressed for its retention after the passage of legislation. It has continued to meet, albeit at less frequent intervals throughout the construction period. Its most lasting effect was the Kent Impact Study of 1987 which was monitored in subsequent years and then fully reviewed again in 1991 (Channel Tunnel Joint Consultative Committee, 1987, 1991). The main thrust of the KIST report was to estimate likely primary and secondary job impacts on the county and to formulate policy responses to these. Table 7.1 shows the estimates made in 1987 and the revised figures in 1991. These show how the early optimism of the Tunnel as a generator of economic activity soon evaporated; job losses in the ferry industry grew in estimated importance whilst induced jobs in such areas as distribution, manufacturing and tourism diminished.

The policy response was to be the creation of an East Kent Development Agency to bring other public and private interests. This ran into early problems as one after the other, the district authorities dropped out feeling they could perform better alone. Central government was also rather lukewarm to such a scheme which appeared to be a formula for spending public money. The increasing gloom by 1991 led to renewed calls for such an agency which was resurrected as the East Kent Initiative (EKI). This time Eurotunnel itself took the initiative in a genuine public-private joint venture. EKI determined that its major brief was to be to identify principal infrastructure, site development and inward invest-

Table 7.1.   Estimates of potential employment changes in Kent to 1996.

	1991 Review Estimates	1987 KIS Estimates
Direct employment effects arising from the operation of the Tunnel		
Port and ferry industries	−7,480	−4,300/−6,600
Tunnel and rail operation	+2,000	+3,200
Sub-total	−5,480	−1,100/−3,400
Secondary employment impacts of Tunnel and related infrastructure		
Producer services	+1,500	+1,800
Manufacturing	+2,760	+5,200
Wholesale distribution and road haulage	+1,000	+2,700
Retail distribution	(incl in tourism)	+1,300
Tourism	+500	+3,000/+2,000
Sub-total	+5,760	+14,000/+13,000
Employment impact of Single European Market		
Custom clearance in freight forwarders	−1,300	(not estimated)
HM Customs & Excise and immigration	−520	(not estimated)
Indirect impact on other sectors (net)	+4,150	(not estimated)
Sub-total	+2,330	(not estimated)
Grand Total	**+2,610**	**+12,900/+9,600**

Source: Channel Tunnel Joint Consultative Committee (1991).

ment needs in the area and to lobby for these. It has played an important role in securing specific EC assistance in the form of RECHAR (for re-development of coal mining areas) funding for the coalfield area and INTERREG funding for a designated Transfrontier Region, as well as in the bids for Assisted Area status and for ERDF Objective 2 status.

Although the uptake of planned development sites in Kent had been poor up to 1992, levels of investment and job creation have improved markedly with £16.8 million investment involving nearly 1,000 jobs in 1993 plus a further £214 million of land and property development pro-viding space for nearly 5,500 jobs (Kent County Council, 1994). A new dimension of development in Kent is that of rural areas. Two large areas have been designated as Rural Development Areas, that for Romney Marsh has been extended to include a large area to the west of Ashford, and a new area created covering the former East Kent Coalfield. This entitles receipt of financial assistance for economic, social and environ-mental projects in both public and private sectors. Further application to the European Commission for Objective 5b status was not successful.

Taken together, however, with the Assisted Area status for the coastal belt, and the Objective 2 status for Thanet, a substantial part of East Kent has now received the injection of regional development assistance needed to start the process of restructuring. Further assistance is also planned for the areas in the north of the county which fall into the East Thames Corridor regeneration area.

Transport policy response has also been divided between central and local government. Roads policy can be reasonably well coordinated with central government responsible for motorways and trunk roads and Kent County Council responsible for other roads, although with much of the finance coming directly from central government through Transport Supplementary Grant. Thus a reasonably effective roads policy was formulated with the completion and upgrading of the M20 motorway as the major route to the Tunnel and the improvement of the A20 Folkestone-Dover road to near motorway standard whilst local road policy concentrated on improving access to these major routes for all regions of Kent, including the provision of much needed local by-passes. A similar pattern emerged in Nord-Pas de Calais with the completion of a core framework of autoroutes supplemented by improved regional roads to ensure improved access to all parts of the region.

The situation for rail is rather different. Here the local authority can only respond to BR proposals, and although central government is the critical paymaster, fixing the external financing limits, it too sees its role as one of reacting to BR investment proposals. This has led to problems in particular with the Ashford International Passenger Station project and the high speed rail link. Kent County Council has committed itself to both of these projects, but has also wished to push for the best deal for Kent residents. This has led to a situation in which by trying to secure high quality environmental treatment and the provision of improved services for local residents the County Council has had to take the position of a major objector. The most interesting contrast is with that of the route through Lille where the local authorities were able to secure their preferred route by the simple expedient of committing the extra funding needed, much of which could be included within the planning contracts and paid by central government (Holliday et al., 1991a; Bruyelle and Thomas, 1994).

The pattern of impact on the regions near to the Tunnel has thus followed the expectation that such regions are not likely to benefit in a large measure, and where they do it will largely be the product of additional investment to capitalize on the new infrastructure. However, the creation of cross-border cooperation and the ability to use the Tunnel as a focus of development activity are starting to pay dividends (Vickerman, 1993). In both regions, however, a relatively small part of this regeneration is directly Tunnel related; the Tunnel may be argued to have acted as a catalyst for change, but it has not induced it directly without further outside assistance.

Regional Impacts in the UK

If the Tunnel has limited impacts on the nearby regions, what can be said of the impacts on the UK as a whole? Two features stand out, that the impact of the Tunnel depends heavily on the structure of local industry and its propensity to trade with particular markets, and that connectivity to Tunnel-related networks (through passenger rail services and freight villages) within regions is critical. Some 80% of UK export trade with European markets originates from regions to the north and west of London. For much of this trade the Tunnel is irrelevant since it involves longer (expensive) land journeys through congested areas to secure shorter sea crossings. For the large bulk of this trade, which is not time sensitive, North Sea and Western Channel ferry routes will continue to offer the most competitive service. It is specialist traffic, such as automobile industry or perishable traffic where the Tunnel has the biggest advantage, and hence the regions specializing in such trade will gain competitive advantage, but also face a shift of the accessibility problem to that of the congestion associated with traffic across London (Vickerman and Flowerdew, 1990).

Until the completion of a new rail link which provides an easy cross-London connection via a new terminal at St Pancras, passenger traffic will face either the conventional change of trains and stations across London or the slow and tortuous journey for the limited number of through trains via the Kensington Olympia route. Freight traffic will suffer from increasing congestion on the routes it will need to share with passenger traffic until the latter can divert to a new route. London therefore presents a major obstacle to other regions in the UK sharing in the potential benefits of the Tunnel.

However, London also stands to be a major beneficiary with the improvement of passenger rail communications with the other major cities of the European Capitals region. Even without a dedicated rail link in the UK, Paris and Brussels will be only a 3-hour train journey away. London's natural advantages as a world financial centre will be supported by this improvement in accessibility and competitiveness. However, this improved potential competitiveness can only be realized if internal accessibility within the region improves. It is of no value having journey times of less than 3 hours from city centre to city centre 500 km or more apart if access to that network over distances of less than 100 km takes up to 2 hours. A similar problem exists with the provision of freight villages in other regions where it is access, by both road and rail, to these multi-modal centres, which may be the critical factor in enabling them to attract adequate trade (McKinnon, 1994).

It is this failure to recognize the importance of supporting infrastructure which is the major failure of UK policy towards the Tunnel. Here there is a major contrast with France. French trade does not need improved communications through a single narrow corridor to the same extent as the UK (whether this is ultimately ferry or Tunnel traffic is irrelevant). In France national and regional policy responses to the Tunnel largely coincide in Nord-Pas de Calais. In the UK the potential beneficiaries are spread out over a large number of more distant regions, but they all need improvements of communications with markets in the same general direction. To this can be added the Irish demands for improved access to continental markets across the UK. In summary, the Tunnel is not just the 50 km of the distance from Folkestone to Calais, it is as important as the total networks it serves.

The Tunnel as an Instrument of European Integration

It would be unreal to consider the decision to construct the Tunnel as being principally an instrument of either government's European policy despite the obviously European context of the UK government's original commitment. The European Commission was also kept at arm's length by the private finance decision, although the Commission continued to seek a role as did the European Parliament. The Tunnel has nevertheless become a symbol of integration through its sheer size, its cross-border context, its role as a pioneer private finance scheme, and its contribution to the increasing emphasis being placed on rail in the development of European networks. Where the Commission has had a direct policy role is in the development of the networks which connect to the Tunnel. New road schemes in both countries have been aided from the Infrastructure Fund, as has a considerable part of the British Rail investment in upgrading infrastructure for initial Tunnel services. This is increasingly dealt with within the context of trans-European networks.

Three broad policy issues emerge at the wider European level: transport policy, regional and cohesion policy, and competitiveness. The transport policy issues concern both infrastructure provision and inter-modal competition. The European Union has begun to recognize the need for a clear framework for both of these because of the important spillovers between member states. We have already discussed the potential for centralization occasioned by the Tunnel and its connecting high speed rail networks, but this has to be set in context, Although there is a bias towards the major metropolitan centres, other parts of the central regions (including Kent and Nord-Pas de Calais) may be disadvantaged. Similarly major centres in more peripheral regions may achieve better accessibility through improved connectivity of networks (Vickerman, 1994*b*). The pattern of change is thus highly dependent on networks at different levels and the degree of connectivity between these. Finally, improved competitiveness of the Union as a whole depends on greater integration of markets which, in turn, depends in a major part on increased transport efficiency. If the Union is to benefit from the potential of the Single Market there has to be a genuine integration of industries in terms of production processes, not just an increase in the intra-Union trade of finished commodities. This requires the provision of transport which is consistent with the logistic needs of modern industry, where speed, efficiency and reliability are critical.

7.6. CONCLUSIONS

The main lesson to be learned from the various aspects discussed in this chapter is the clear need to consider transport infrastructure investments in terms of networks. This aspect is clearly omitted from the contractual structure of the Channel Tunnel project. The second key issue, which is still unresolved, is the appropriate degree of risk which can be shifted to the private sector when the public sector still has control of the environment in which the privately provided infrastructure is situated. The third major issue is the extent to which major infrastructure has only limited impacts in regions near to its location, but can have much more substantial effects on more distant locations, depending critically on accessibility to networks.

Perhaps the nature and scale of the Channel Tunnel has always made it unlikely to be a precise model for future private sector infrastructure projects, but nevertheless there are several lessons relevant to the private sector model and to the impact of infrastructure which can be learned. The main one of these has been the need for better definition of accessibility to allow for such infrastructure, reflecting the demands made on transport networks as well as simple distance related measures. There is already evidence that these lessons have not been learned with respect to investment in the CTRL, which at £3 billion is smaller, but with potentially more important economic and environmental effects at local, regional, national and European levels.

References

Bonavia, M. (1987) *The Channel Tunnel Story*. Newton Abbot: David and Charles.
Bruyelle, P. and Thomas, P.R. (1994) The impact of the Channel Tunnel on the Nord-Pas de Calais. *Applied Geography*, **14**, pp. 87–104.

Channel Tunnel Joint Consultative Committee (1987) *Kent Impact Study: Overall Assessment*. London: HMSO.

Channel Tunnel Joint Consultative Committee (1991) *Kent Impact Study 1991 Review: The Channel Study – A Strategy for Kent*. Report by PA Cambridge Economic Consultants, Halcrow Fox and Associates and MDS Transmodal. Maidstone: Kent County Council.

Commission of the European Communities (1980) *The Nature and Extent of a Possible Community Interest in the Construction of a Fixed Link across the Channel*, Some Results of a Study for the EEC by Coopers and Lybrand Associates and SETEC-Economie. Brussels: European Commission.

Department of the Environment (1973) *The Channel Tunnel Project*, Cmnd 5256. London: HMSO.

Department of the Environment (1975) *The Channel Tunnel and Alternative Cross-Channel Services*, Report to the Secretary of State for the Environment by the Channel Tunnel Advisory Group (Chairman, Sir Alec Cairncross). London: HMSO.

Department of Transport (1982) *Fixed Channel Link: Report of UK/French Study Group*, Cmnd 8561. London: HMSO.

Department of Transport (1986a) *The Channel Fixed Link*, Cmnd 9735. London: HMSO.

Department of Transport (1986b) *The Channel Fixed Link: Concession Agreement*, Cmnd 9769. London: HMSO.

Gibb, R., Knowles, R.D. and Farrington, J.H. (1992) The Channel Tunnel Rail Link and regional development: an evaluation of British Rail's procedures and policies. *The Geographical Journal*, **158**, pp. 273–285.

Hall, P. (1980) *Great Planning Disasters*. London: Weidenfeld and Nicolson.

Helm, D. and Thomson, D.R. (1991) Privatised transport infrastructure and incentives to invest. *Journal of Transport Economics and Policy*, **25**, pp. 231–246.

Holliday, I.M., Langrand, M. and Vickerman, R.W. (1991a) *Nord-Pas de Calais in the 1990s*, Special Report M601. London: Economist Intelligence Unit.

Holliday, I.M., Marcou, G. and Vickerman, R.W. (1991b) *The Channel Tunnel: Public Policy, Regional Development and European Integration*. London: Belhaven.

House of Commons (1981) *The Channel Link*, Second Report of the Transport Committee, session 1980/81, HC 155. London: HMSO.

Kent County Council (1994) *Strategy for Economic Development: Consultation Document*. Economic Development Department, Maidstone: Kent County Council.

Le Maire, D. and Pevsner, M. (1992) Eurotunnel: the development of traffic forecasts for a private sector project, in Bovy, P.H.L. and Smit, H.G. (eds.) *Financing European Transport*. Delft: European Transport Planning Colloquium Foundation.

McKinnon, A. (1994) Channel Tunnel freight services between Scotland and continental Europe. *Applied Geography*, **14**, pp. 68–86.

Ministry of Transport (1963) *Proposals for a Fixed Channel Link*, Cmnd 2137. London: HMSO.

Szymanski, S. (1991) The optimal timing of infrastructure investment. *Journal of Transport Economics and Policy*, **25**, pp. 247–258.

Thatcher, M. (1993) *The Downing Street Years*. London: Harper Collins.

Vickerman, R.W. (1993) The Channel Tunnel and trans-frontier cooperation, in Cappellin, R. and Batey, P. (eds.) *Regional Networks, Border Regions and European Integration*. European Research in Regional Science 3. London: Pion.

Vickerman, R.W. (1994a) The Channel Tunnel and regional development in

Europe: an overview. *Applied Geography*, **14**, pp. 9 –25.

Vickerman, R.W. (1994*b*) Transport infrastructure and region building in the European Community. *Journal of Common Market Studies*, **32**, pp. 1–24.

Vickerman, R.W. (1994*c*) Transport policy and the Channel Tunnel: UK, French and European perspectives, in Gibb, R. (ed.) *The Geography of the Channel Tunnel*. London: John Wiley, pp. 217–237.

Vickerman, R.W. (1995) The regional impacts of trans-European networks. *Annals of Regional Science*, forthcoming.

Vickerman, R.W. and Flowerdew, A.D.J. (1990) *The Channel Tunnel: The Economic and Regional Impact*, Special Report 2024. London: The Economist Intelligence Unit.

Young, H. (1990) *One of Us: A Biography of Margaret Thatcher*. London: Macmillan.

Acknowledgements

The original research for this chapter was undertaken in 1988–90 with the help of an ESRC Grant (YD00250018) and has benefited immeasurably from the work of my co-researchers Ian Holliday, now of the University of Manchester, and Gerard Marcou, of the Université de Lille II. Current work reflected in this chapter is aided by grants under the Transport and the Environment Programme of ESRC (L119251008 and L119251009).

CHAPTER 8

CRITICAL ISSUES IN REGIONAL RAIL INVESTMENT

Michael Edwards

Roger Vickerman's chapter is a fascinating critical narrative packed with expertise and is clearly the tip of an iceberg of experience and knowledge. It promises to evaluate whether the decision to make the Tunnel a private project has been a success, and to draw lessons from it.

A first issue to discuss is the question whether – or rather in what sense – such a question is *capable* of being answered. Surely the decision to make this project so strongly a private one (and embed this in statute law) was a purely ideological one, at least on the UK side. Insofar as this is the case, the 'success' of the decision is a question which social scientists must find almost impossible to answer contemporaneously. It would have to join the Falklands War, the Poll Tax, the abolition of metropolitan counties and the rest of the saga as raw material for an essentially *historical* evaluation.

There are, however, areas in which we could perhaps draw some conclusions from the experience so far, both for what this private approach has meant and to shed light on future cases. The following points are proposed as key issues for debate.

As a matter of context we must not make the textbook error of assuming too much rationality or co-ordination capacity in the investment fraternity.

1. Rationality is limited. We know that investors and their institutions are constantly searching for places to invest the flood of the world's investible funds. Despite a lot of impressive talk about portfolio management, it is evident that some rather unscientific herd behaviour goes on, with money flooding into Latin American public debt and Poland, then into North Atlantic and Japanese real estate, and into equities, now into the so-called 'emerging markets' and after that eventually into the ruins of

the USSR and Eastern Europe. There is a lemming-like quality to this investment management and, as with lemmings, wealth is destroyed as well as created.

2.   Opportunities are limited. Good returns combined with low risk are always hard to find and we have a paradox here: the pressures on governments to cut public borrowing through balanced budgets, privatizations and so on, have created new opportunities for private investment – like the Tunnel – but at the same time cut back on what was always the most secure of the investment avenues available: the mass of government stocks. Periodically we hear complaints that government stocks are in short supply and perhaps we should start thinking of certain types of infrastructure and utility investments as modern substitutes for gilt-edged stock.

3.   The investors are a heterogeneous and ill-coordinated group as we can see from the experience of our property markets where the 1980s boom was fuelled by floods of money from international banks (including a lot of lemmings); after the resulting crash some rather different banks (notably German) came in and picked up some bargains; now that the markets are rising again, some of the insurance companies and pension funds who largely stood aside from the 1980s boom and crash are buying again. There is very little coordination among these investors. The market does not coordinate, nor do governments. Investors themselves do not seem to have effective cartels to protect themselves against excessive lending into fashionable markets.

The Tunnel project emerges from Vickerman's analysis as a special case in at least two key respects:

1.   The financial arrangements are fairly transparent and unusually co-ordinated. This is in contrast to most smaller, lower-profile types of lending markets, and in contrast even to some other large projects like EuroDisney. Vickerman's chapter is very instructive on the ease with which the banks were able to coordinate and act together on the Tunnel.

2.   It is the building of a near-monopoly. Once the thing is fully operative, it is capable of being used in such a way as to defeat competition through predatory pricing. Depending on the degree to which this power is used, the proprietors will have something close to a power of taxation on cross-Channel activity so it will become a cash cow[1] – just a year or two later than planned. Clearly, attracting private investors to projects with *this* potentiality is much simpler than attracting them to links in denser networks where closer competing substitutes (other routes, other modes, other operators) will always threaten to devalue their capital.

Whatever Section 42 said, it is clear that the governments, even the British, were and remain very much committed to the Tunnel and Roger Vickerman's chapter is fascinating in pointing out (i) how active the Bank of England has been on a number of occasions and (ii) how at the outset the key decisions and authorizations were linked and orchestrated in such a way as to remove most of what we might call the decision-making risk. I would add that if any costs arise from terrorism risks they are likely to be shouldered by government, as was the case for the City of London building reinsurance.

But the most important contribution from the Vickerman analysis is in pointing out how widely distributed the enduring effects are likely to be. The direct effects impact upon accessibility for those who use the new route. The indirect effects impact more widely through enhancing the viability of other links in the European networks such as the Bruxelles-Köln line, and this will benefit those who will not be using the Tunnel itself. Indirect effects will also be felt by those who benefit from the diversion of traffic from roads, airways and airports.[2] Finally, there are the wider benefits generated by all these transport changes, such as the economic and social repercussions on production, consumption and real estate throughout Europe.

Because of the wide spread of benefits which transport projects can generate, it is almost inconceivable that user charges (i.e. fares) could ever be the basis for financing an *optimum* level of investment in the networks. As Foster and Beesley (1963) showed for the Victoria Line, if fares were high enough to give a market rate of profit on the investment, ridership would probably fall to a level where the benefits which justified the construction were simply not being realized. Although it may be possible to secure some private investment in networks, remunerated from fares or line rental (and it will be easiest in the quasi-monopoly situations of sea crossings or Alpine tunnels), this will never be up to the optimum level. This must be in every first year transport economics course.

As a result of this inherent problem of capturing benefits through fares, we are seeing attempts to bump up the profitability through property development profits. Vickerman does not say much about this but two comments need to be added:

1.   To try and capture significant parts of the benefits from transport network improvements through land values at nodal points like stations is a pretty hopeless prospect as Olberg (1990) has argued. Collecting profit through consolidated land ownership in a broad corridor would be much easier but that would need a government to do compulsory purchase on a large scale first – hardly part of the current ideological programme.

2. Efforts to maximize the contribution to railway profits from property developments at international stations does seem to me a serious threat which the social science community should alert people to.

First of all there will tend to be very concentrated over-development at the stations, and the mixed-class populations and small firms who tend to occupy the space round stations are liable to resist or suffer severe displacement effects – as we know from King's Cross. Preconditions exist for the same sorts of conflict at Zürich, Frankfurt, Brussels, and a number of Italian and other cities.

Second there seems to be a tendency in the planning for our own benighted Channel Tunnel Rail Link (CTRL) to restrict the number of passenger stations and to maximize the certainty of development profit at those that do go ahead. This has resulted in an intermediate station being located at Ebbsfleet where Blue Circle owns a substantial amount of land. It is here that the clearest estimates of the development potential and profit can be made. This could well prevent the international links playing the intended role in regional regeneration (e.g. of Stratford and Rainham) and really impede the implementation of the whole East Thames Corridor (ETC) plan.

This is not the tail wagging the dog. It is the fleas.

We can see the Anglo-French approaches presented in the chapters by Vickerman and Ampe as being diametrically opposed. Ampe refers to the prospect of rising land and property prices in passing as a dangerous threat to be avoided. Yet the British view is that these prospects are one of the main justifications for private sector involvement. Four critical issues for discussion are:

1. What we could do as social scientists is help indicate the conditions under which private investors might invest.

2. This will always be very approximate because investors vary so much, the investment climate and fashions change and rationality is limited.

3. Private agents will seek to minimize risks, and especially risks of political, democratic and consultation delays or cancellations. These are some of the most hazardous speculations available in the UK situation and we should not expect them to be shouldered without guarantees – which might well include power to claim reimbursement for abortive work. This would be a very high price for public funds to pay and is hardly an example of 'risk-sharing'.

4. Efforts to select station sites to maximize development profits will distort decisions and may well court local resistance.

Notes

1.   We should probably be treating such cases in the framework of absolute rent analysis.

2.   Concerning these 'conventional' transport benefits however, there is a major issue which none of the present chapters confronts: whether more transport output in GNP is a benign form of growth. In a world where low oil prices, GATT, the IMF, the Single Market and most transport investment are boosting the transport content in global output, we are simultaneously told that pollution trends must actually be reversed. The implications do not yet seem to have been worked through by transport analysts.

References

Foster, C.D. and Beesley, M.E. (1963) Estimating the social benefits of constructing an underground railway in London. *Journal of the Royal Statistical Society A,* **126**(1), pp. 46–92.

Olsberg, S. (1990) Gains for Trains: Land Value Capture and the Financing of Urban Transport Improvements. Unpublished MPhil Thesis in Town Planning, University College London.

CHAPTER 9

TECHNOPOLE DEVELOPMENT IN EURALILLE

Francis Ampe

9.1. INTRODUCTION

In France a very different approach to development and transport infrastructure investment has been adopted. The planning, finance and rationale for such schemes are carried out with a much greater emphasis on regional and local benefits. One example of such a development is Euralille in Northern France. It acts as a clear counter to the priorities for development in Kent and the two regions are now linked by the Channel Tunnel.

Lille is the capital city of the Nord Pas de Calais, which has a population of 4 million inhabitants. Previously, it was a centre for heavy industry and textiles. Its conurbation incorporates cities on both sides of the Franco-Belgian frontier. Within a radius of 25 km around the centre of Lille there are about 1.5 million inhabitants. Co-operation agreements have been signed (1990) between the Metropolitan Council of Lille and the local governments of Tournai, Courtrai, Mouscron and Ypres to assist in the development of the region. In addition, the Channel Tunnel and the TGV interconnections will allow the Lille region to be connected to Europe. At the heart of the TGV hub is the Euralille project which will provide a unique opportunity to capitalize on the new accessibility within the region. The Euralille project opened in mid-1994.

The city of Lille is in the centre of a triangle between London, Paris and Brussels (figure 9.1). It is also located at the junction between the new routes on the high speed rail network in Northern Europe. To take advantage of this radically improved accessibility, Lille needs to optimize the use of the existing and new transport infrastructures.

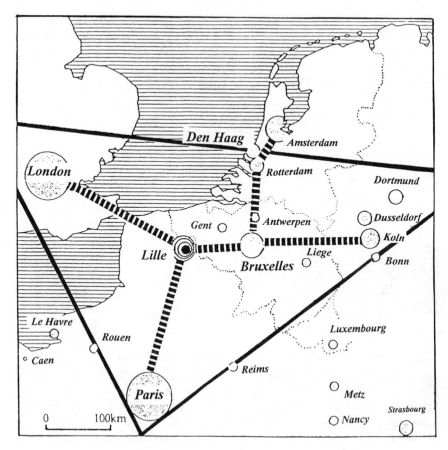

Figure 9.1   Lille at the crossroads within the Golden Triangle.

9.2.   THE TGV STRATEGY

The decision to construct the Channel Tunnel in 1986 was quickly followed by the agreement to construct the North European TGV network. Extensive local lobbying ensured the position of Lille as a key hub in this network. The convergence of time and space now means that Paris is only one hour from Lille by rail. This link was opened in May 1993. It will be followed by high speed rail connections to Brussels (30 minutes in 1996) and London, Amsterdam and Cologne in two hours. In addition, high speed trains will leave Lille-Europe station for the South East, the South of France and Southern Europe. However, there will be direct links to the Roissy-Charles de Gaulle Airport. Times and links are given in figure 9.2.

These new links will allow frequent daily connections from Lille to a

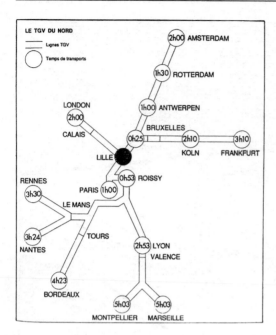

Figure 9.2   Travel times from Lille to major European cities by TGV.

range of European cities. From 1994 onwards, there will be eight trains a day to London, eight to Brussels, 15 to Paris and up to 20 direct trains bound for southern Europe. Recent studies have concluded that TGV towns do not benefit automatically from having a TGV station, but that a strategy has to be developed to take advantage of the opportunities offered by substantially improved transport links. The TGV strategy for Lille includes the following elements:

• a business bridge-head on the continent for London;

• provision of a service function to the European Union capital, Brussels;

• attraction of relocations from Paris.

The different strategy for each of the three capitals is summarized in figure 9.3.

9.3.   TGV AND AIRPORTS

In addition to the high speed rail links and the improved accessibility resulting from this investment, there is potential to link in the rail hub with the local and regional airports. Lille-Lesquin airport accommodates 832,000 passengers a year, but it is only 10 km from the city centre (figure 9.4). It also suffers from being only two hours drive from the major

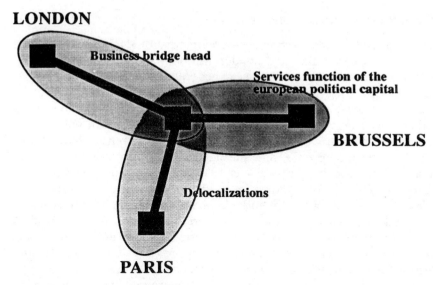

Figure 9.3   The Lille TGV strategy.

international airports at Paris-Roissy and Brussels-Zaventem. To achieve its status as a major international city, Lille must also develop its international airport. Discussion is underway on the long term possibility (30 years) of a new international airport halfway between Lille and Brussels on the high speed rail link and the motorway. In the short term, the existing capacity of Lille-Lesquin will be expanded (figure 9.4).

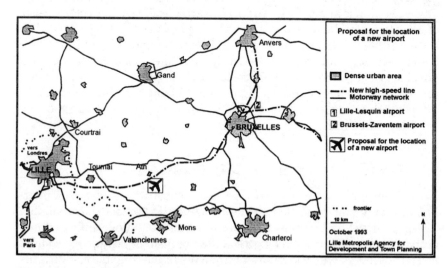

Figure 9.4   Proposals for the new airport at Lille.

9.4. ROAD CONNECTIONS IN LILLE

Lille is also at the intersection of several international motorways to Paris (A1), to Dunkirk, Calais and London (A25), to Antwerp and Rotterdam (E17), to Brussels (A27), to Valenciennes (A23) and to Reims and la Côte d'Azur. Clear objectives need to be established to allow for efficient regional and local accessibility without the necessity for relocation from other towns (e.g. Douai or Valenciennes) or an over concentration of activity in the centre of Lille. The Regional Express Transportation (TER) needs to be modernized, and the new levels of accessibility by road matched against the expected increases in demand for road transport. This problem is being studied, in particular the key position that Lille plays at the centre of the network. At present there is substantial congestion at the key entry points to the city and this reduces the attractiveness of Lille as an international centre. A ring road has to be built around Lille, and in the longer term a regional ring road will be built to link Armentieres, Valenciennes, Douai, Tournai and Courtrai.

The public transport system in the Lille metropolitan area has already proved its efficiency. Today, the urban network consists of two metro lines, one tramway line and 32 bus routes. The traffic has increased rapidly from 50 million passengers in 1982 to 95 million in 1991 since the metro has been put into service. In 1991, trams and the metro carried 60% of the total traffic, and the bus took the remainder. The VAL (Light Automatic Vehicle) system is a fully automatic driverless metro system pioneered in Lille. It was locally designed and built entirely in Lille, and opened in 1983. VAL was the first system of its kind and the technology has now been widely applied in other cities (e.g. Chicago, Jacksonville, Taipei, Toulouse and at Orly Airport in Paris). The VAL network consists of 36 stations and carries over 45 million passengers a year (1993). The system is being extended to Roubaix, Tourcoing and Belgium. Lille also has an extensive tram and bus network. Investment has been funded in a novel way. Local companies have financed improvements in the tram service and the new Franco-Italian trams (Breda) are now in operation (May 1994). In return for the financial assistance, the employees of the firms have free transport on the system.

9.5. EURALILLE – A MULTI-MODAL TRANSPORT CENTRE

At the centre of the strategy in Lille is the construction of a new international TGV station (Lille-Europe) to handle 15,000 passengers a day. The multi-level and largely transparent station building will provide a dramatic setting for the TGV trains, allowing them to be seen from street level. Passengers will also have a clear view of Lille from the station. This

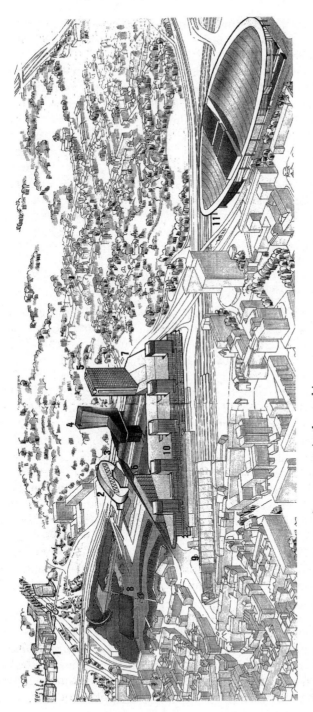

Figure 9.5   Euralille – the twenty-first century in the making

1. The Romarin Development
2. Four Star Hotel
3. Lille Europe Station
4. Crédit Lyonnais Tower

5. Lilleurope Tower
6. Le Corbusier Bridge
7. Atrium World Trade Centre
8. Urban Park

9. Existing Station (Lille Flandres)
10. Euralle Centre
11. Grand Palais Exhibition and Congress Centre

new interchange will have a direct connection to the VAL metro system and the local tram network. The station will have full customs facilities for international travellers.

Lille-Flandres station will continue to serve the internal French rail network, and it will handle 70,000 passengers a day. It is located next to the Euralille development (figure 9.5). The key design concept is the multi-modal transfer point at the Euralille development which permits easy and efficient transfer. Euralille has also been designed as a car-accessible development with direct links to the inner-city ring road. In the development there are three car parks with 6,000 spaces. Euralille is located as the gateway to the whole city and it is in an ideal situation for a major development project based on accessibility. Although the planning policy for the city is global when transport is concerned, its aims are very specific: to ensure the potential advantages of Lille's location at the strategic crossroads of Northern Europe are fully realized.

9.6.   EURALILLE – A MULTI-PURPOSE BUSINESS COMPLEX

There is a strong expectation that companies will relocate from Brussels, Paris and London to Euralille. The Euralille business complex consists of two landmark tower buildings designed by the Dutch architect and planner Rem Koohlaas. The Crédit Lyonnais Tower cost £33.5 m and has 20 floors with 14,600 m² of office space. About 41% of the available floor space (6,000 m²) will become the northern headquarters for the Crédit Lyonnais bank and the rest will be available for rent. The Lille-Europe Centre and the World Trade Centre Atrium cost £65 m and has 25,124 m² of offices on 25 floors. At the foot of this tower is a huge Atrium which opens out onto the Lille-Europe station, and the Euralille Centre covers 15,000 m². This space will accommodate a wide range of services for businesses including those located in the World Trade Centre. Euralille's Grand Palais will provide the following accommodation: Congress (20,000 m²); exhibition (20,000 m²), and concert (5,000 seats – similar to the Zénith in Paris), all of which can be used simultaneously. These facilities opened in (June 1994). When the ring road is re-routed in 1998, these facilities will become an integral part of the Euralille development (figure 9.5). The construction of a new international hotel has been delayed due to a lack of investors.

Apart from its main functions as a key transport interchange and business complex, Euralille has close links with the existing town centre where most of its workforce will still live. Other facilities have been provided as an integral part of the development. The Euralille Centre linking the two railway stations has a Carrefour hypermarket, Lille Business School, about 150 shops, a concert hall, leisure facilities and public services. It will also include housing (134 flats for sale or rental), a hotel, three serviced apartment units and offices. It is also possible that the European Foundation for Urban Studies and Architecture will set up near the Urban Park (figure 9.5). The Urban Park will be located on a 10 hectare site at the Porte de Roubaix, one of Lille's historic gates in the town fortifications. The Le Corbusier Viaduct links the Euralille development to the historical centre.

9.7. CONCLUSIONS: EURALILLE TO EUROCITY

The example of Euralille demonstrates the means by which transport and related urban development can proceed simultaneously. Development does not take place automatically when there are significant improvements in the quality of the road, rail and air infrastructure, but it provides an opportunity. One crucial component in the Euralille development has been the availability of funding, even when public budgets are limited and there has been a substantial downturn in the real estate market. Euralille is managed by a *Société d' Economie Mixte* (SEM), which is a semi-public company. The public sector has funded 54% of the development with the private sector, mainly through loans from international banks, funding the remaining 46% of the FF50 million capital. The public sector contributions have been directed towards the transport infrastructure, whilst the private sector has financed the business complex, housing and shops.

The transport infrastructure is now fully operational before the overall completion of the project. This again gives clear messages to the private sector concerning the public commitment to the project and consequently may reduce the perceived risk of the investment. Land has also been made available for a further extension of the Euralille project south of the TGV station towards the Grand Palais and then towards the Saint Sauveur goods station. Perhaps the French model for comprehensive transport and urban development with the use of semi public SEMs is one type of partnership between the public and private sectors which could be adopted in the UK and elsewhere. At the very least, it is expected that Euralille may become a Eurocity.

CHAPTER 10

DEVELOPMENT IMPACTS OF URBAN TRANSPORT: A US PERSPECTIVE

Bob Cervero and John Landis

10.1. INTRODUCTION

Any discussion of how urban transport investments shape, both economically and spatially, cities and regions of the US must initially be framed in terms of the overwhelming dominance of the private automobile. In 1990, 84.6% of journeys-to-work in the 50 largest metropolitan areas in the US were by private automobile (Pisarski, 1992; Cervero, 1994a). A host of well-documented historical, cultural, and contextual factors account for America's high degree of automobile-dependency (estimated to be 2–3 times higher than comparable settings in Europe), though according to some observers (Pucher, 1988; Newman and Kenworthy, 1989) deliberate public policies, such as artificially cheap fuel prices, have had a direct and traceable hand in this outcome.

In large part because of its ubiquity and high performance features, the private automobile and the massive freeway construction programmes that were initiated to accommodate it, helped usher in an era of seemingly unrelentless population and employment decentralization following the Second World War. In 1990, over half of the nation's population lived in the 39 metropolitan areas containing over one million residents (Hughes, 1992). The suburban population in these areas increased 55% between 1970 and 1990, while the traditional, central city population increased only 2%. By 1990, moreover, around two-thirds of all jobs in US metropolitan areas were outside of central cities, up from 45% just a decade earlier (Hughes, 1992). In recent years, most development has been occurring on the outer fringes of US metropolitan areas. In greater Atlanta, Boston, Houston, Los Angeles, and Phoenix, population and employment growth in the outer suburbs exceeded that of inner suburbs and inner cities, on average, by a factor of three (Speare, 1993). A detached single-family home with a two-car garage on a quarter acre lot, even if an hour away from a central city, has become the domicile of choice of more and more of America's burgeoning middle class. Corporate America has likewise taken up suburban and exurban addresses, often in campus-style office parks designed for cars, not pedestrians (Cervero, 1986a, 1989).

It is against this backdrop of the automobile's ascendancy and American-style sprawl that the development impacts of contemporary urban transport investments must be understood. Because most Americans already enjoyed unprecedented mobility and any new large-scale transport investments, such as heavy rail projects, provided only small incremental gains in regional accessibility, the development impacts of such investments have, to no great surprise, tended to be small and incremental also. Certainly no grand lessons into the art and science of city building can be gained by studying America's experiences with urban transport development over the postwar era, especially among a European audience. Despite the lack of significant and sustainable macro-development effects, there is nonetheless some evidence that urban transport investments have induced highly localized land-use changes and sparked real estate activities in isolated settings, especially in fast-growing suburbs. Moreover, some American transport authorities have sought to capitalize proactively on localized impacts by introducing a host of joint-development schemes aimed at recapturing some of the value added by public transport investments. Since we believe these are some of the most valuable policy insights America has to offer, we have framed our discussion largely around the themes of value capture and private-sector participation.

The first part of this chapter summarizes the results of several recent research projects that examined the development impacts of new-generation rail transit investments in the US, drawing on experiences principally in the San Francisco Bay Area and other parts of California as well as from the Washington, DC and Atlanta metropolitan areas. Evidence on the capitalization effects of transit investments on both residential and commerical-office real estate markets is also presented. Preliminary findings from the 20-year update study on the development impacts of BART (Bay Area Rapid Transit) are also discussed. The chapter then turns to the question of how successful urban transit agencies have been in recapturing some of the development benefits of transit through various leasing and special assessment tactics. The effects of transit-focused development on ridership are also summarized. The chapter ends with several observations on what steps might be necessary to stimulate value recapture programmes of urban transport investments in the US and elsewhere.

10.2. Overview of North American Studies on Urban Transport and Development

Recent Heavy Rail Systems

Most research attention on development impacts of urban transport investments has focused on newer generation heavy rail systems since these technologies have provided the largest incremental increases in regional accessibility and thus could be expected to induce the most measurable land-use impacts. The land-use impacts of modern rail systems built since 1960 in Atlanta, Philadelphia, Montreal, San Francisco, Toronto, and Washington, DC have varied widely, both between and within metropolitan areas. Overall, *ex post* evaluations of the land-use impacts of BART (Webber, 1976; Dyett *et al.*, 1979), Philadelphia's Lindenwold line (Boyce *et al.*, 1972), and Washington Metrorail (Lerman *et al.*, 1978; Paget Donnelly, 1982) found that, consistent with location theory, regional rail systems have been a force toward decentralization of both population and employment. Inter-city comparisons with 'control' cities without regional rail systems suggest these rail investments probably had some 'clustering' effects, leading to perhaps a more polycentric metropolitan form than would have existed had any of these rail transit systems not been built (Hilton, 1968; Meyer and Gomez-Ibanez, 1981; Smith, 1984).

Toronto is often heralded as the best North American example of rail transit's city-shaping abilities. A frequently cited statistic is that during the early 1960s following the opening of Toronto's Yonge Street subway line, around one-half of high-rise apartments and 90% of office construction in the city of Toronto was within a five minute walk of a train station (Heenan, 1968). Stringent land-use controls and various pro-development forces (e.g., regional government that promoted coordinated planning, rapid growth of immigrant populations) were largely responsible for intensive development around Toronto's subway lines (Knight and Trygg, 1977). Besides complementary zoning and taxation policies, the consensus of North American studies is that a number of other conditions are necessary for rail transit to exert a strong and lasting influence on urban form and land uses: a healthy and buoyant regional economy, the availability of land that is easily assembled and developed, a hospitable physical setting (in terms of aesthetics, ease of pedestrian access, etc.), and the existence of some automobile restraints (such as parking restrictions) (Knight and Trygg, 1977; Dear, 1975; Dingemans, 1978; Cervero, 1984).

Past work also suggests that rail transit investments do not stimulate real economic growth; rather they only help guide where already committed growth takes place. (All rail investments, of course, induce construction-related employment growth, which in the case of Buffalo and other areas with fairly stagnant regional economies can be significant [Paaswell and Berechman, 1981].) Overall, then, the development impacts of urban rail systems are largely distributive – e.g., in favour of one radial corridor instead of another. There is less evidence, by contrast, that North American transit investments cause shifts in population and employment between downtowns and suburbs (Knight and Trygg, 1977).

Regarding capitalization effects, previous studies have likewise shown fairly modest impacts. One study concluded that San Francisco's BART 'had a small but significant positive effect on the price of single family dwellings' (Blayney Associates, 1978). This study found a positive effect on housing prices at 1,000 feet from BART stations of between 0% and 4% which diminished rapidly with increasing distance from the station. In no case did the BART effect extend beyond 5,000 feet. Similar studies of Atlanta's MARTA (Metropolitan Atlanta Rapid Transit Authority) also concluded that transit station proximity is beneficial to residential values when stations are designed with sensitivity to surrounding neighbour-hoods (Nelson and McClesky, 1990). The potential negative effects of proximity to rail transit have likewise been studied. Indeed, an opinion survey conducted by Baldasarre *et al.* (1979) found less preference for homes near elevated BART stations. Burkhardt (1976) and Dornbush (1975) also note value decreases around BART due to such nuisances as noise and vibration, increased automobile traffic, and the perceived acces-sibility of different social classes and ethnic groups to otherwise homog-enous neighbourhoods.

Other Transit Technologies

Few macro-level impact studies of other transit technologies in North America have been conducted to date. The few that have been conducted suggest that for flexible technologies like the modern motor bus, impacts tend to be far more diffuse relative to heavy rail investments. Studies of the Shirley Highway dedicated busway system (with an exclusive lane in the freeway median) found it enabled many Washington, DC workers to reside farther away than they would have without the busway. While several suburban stations on Ottawa's dedicated busway are surrounded by mid-rise apartments and offices, interviews with developers found that the growth would have occurred regardless and that the busways merely accelerated the timing of development (Bonsall, 1985; Cervero, 1986b). In the case of Houston's bus transitway, Mullins *et al.* (1989) found relatively few impacts – developers stated it had no influence on their locational choices, and before-and-after studies at park-and-ride lots near the busway found few land-use conversions.

Investigations of light rail transit (LRT) systems in the US have similarly recorded modest land-use impacts because most LRT lines follow abandoned rail rights-of-way with minimal development potential and they also rely heavily on park-and-ride access (Cervero, 1984). LRT has been most helpful in downtown areas. In the case of Buffalo, San Jose, Sacramento, and Portland, LRT lines that operate in a downtown pedestrian mall have been important catalysts to office and retail redevelopment. Outside of downtowns, however, light-rail systems have induced few significant land use changes.

Highway System Impacts

Sprawling metropolises like Los Angeles, Phoenix, and Houston stand as testaments to the powerful decentralizing effects of highway and freeway investments. Early studies conducted in the 1950s and 1960s confirmed that freeway systems built at the time increased accessibility which lead to higher land prices near interchanges (Adkins, 1959; Mohring, 1961; Golden, 1968). However, a study of 54 US cities, including 27 with beltways, found that the greatest proportion of suburban residential developments occurred in cities without beltways (Payne-Maxie Consultants, 1980). It also showed that low-density residential developments tended to occur away from beltway areas, and medium- and high-density development clustered closer to beltways.

10.3. CAPITALIZATION OF URBAN TRANSPORT IN SINGLE FAMILY HOME VALUES: EXPERIENCES IN CALIFORNIA

In theory, to the degree that regional transportation investments provide accessibility advantages to sites served, this benefit should get capitalized into higher rents, all else being equal. As part of the 'BART at 20' update study, the capitalization effects of proximity of single-family homes to BART as well as several other California rail systems were recently studied (Landis *et al.*, 1994). Based on 1990 sales transaction data, hedonic price models were estimated, using ordinary least squares (OLS) techniques, to isolate the discrete effect of distance from transit and highways on single-family home prices, controlling for other factors that affect value. The analysis also examined the potential disamenity effect of a 300 metre buffer zone around rail lines and highways. For each home sales transaction, GIS was used to address-match a housing unit to a computerized street map, and then to measure the street distance of address-matched homes to transit stops and highway interchanges. Table 10.1 lists the variables used in the analysis.

The hedonic model, summarized in table 10.2, suggests that there is a premium on homes in Alameda and Contra Costa Counties with good

Table 10.1.   Variable descriptions and sources.

Variable	Definition	Units	Source
Dependent:			
SALEPRICE	Sale price of single family homes	$	TRW-REDI
Independent – Housing Characteristics:			
LOTSIZE	Lot size	acres	TRW-REDI
SQRFT	Total built-up living space	sq. ft.	TRW-REDI
BEDROOMS	Number of bedrooms	number	TRW-REDI
BATHS	Number of Baths	number	TRW-REDI
AGE	Age of the structure	years	TRW-REDI*
Independent – Neighbourhood Quality:			
PCTWHITE	Percent White in census tract	%	1990 Census
PCTBLACK	Percent Black in census tract	%	1990 Census
PCTHISPN	Percent Hispanic in census tract	%	1990 Census
PCTASIAN	Percent Asian in census tract	%	1990 Census
PCTOWNER	Percent homeowners in census tract	%	1990 Census
MEDHHINC	Median household income in census tract	$	1990 Census
Independent – Transportation Access:			
TRANDIST	Distance along streets to transit station	metres	ArcInfo*
HIWYDIST	Distance along streets to highway nodes	metres	ArcInfo*
NEARTRAN	Direct distance to transit line (for buffering)	metres	ArcInfo*
NEARHIWY	Direct distance to highway (for buffering)	metres	ArcInfo*

* Derived from the system or from other variables.

access to the BART system (signified by the variable, TRANSDIS). These are the two East Bay counties, outside of the city of San Francisco, served by BART. In Alameda county, for every metre a home is closer to the nearest BART station, its selling price increases by $2.29, all else being equal. A similar rise in the sales price of homes is observed in Contra Costa county, but the rate of increase is a little lower at $1.96. Contrary to expectations, an average home within the 300 metre buffer zone (signified by the variable, NEARTRAN) did not sell for a lower price compared to a similar home outside the buffer.

The model also shows that, in contrast to the influence of rail transit, proximity to highways has a depressing effect on home prices in both Alameda and Contra Costa counties. The sales price of a home in Alameda County is $2.80 lower for every metre it is closer to a highway access point, all else being equal. Additionally, being within the 300 metre zone of a highway had no appreciable effect on home sales prices. By and large, the disamenity effects of both the BART line and highways are non-existent.

Hedonic models were also estimated for single-family home sales near

Table 10.2.   Capitalization effects of transit investments on single-family home prices: BART-served Alameda and Contra Costa Counties, California

| | Dependent: SALEPRICE (Single Family House: 1990) | | | |
| | Alameda | | Contra Costa | |
	Coefficient	t-stat	Coefficient	t-stat
Home Characteristics:				
LOTSIZE	**$1.81**	**5.79**	**$2.51**	**12.71**
SQRFT	**$110.62**	**27.48**	**$107.37**	**22.91**
BATHS	$3,768.88	1.23	$297.03	0.07
AGE	$91.63	1.00	$2.08	0.02
BEDROOMS	**($5,523.37)**	**−2.20**	**($13,335.03)**	**−4.60**
Neighbourhood Characteristics:				
PCTWHITE	($125,164.75)	−1.62	($88,629.47)	−1.02
PCTBLACK	**($214,791.49)**	**−2.66**	($138,114.63)	−1.55
PCTASIAN	**($175,514.43)**	**−2.21**	($61,199.46)	−0.70
PCTHISPN	**($225,039.93)**	**−4.14**	**($143,943.67)**	**−2.78**
PCTOWNER	**($57,769.56)**	**−4.92**	**($85,097.96)**	**−4.73**
MEDINCOM	**$2.10**	**12.02**	**$2.21**	**10.81**
Locational Characteristics:				
HIWAYDIS	**$2.80**	**2.30**	**$3.41**	**6.48**
TRANSDIS	**($2.29)**	**−10.50**	**($1.96)**	**−8.78**
NEARHIWY	($108.43)	−0.03	$631.86	0.11
NEARTRAN	$5,240.62	0.81	$10,484.16	1.00
CONSTANT	**$182,376.87**	**2.23**	$138,127.16	1.58
R Square	0.80		0.76	
Observations	1,131		1,228	

Note: Coefficients in **bold print** are significant at the 95% confidence level.

other California rail systems – the CalTrain commuter line in San Mateo County (south of San Francisco) and three LRT lines (Sacramento, San Jose, and San Diego). A similar capitalization rate was found for the CalTrain commuter line as for BART, and more consistent with expectation, a disamenity effect was found for parcels within 300 metres of the commuter station. Since CalTrain relies on conventional railway technology and, as a commuter service, is reached mainly by auto-motorists who park-and-ride, the combination of noisier trains and heavy auto traffic seems to have a significant negative effect on home values for nearby properties.

In terms of the three light rail lines, which extend only around one-third the distance of BART and one-half the distance of CalTrain, no appreciable capitalization was found. In the case of hedonic models estimated for single-family homes near Sacramento and San Diego LRT stations, the variable measuring proximity was statistically insignificant.

In the case of the San Jose LRT, the hedonic model showed that transit actually takes away value from properties that are located within easy reach of its station. The decline in average home prices in San Jose is about $2 for each metre a home is closer to a transit station. Locations close to highways also appear unpopular in San Jose – on average, homes within 300 metres of a highway sell for $11,000 less than similar homes outside the buffer.

One inference of these findings is that the type of rail technology and extensiveness of the system has some bearing on home values. BART, as a relatively large system that operates modern trains that serve major urban centres, seems to exert positive influences on nearby single-family homes. As mainly single lines that serve a limited number of destinations, California's LRT lines, on the other hand, impart little value. Ostensibly, BART's value added stems from providing regional access that is some-what competitive with the auto-highway system; where transit services are far more limited, as with LRT, capitalization does not seem to occur. Additionally, the nuisance effects of the transit line in terms of noise and vibration levels, congestion, and reduced parking availability in neighbourhoods appear limited to systems that are similar to conventional railroads.

10.4.   OTHER RECENT DEVELOPMENT IMPACTS OF BART

The original BART Impact Study, carried out in the mid-1970s only a few years after the 1972 opening of the 140-mile BART system, is the most extensive study carried out to date on the development impacts of a US transit system. While the study found BART did not induce significant development impacts, especially outside of downtown San Francisco, it was perhaps premature to expect BART to have exerted meaningful land-use changes in such a short period of time. It is important to revisit BART's impacts on land-use patterns because a premise of the entire project was that it would eventually lead to mini-communities mush-rooming around suburban rail stations, thus helping to create a more multi-centric, and thus ostensibly more sustainable, settlement pattern. Indeed, the $1 billion (1967 currency) property-tax bond issue that was sold to the Bay Area public was based partly on the argument that BART would enhance quality of life in the region. Some preliminary findings of the BART at 20 update study are provided in this section. (See figure 10.1 for a map of the BART system.)

Residential Location and Densities

Between 1970 and 1990, residential population grew, on average, 20% faster in corridors not served by BART (I-580 and I-680 corridors and

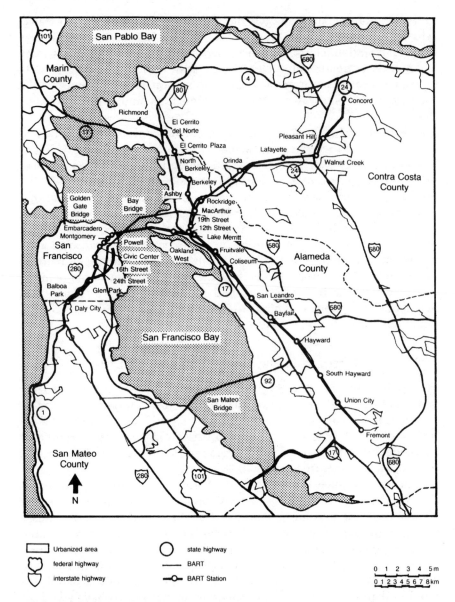

Figure 10.1   BART transit system.

Highway 1 Marin corridor) than those served by BART. Moreover, density gradients along the Fremont and Richmond lines were slightly flatter in 1990 than they were in 1980. Also, a matched-pair analysis of 1970–90 population growth within one-half mile of BART stations along the

Fremont-Richmond lines revealed growth rates were only around 5% higher for zones lying within one-half mile of nearby freeway interchanges. Overall, BART appears to have done little to channel population growth over its first twenty years of operation.

Office Development

BART's impact on office development has been spotty. Its major influence has been in downtown San Francisco, where around 40 million square feet of office inventory was built within one-quarter mile of BART from 1975 to 1992. (This compares to an addition of only 12 million square feet of office space elsewhere in San Francisco over the same period.)

In contrast, BART's influence on office development in the East Bay has been weak. The major changes have been in downtown Oakland, where around 4 million square feet of office space was added between 1975 and 1992; most of this has been for public buildings, including government offices. The only significant office cluster in the suburbs has been around the Walnut Creek station, which added around 2.5 million square feet of office space since 1975. However, this amount pales in comparison to the 22 million square feet of office space added to the I-680 freeway corridor in the suburbs of Alameda and Contra Costa County. Overall, 35 million square feet of office space was built in areas unserved by BART since BART's 1972 opening, compared to only 9 million square feet within one-half mile of an East Bay BART station.

Employment Growth

With most suburban office growth having turned its back on BART, employment growth during the 1980s has generally occurred in non-BART-served corridors. Figure 10.2 shows that, using data from *County Business Patterns* recorded at the zip code level, employment growth rates did vary dramatically by sector. BART's locational advantage seems to be predominantly in the FIRE (finance-insurance-real estate) and non-business service sectors. This is especially the case for the Fremont-Richmond lines that do not lie in the median of the freeway (unlike the bulk of the Concord line).

In terms of occupational breakdowns, BART seems to have induced businesses that hire high shares of professional, technical, and administrative/clerical workers, consistent with the finding that BART's primary locational influence was in the FIRE sectors. Along the Fremont-Richmond line, for instance, BART station areas consistently average around 20–30 percentage points more of professional, technical, and administrative/clerical workers than do businesses around nearby free-

Employment growth differential

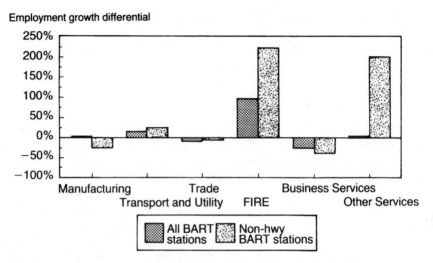

Figure 10.2 1981–1990 percentage employment growth differentials: BART station zipcodes versus 3-county region.

way interchanges. Employment densities (in workers per acre) around BART stations versus matched-paired freeway interchanges also tend to be around 12% higher in the suburbs, and around 28% higher in the more urbanized parts of the East Bay (Berkeley and Oakland).

Full asking rent (per square foot)

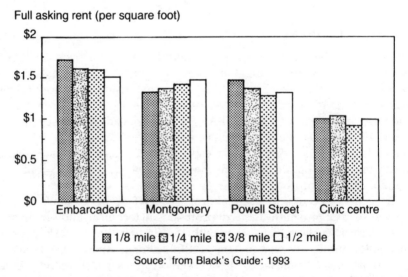

Souce: from Black's Guide: 1993

Figure 10.3 Average 1993 office rents in 1/8 mile distance rings from BART stations: Downtown San Francisco.

Full asking rent (per square foot)

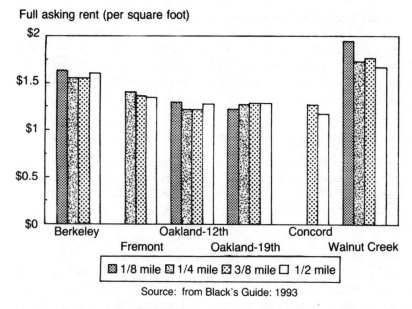

Figure 10.4   Average 1993 office rents in 1/8 mile rings from BART stations: East Bay.

Office Rents

In downtown San Francisco, BART seems to command higher office rents for buildings closest to stations (figure 10.3). This is only so for the Embarcadero and Powell Street station; in the case of the Montgomery Street station, which directly serves the priciest real estate market in San Francisco, the Financial District, rents actually increase with distance to BART. Thus, the impacts of BART on office rents in downtown San Francisco are not consistent or easily generalizable. In Berkeley, Walnut Creek, and Oakland, proximity of offices to BART seems to get capitalized into higher rent premiums (figure 10.4).

10.5. Capitalizing on Transit Investments: US Experiences with Joint Development

To the degree urban transport investments create demonstrable benefits, public agencies should be able to share in these benefits. In the US, around 115 joint development projects, mainly involving commercial and office buildings, were constructed in more than two dozen cities as of 1990 (Cervero et al., 1992); since commercial real estate markets have been fairly flat since 1990, this number probably still holds as of the mid-1990s. In enumerating joint development experiences, a fairly limited definition was applied: projects had to be in the form of a legally binding agreement between a public transit authority and private real estate developer that was voluntarily entered into, and involve some form of remuneration from the private to the public sector, either in the form of revenue-sharing or cost-sharing.

Types of Joint Development Projects

Of the 115 joint-development projects completed by 1990, around two-fifths involved cost-sharing – public-private sharing of such costs as those for excavation, construction staging sites, labour and heavy equipment, heating/ventilating/air-conditioning systems, and parking lots. Rail operators in New York City (MTA) and Philadelphia (SEPTA) have entered into by far the most cost-sharing agreements to date. New York uses zoning incentives such as density bonuses to encourage developers to renovate subway stations and relocate passageways; Philadelphia leases commercial space in suburban rail stations at favourable rates, and in return building tenants upgrade and maintain public concourses and passageways.

Around one out of four joint development projects in the US have used revenue-sharing in the form of air-rights and property leasing, connection fees (for physically linking a retail store to a station) or benefit-assessment financing. Washington's Metrorail is the national leader in striking revenue-sharing deals, having entered into nine separate station leases and eleven station connections by 1992. Atlanta ranks second; to date, MARTA has received revenues from three air-rights leases (IBM Tower, Southern Bell Tower, and Georgia State Office Building) and three station connection projects (Atlanta Plaza, Resurgens Plaza, and Rich's Department Store).

The only significant examples of benefit assessment financing so far have been for downtown people-mover systems, principally in downtown Detroit and Miami. This is largely because downtown business merchants felt the need to improve circulation so as to make the central cores more competitive with suburban shopping malls and other commercial districts, and thus willingly formed assessment districts to tax themselves to build people-movers. Over 80% of capital funds for these projects, however, have come from federal and state grants rather than assessment fees, so the level of value recapture has been fairly modest in these instances. The only US city that has aggressively pursued benefit-assessment financing for heavy rail transit is Los Angeles, which originally planned to finance upwards of 15% of capital construction projects for the planned 200-mile Metrorail through special assessments. The region's economic downturn, coupled with court challenges by some property owners over perceived inequities of benefit assessments, has stalled efforts to introduce effectively this form of value capture.

Benefits to Public Transit Agencies

To date, joint-development schemes have brought only modest benefits to US transit agencies. Although between 1979 and 1989, New York's MTA received over $63 million in capital contributions (in 1989 dollars), when these funds are amortized over the typical 30-year bond period for transit projects at an interest rate of 12.5%, they amount to only about 3% of MTA capital expenditures. Examined this way, contributions from joint-development projects accounted for, respectively, only 0.7% and 0.2% of rail capital expenditures in Washington, DC and Atlanta over the same period. Leasing and fee revenues have generally been a smaller percentage of each rail system's annual operating budget. Over the 1979–89 period, Washington's rail authority received over $20 million in leasing revenues and station-connection fee income, but these payments have never amounted to more than 0.7% of annual income. One explanation for these meagre results may be that most US transit agencies, with the possible exception of WMATA, have had limited experience in appraising the potential market value of joint-development sites and in negotiating favourable real estate deals. The modest earnings may also reflect the reluctance of most US transit boards to engage in real estate transactions and other entrepreneurial pursuits; in fact, legal restrictions often bar transit authorities in the US from land banking and from recapturing transit-induced rises in land value by acquiring excess land.

Besides lease income, joint development projects generate more fare revenues to the extent they attact more people to transit. Washington Metrorail officials calculate that the annual worth of an easement and private construction of a passageway to the Fashion Center mall near the Pentagon City station is more than $250,000, but that the annual gains in farebox revenues from being near the mall have been easily twice that amount. In all, 4.2 million Washington Metrorail riders annually have as their destinations buildings directly connected to Metro stations.

Private Benefits from Joint Development

The effects of joint development on office-commercial rents near suburban rail stations in Washington, DC and Atlanta were examined by pooling data across five station areas over the 1978–89 period (Cervero, 1994b). The station areas studied were Ballston, Bethesda, and Silver Spring (on Washington Metrorail) and Arts Center and Lenox (on Atlanta's MARTA). Real estate market impacts were measured for all commercial and office projects having over 100,000 square feet of floorspace and sited within a one-quarter-mile radius of one of the five transit stations.

Controlling for other variables, including ridership levels, type of station, and regional growth rates over time, the pooled time series/cross-sectional analysis found that the presence of joint-development projects at stations increased rents – about 15% above office projects that were not jointly developed, or at a annual rental premium of around $3 per square foot. This finding underscored the fact that joint-development projects tend to be of a high quality – typically dense, mixed use projects that enjoyed agglomeration economies and that benefited from extensive land-scaping and attractive urban designs.

Matched-pair comparisons of rents at these five stations with nearby commercial-office developments served only by freeways similarly re-vealed around a $3 per square foot rent premium. Office projects immedi-ately adjacent to Washington Metrorail stations, moreover, commanded up to 10% more in rents than did similar buildings two blocks away. Besides higher quality designs, part of the difference is due to the fact that joint-development projects usually feature more retail space than high-way-served office projects do; retail space typically leases for twice as much as office space. Mixed-use projects, moreover, have outperformed single-use office buildings in recent years, leasing new space more quickly and at higher rents. Additionally, the net leasable space can often be greater in joint-development projects because on-site tenants require less parking space, and mixed-use projects make shared parking possible. A reflection of the fact that joint-development projects command rent pre-miums is the favourable treatment they often receive in securing perma-nent financing. Long-term real estate lenders now assign credit in their loan evaluations for joint development projects because of their proven ability to generate top rents over long periods.

Due to changes in national tax laws and a notional recession, commer-cial and office real estate markets have largely dried up in the past few years in most US cities. With office and retail vacancy rates today hover-ing around 15% to 20% in most places, there will likely be few oppor-tunities for commercial joint development projects during the 1990s. Residential real estate markets, however, have been far more healthy in much of the US, providing a potentially new market niche for applying joint development practices. BART, in cooperation with local redevelop-ment authorities, has recently negotiated several joint development deals with private builders to construct mid-rise housing complexes on or near existing parking lots at the Pleasant Hill and El Cerrito stations. Rising land values and pressures for affordable housing have prompted BART seriously to consider converting parts of its vast inventory of park-and-ride lots to mid-rise housing (Bernick, 1993). Whether transit-based housing might attract significant shares of station-area residents to transit is addressed in the next section.

10.6. RIDERSHIP IMPACTS OF TRANSIT-LINKED DEVELOPMENT IN CALIFORNIA

Nowhere in the US has there been more interest in clustering housing and commercial development around rail transit stations in recent years than in California. A recent survey found that 10 of the 36 northern California jurisdictions with rail transit stations have undertaken major planning activities to attract housing and commercial development around stations, including introducing such development incentives as density bonuses, lower minimum parking requirements, tax-increment financing, and industrial development bonds. In the case of the San Jose LRT system, plans are underway to build over 13,000 units of moderate-density housing (at blended densities of 12 to 40 dwelling units per acre) near the LRT line. Besides accommodating growth and reducing traffic congestion, planners hope that focusing more growth around rail lines will improve air quality over the long run. The potential of transit-oriented development to reduce exhaust emissions is particularly important in California in that the state's largest cities currently exceed federal and state clean air standards for ozone and carbon monoxide.

Transit-based development yields benefits only to the degree that it attracts riders from automobiles to trains and buses. A recent survey of over 900 dwelling units near rail systems in California found that only 15% of all trips (and 18% of work trips) by adults residing within one-quarter mile of a rail station were by transit; three-quarters of motorized trips were by drive-alone private automobile (Cervero, 1994c). In the case of adults living near BART, they were, on average, 5 times as likely to commute by rail transit as those living in the same city but beyond one-quarter mile of BART.

The results of logit model of mode choice found that the two key factors that influenced how station-area residents commuted was their destination and availability of free parking at the workplace. Figure 10.5, which summarizes the results of the logit model in graphic form, shows that if someone living near a Bay Area rail station owns no car, works in downtown San Francisco, and has to pay for parking, there is an 88% likelihood that he or she will commute via rail transit. At the other extreme, if they have three cars available, can park free, and are destined anywhere other than San Francisco, there is only about a 1% probability they will opt for rail travel.

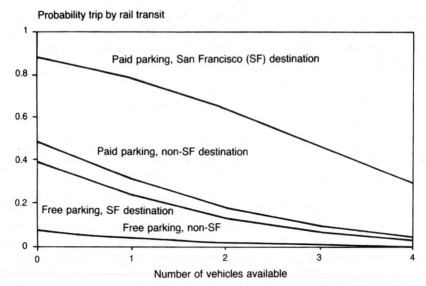

Figure 10.5   Relationship of rail commuting to parking prices, destination city, and vehicle availability: BART, 1992.

Clearly, clustering housing around rail stations will do little good if, as has been the case in California's metropolises over the past decade, most job growth occurs in the suburbs far removed from rail stations and suburban workers continue to park for free. A built form, similar to that of Stockholm or Toronto, where many offices and workplaces in addition to residences are within walking distance of rail will be necessary if California's effort to promote transit-based housing projects is to have much payoff. In addition to higher fuel prices and possibly road pricing, a stronger regional planning effort will be necessary in order to produce such a built form. To date, this has proven to be an elusive goal in the US.

Stockholm, Sweden provides perhaps the best example anywhere of the potential benefits of integrating rail transit and regional development. Stockholm is an appropriate comparison, we would argue, in that Sweden is one of the world's most affluent countries and has a high automobile ownership rate (2.1 persons/vehicle) (Westin, 1993). Moreover, greater Stockholm is surrounded by vast open spaces and experienced rapid growth following World War II, meaning that it could easily have followed an American-style highway-oriented development pattern. Instead, Stockholm's City Council built a number of satellite new towns over the past three decades, most surrounded by greenbelts and connected to Stockholm city by rail. An overriding principle was to distribute industry and offices to satellites roughly in proportion to residential population in order to avoid a 'dormitory town environment' (Hall, 1988; City of Stockholm, 1989; Cervero, 1993).

The impact of this built form on travel choices has been unmistakable. In 1990, 38% of the residents and 53% of the workers of Stockholm's rail-served new towns commuted by rail transit. For all of Stockholm County, rail accounted for 42% of commute trips (Cervero, 1993). Urban development patterns, alone, did not produce these results, however. Parking and motoring are expensive in all Swedish cities, and nearly all appartments are publicly subsidized. Cities like Stockholm are testaments to how integrated rail and land-use planning in combination with market-rate pricing of automobile travel and other transportation demand management strategies can reduce auto-dependency.

10.7. CONCLUSION

This chapter has summarized urban transport and development relationships in the US. Recent evidence from California revealed some degree of capitalization benefits, which over the long run could be expected to induce clustering around rail stations. However these impacts are not easily generalizable. The type of transit technology and the spatial extent of the system seems to have some bearing on rates of capitalization. In the case of BART, closeby properties enjoyed a value premium; for more modest LRT systems, proximity played little role in influencing residential property values. In general, the capitalization effects of rail transit seem highly localized and contextual. The inability to generalize easily could render the introduction of value capture mechanisms more difficult.

To date, the most progress in recouping some of the benefits induced by public investments in transport has been through various joint-development schemes tied to local commercial real estate projects. While value capture is a conceptually elegant mechanism for co-financing public transport investments, in practice it is fraught with implementation difficulties. For the most part, benefit assessment schemes, which are the purest form of value capture among joint-development approaches, have been limited to a handful of people-mover systems. Value capture approaches seem most feasible in settings with an expanding, buoyant macro-economy and where the distinction between benefiting and non-benefiting property-owners can be easily delimited. Some land-owners have argued that proximity to transit can be a disbenefit (e.g., more security expenses), and thus suggest that some form of 'disvalue compensation' be provided. In the case of BART, little evidence of a disamenity effect was found. For conventional railroad systems, however, some disvalue effect seems to hold for residential percels within a 300 metre zone of a station.

Attempts by US transit properties to leverage transit investments through value capture have been significant in number, but in terms of revenue generation, these efforts have yielded meagre results. Cost-sharing seems to be the most popular form of joint-development, in part because it is easiest for all parties to agree upon the terms. Regions with no prior joint-development experience might consider first initiating cost-sharing programmes on these very grounds; with time, the more difficult practice of revenue-sharing might later be introduced.

The potential of rail transit to lure motorists to trains has spawned a series of transit-based housing projects in the US in the past few years, especially in California. The ridership impacts of transit-based housing have generally been modest. With most employment growth occurring away from rail transit stations and motorists continuing to receive subsidies (mainly in the form of free parking), the ability of transit-based housing programmes to induce significant ridership increases seems in doubt. Experiences in other countries suggest that rail transit planning must be coordinated on a regional scale, and matched with constraints on automobile usage, to yield significant ridership and social benefits.

In short, urban transport and land development have had a rather tenuous relationship in the US over the postwar period. In isolated settings, rail transit seems to have produced value gains and induced growth. However the circumstances that brought about these changes are not easily generalizable. Perhaps the best lessons from the US are in the area of leveraging public transport investments through joint-development initiatives. While these efforts have failed to generate substantial income for US transit properties, to the degree they represent initial efforts at recapturing publicly created added value, every effort should be made to expand these programmes – both as an aid to cash-strapped governments and as a lever to coordinated transport and land development.

References

Adkins, W. (1959) Land Value Impacts of Expressways in Dallas, Houston, and San Antonio, Texas. *Highway Research Board, Bulletin 227*, pp. 50–65.

Baldassare, M., Knight, R. and Swan, S. (1979) Urban service and environmental stressor: The impacts of the Bay Area Rapid Transit System on residential mobility. *Enviroment and Behavior*, **11**(4), pp. 125–141.

Bernick, M. (1993) The Bay Area's emerging transit-based housing. *Urban Land*, **52**(7), pp. 38–41.

Blayney Associates (1978) *The Study of Proprety Prices and Rents: BART Impact Study*. Berkeley: Metropolitan Transportation Commission.

Bonsall, J. (1985) *A Bus for All Seasons*. Ottawa: Ottawa-Carleton Regional Transit District.

Boyce, D., Allen, W., Mudge, R., Slater, P., and Isserman, A. (1972) *Impacts of Rapid Transit on Suburban Property Values and Land Development: Analysis of the Philadelphia-Lindenwold High-Speed Line*. Philadelphia: University of Pennsylvania.

Burkhardt, R. (1976) *Summary of Research: Joint Development Study*. New York: Administration and Managerial Research Association.

Cervero, R. (1984) Light rail transit and urban development. *Journal of the American Planning Association*, **50**(2), pp. 133–147.

Cervero, R. (1986a) *Suburban Gridlock*. New Brunswick, Connecticut: Center for Urban Policy Research.

Cervero, R. (1986b) Urban transit in Canada: Integration and innovations at its best. *Transportation Quarterly*, **43**, pp. 46–57.

Cervero, R. (1989) *America's Suburban Centers: The Land Use-Transportation Link*. Boston: Unwin Hyman.

Cervero, R. (1993) *Transit-Supportive Development in the United States: Experiences and Prospects*. Washington, DC: U.S. Department of Transportation, Federal Transit Administration.

Cervero, R. (1994a) Changing live-work spatial relationships: Implications for metropolitan structure and mobility, in Brotchie, J. et al. (eds.) *Productive and Sustainable Cities*. Sydney: Longman Cheshire.

Cervero, R. (1994b) Rail transit and joint development: Land market impacts in Washington, DC and Atlanta. *Journal of the American Planning Association*, **60**(1), pp. 83–94.

Cervero, R. (1994c) Transit-based housing in California: Evidence on ridership impacts. *Transport Policy*, **1**(3), pp. 174–183.

Cervero, R., Hall, P. and Landis, J. (1992) *Transit Joint Development in the United States: A Review of Recent Experiences and an Assessment of Future Potential*. Washington, DC: Urban Mass Transportation Administration, U.S. Department of Transportation.

City of Stockholm (1989) *The Development of Stockholm*. Stockholm: City of Stockholm.

Dear, M. (1975) Rapid transit and office development. *Traffic Quarterly*, **29**(2), pp. 223–242.

Dingemans, D. (1978) Rapid transit and suburban residential land use. *Traffic Quarterly*, **32**(2), pp. 289–306.

Dornbush, D. (1975) BART-induced changes in property values and rents, in *Land Use and Urban Development Projects, Phase I, BART Impact Study*. Washington, DC: U.S. Department of Transportation and U.S. Department of Housing and Urban Development.

Dyett, M., et al. (1979) *The Impact of BART on Land Use and Urban Development: Interpretative Summary of the Final Report*. Washington, DC: U.S. Department of Transportation.

Golden, J. (1968) *Land Values in Chicago: Before and After Expressway Construction*. Chicago: Chicago Area Transportation Studies.

Hall, P. (1988) *Cities of Tomorrow: An Intellectual History of Urban Planning and Design in the Twentieth Century*. Oxford: Basil Blackwell.

Heenan, W. (1968) The Economic Effect of Rapid Transit on Real Estate Development. *The Appraisal Journal*, **36**, pp. 212–224.

Hilton, G. (1968) Rail transit and the pattern of cities: The California case. *Traffic Quarterly*, **67**, pp. 379–393.

Hughes, M. (1992) Regional economics and edge cities, in *Edge Cities and ISTEA: Examining the Transportation Implications of Suburban Development Patterns*. Washington, DC: U.S. Department of Transportation, Federal Highway Administration.

Knight, R. and Trygg, J. (1977) Urban mass transit and land use impacts. *Transportation*, **5**(1), pp. 12–24.

Landis, J., Guhathakurta, S. and Zhang, M. (1994) Capitalization of Transportation Investments into Single Family Home Prices: A Comparative Analysis of California Transit Systems and Highways. Berkeley: Institute of Urban and Regional Development, University of California, Working Paper.

Lerman, S., Damm, D., Lam, E. and Young, J. (1978) *The Effects of the Washington Metro on Urban Property Values*. Washington, DC: Urban Mass Transportation Administration, U.S. Department of Transportation.

Meyer, J. and Gomez-Ibanez, J. (1981) *Autos, Transit, and Cities*. Cambridge: Harvard University Press.

Mohring, H. (1961) Land values and the measurement of highway benefits. *Journal of Political Economy*, **79**, pp. 236–249.

Mullins, J., Washington, E., and Stokes, R. (1989) Land use impacts of the Houston transitway system. *Transportation Research Record*, No. 1237, pp. 29–38.

Nelson, A. and McClesky, S. (1990) Improving the effects of elevated transit stations on neighborhoods. *Transportation Research Record*, No. 1266, pp. 174–180.

Newman, P. and Kenworthy, J. (1989) Gasoline consumption and cities: A comparison of U.S. cities with a global survey. *Journal of the American Planning Association*, **56**(1), pp. 24–37.

Paaswell, R. and Berechman, J. (1981) *An Analysis of Rapid Transit Investments: The Buffalo Experience*. Washington, DC: U.S. Department of Transportation, Urban Mass Transportation Administration.

Paget Donnelly (1982) *Rail Transit Impact Studies: Atlanta, Washington, San Diego*. Washington, DC: U.S. Department of Transportation, Urban Mass Transportation Administration.

Payne-Maxie Consultants (1980) *The Land Use and Urban Development Impacts of Beltways*. Washington, DC: U.S. Department of Transportation, Federal Highway Administration.

Pisarski, A. (1992) *New Perspectives in Commuting*. Washington, DC: Federal Highway Administration, U.S. Department of Transportation.

Pucher, J. (1988) Urban travel behavior as the outcome of public policy: The example of modal-split in Western Europe and North America. *Journal of the American Planning Association*, **54**(4), pp. 509–520.

Smith, W. (1984) Mass transit for high-rise, high-density living. *Journal of Transportation Engineering*, **100**(6), pp. 521–535.

Speare, A. (1993) Changes in Urban Growth Patterns: 1980–90. Cambridge, Massachusetts: Lincoln Institute of Land Policy, Working Paper.

Webber, M. (1976) The BART experience – What have we learned? *The Public Interest*, **12**(3), pp. 79–108.

Westin, K. (1993) Sweden: Moving towards a safer environment, in Salomon, A. *et al*. (eds.) *Billions of Trips a Day*. Dordrecht: Kluwer, pp. 367–385.

Chapter 11

Accessibility and Development Impacts

Michael Wegener

There is broad agreement that transport is one of the major factors determining the spatial organization of urban areas. Medieval cities were built for walking, and this required that living and working were close together. The railway made spatial division of labour possible and so opened the way for the growth of cities. Rapid transit and the private car have facilitated the expansion of metropolitan areas over wider and wider territories. However, the growing separation of human activities demands ever longer trips and greater volumes of traffic with all their associated problems of congestion, traffic accidents, energy use, pollution and land consumption.

In the 1950s first efforts were made in the United States to study systematically the interrelationship between transport and location in cities. Hansen (1959) demonstrated for Washington, DC, that locations with good accessibility had a higher chance of being developed, and at a higher density, than remote locations ('How accessibility shapes land use'). The recognition that trip and location decisions co-determine each other and that therefore transport and land-use planning needed to be coordinated, quickly spread among American planners, and the 'land-use transport feedback cycle' (figure 11.1) became a commonplace in the American planning literature.

The set of relationships implied by the land-use transport feedback cycle can be summarized as follows:

1.   The distribution of *land uses* such as residential, industrial or commercial across the urban area determines the locations of human *activities* such as living, working, shopping, education or leisure.

2.   The distribution of human *activities* in space requires spatial interactions or trips in the *transport system* to overcome the distance between the locations of activities.

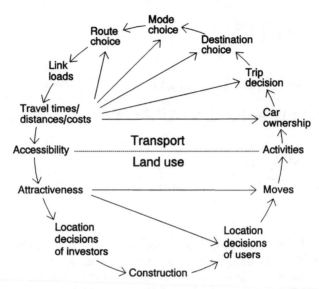

Figure 11.1   The 'land-use transport feedback cycle'.

3.   The distribution of infrastructure in the *transport system* creates opportunities for spatial interactions that can be measured as *accessibility*.

4.   The distribution of *accessibility* in space co-determines location decisions and so results in changes in the *land-use* system.

Thirty-five years later, Robert Cervero and John Landis inform us that all this may be wrong. According to their impressive collection of evidence from North American cities, locations close to rail stations in general have not attracted more development and not generated higher land values than more remote locations; transit investments have not caused shifts in population and employment between downtowns and suburbs; and the greatest proportion of suburban residential development occurred in cities without freeways. If rail transit and freeways are compared, rail is losing out. In the San Francisco Bay area, residential population grew, on average, 20% faster in corridors only served by freeways than in those served by BART, and also employment growth occurred mostly in non-BART-served corridors, except office development with professional, technical and administrative/clerical employment. And even the reverse relationship from land use to transport, that land use determines travel behaviour, does not seem to work any longer, as witnessed by only 15% of all trips of adults residing near rail stations in California being by transit.

The evidence is disturbing. It seems to undermine the body of theory expressed by the land-use transport feedback cycle and embedded in all land-use transport simulation models dating back to the seminal *Model of*

Metropolis by Lowry (1964): that transport shapes cities and that therefore transport policy is the right way to influence spatial urban development, and that transport is a function of land use, and that therefore land-use policy is the right way to influence transport.

The apparent dissolution or at least weakening of the interdependency between land use and transport comes very inconvenient at a time when planners are desperately looking for ways to come to grips with the negative environmental impacts of car traffic in cities under the threat of long-term climate change. Will higher-density, mixed use development projects near rail transit stations make much difference if they are dwarfed by concurrent much larger growth near expressway interchanges, and even if transit-oriented projects are implemented, will their residents ride by rail or continue to use their cars? As Cervero himself has been one of the most eloquent promoters of transit-oriented land-use policies (Cervero, 1991), the evidence presented here deserves attention.

The key to understanding why in contemporary North American cities the interaction between land use and transport has become so weak lies in the socioeconomic conditions under which it takes place. It is useful to remember that the land-use/transport feedback cycle was proposed at a time when accessibility was still a scarce resource (Hansen used data of Washington, DC between 1948 and 1955). Today all parts of North American metropolitan regions are served by freeways and are almost equally accessible. Most roads are free and fuel is ridiculously under-priced, so the cost of car driving is negligible. The small differences in accessibility are usually more than compensated by amenities such as clean air, quietude, closeness to nature or social prestige, and whatever differences in attractiveness remain are levelled off by the price elasticity of the real estate market. Furthermore, in the most advanced metropolitan regions, employment is rapidly decentralizing into the residential suburbs and beyond. Most importantly, there is little development control and strong competition between municipalities and rarely any regional planning.

It is not surprising that, under conditions of ubiquitous accessibility, incremental transport improvements have little effect on location. It is interesting to look at a perhaps extreme counter example. In Tokyo, one of the most decentralized cities in the world, suburbanization is almost totally led by rail transit, and residential land values are largely a function of rail travel time to Tokyo Station. This is so because in Tokyo employment is still highly centralized and central parking is unaffordable. So for most people, the car is no alternative for suburb-to-centre journeys. With commuting by rail of more than one hour one-way being common, accessibility remains a primary value strongly determining all location and travel decisions.

The lesson from the Tokyo example is that the land-use transport feedback cycle remains in effect only where accessibility is a scarce commodity. This implies that in metropolitan areas with inexpensive transport, little planning control and a deregulated land market, policies to influence location or travel behaviour only by incentives must fail. This explains why public transport investment alone does not lead to concentrations of development near transit stations and why transit-oriented mixed-used development alone does not lead to significant reductions of car use. The consequence is that a synergistic mix of incentives *and* restrictive measures seem necessary: incentives to promote higher-density mixed-use development and environment-friendly modes such as public transport, cycling and walking, and constraints on urban sprawl through stricter land-use control and on car driving through speed limits, parking restrictions and higher fuel taxes.

This policy mix has become standard practice in many European countries. The achievements of the Netherlands in introducing car restraint schemes in residential areas, extensive networks of cycling lanes and pedestrianized neighbourhood shopping centres are well known. The Netherlands, Britain and the Scandinavian countries pioneered public-transport oriented new towns centred around commuter rail stations. In general, countries with the strongest interventionist planning system have been more successful in containing dispersal. In the Netherlands, for instance, most residential land passes through public ownership before being released for development with the effect that residential development occurs only where and when the community decides. Germany has introduced area-wide speed limits of 30 km/h in residential neighbourhoods. All European countries have fuel prices about four times as high as the United States or Canada.

The combined results of these policies is that European cities on average use only one quarter of the per capita transport energy consumption of North American cities (Newman and Kenworthy, 1989). The main causes for this difference are controversial. Most experts agree with Newman and Kenworthy that urban density is the key variable (Hall, this volume). Following this line of argument, higher densities are more suited for public transport and walking and cycling. The average density of European cities is in fact twice as high as that of North American cities. That seems to correspond to their higher share of public transport use. However, from a policy point of view it is more useful to relate the difference in transport energy consumption to fuel cost. From that perspective both high transport energy consumption and low urban densities in North American cities are a consequence of inexpensive transport – people drive more because travel is cheap, which is in line with economic theory, and so can afford to live in low-density suburbs.

The implications of this economic explanation for policy analysis are profound. The message is that higher densities combined with low fuel cost will not lead to significant energy savings, whereas increased fuel taxes will achieve significant energy savings without unacceptable sacrifices in mobility, even if current densities are not changed. This has been demonstrated in simulation experiments for Dortmund in Germany (Wegener, 1995). In fact, to increase fuel taxes by between 5% and 8% per year in the future has been seriously discussed by the Green parties in several European countries. It is one of the advantages of this strategy that it can be immediately implemented, whereas introducing higher densities – by infill or in new residential areas – will affect only a very small proportion of the total building stock per year.

Cervero and Landis are perfectly aware that only a comprehensive mix of policies including regulatory and financial restrictions on the car and stronger regional planning will lead to sustainable cities. From the point of view of the Unites States they call this an elusive goal. The Intermodal Surface Transportation Efficiency Act (Paaswell, this volume) seems to herald a paradigm shift in transport planning in the United States. The European experience indicates that there may be no alternative.

References

Cervero, R. (1991) Congestion relief: the land use alternative. *Journal of Planning Education and Research*, **10**(2), pp. 119–129.

Hansen, W.G. (1959) How accessibility shapes land use. *Journal of the American Institute of Planners*, **25**, pp. 73–76.

Lowry, I.S. (1964) *A Model of Metropolis*. RM-4035-RC. Santa Monica, CA: Rand Corporation.

Newman, P. and Kenworthy, J. (1989) *Cities and Automobile Dependence. An International Sourcebook*. Aldershot: Gower Technical.

Wegener, M. (1995) Reduction of CO_2 emissions of transport by reorganisation of urban activities, in Hayashi, Y. and Roy, J. (eds.) *Land Use, Transport and the Environment*. Dordrecht: Kluwer (forthcoming).

CHAPTER 12

THE COMING OF SUPERTRAM: THE IMPACT OF URBAN RAIL DEVELOPMENT IN SHEFFIELD

Peter Townroe

12.1. INTRODUCTION

The South Yorkshire Supertram started to take fare-paying passengers at the end of March 1994. Running at six minute intervals through most of the day, from 6.00 am to 10.00 pm, a service began between the city centre in Sheffield and the Meadowhall shopping centre, a distance of 7 km. The complete 29 km network has three arms stretching north-west, north-east and south-east of the city centre. This is the initial Supertram investment, planned to be fully operational by the end of 1995. Further extensions, within Sheffield and to Rotherham, and possibly to Barnsley, are at a planning stage only. The current investment is £240m.

Each of the 25 trams can carry 256 people, with seating for 88. The vehicles are electrically powered from an overhead catenary, on a 750 volt d.c. system. Built by Siemens in Dusseldorf, they are very quiet and smooth running. The fares are at a small premium over the equivalent bus fare, using tickets purchased from machines at the stations. Discount tickets are available for advance purchase from local retailers, such as newsagents, with concessions for children and for pensioners. The forecast ridership, when in full operation, is 20 million trips per annum with an average trip length between 4 and 5 kilometres.

The 50 stops are at approximately 500 m intervals, with a stopping time of only 20 seconds. The lines are on-street for nearly half of their length, entirely so across the city centre. This contrasts with other current British light rail schemes. However, the vehicles and the station platforms have been designed for level entry. The initial seven-year operating franchise is held by a subsidiary company of the South Yorkshire Passenger Transport Executive, the agency responsible for the investment.

This chapter briefly describes the history of the system, including the various analytical and legislative stages of scrutiny of the investment. It then describes the various categories of urban development impact that will be felt alongside its transport impact within Sheffield. From this a number of methodological issues arise for research into these impacts, and progress made into this research is reported.

12.2. SOME HISTORY

For a British city of more than 500,000 residents, Sheffield always had an underdeveloped suburban rail system. This was partly because of topography, but also because it was not a regional centre in the sense of equivalent sized cities. It did not have a wide-spread commuter, shopping and service catchment. The city is bounded to the west by the Pennines where the city boundary meets the boundary of the Peak District National Park, and there are significant urban centres close to the north, the south and the east. Travel to work was always concentrated within the city boundaries. In the first half of the twentieth century this concentration fostered the development of a local on-street tramway system, and the growth of a prized municipal bus company with a very strong local service ethos.

By 1960 the on street trams were gone, along with associated trolley buses, swept away to provide greater flexibility in the use of road space – for private cars and commercial vehicles as well as for the buses. At the same time, post-war reconstruction had resulted in limited investments in major urban road schemes:

- two-thirds of an inner-ring road, half of which is dualled;
- a major dual route across the city centre;
- the 5 km Parkway, joining the city centre to the M1 from 1968;
- stretches of outer-ring road to dual standard in the south east of the city.

Compared with other major cities, Sheffield did not receive major investments on its principal radial arterial routes. The car culture did not press politically,[1] there were relatively few long distance commuters, and Sheffield was not on major inter-urban axes, especially after the M1 and M62 motorways were constructed.

By the late 1970s, with the growth in car ownership and car usage starting to exert a measure of rush-hour pressure in the city, thought was being given to further transport investment – to the 'missing link' in the inner ring road, to upgrading key arterial roads, to using traffic management and subsidy measures to foster the use of buses, and to a possible investment in an urban light rail system to complement the limited commuter potential of the local heavy rail lines (SYPTE, 1978). A joint land-use/transportation study was presented by consultants in 1976. A strategy based on new suburban mainly segregated tram lines was rejected at that time on grounds of capital expenditure, although the study did recommend safeguarding possible routes.[2]

By 1985 however, consideration of an urban light rail system had turned into a specific proposal, with a technical evaluation of a cross city centre route for what was subsequently referred to as Supertram (SYPTE, 1985). This was against the background of a successful subsidy policy towards the local bus service, then operated by the South Yorkshire Passenger Transport Executive. This policy was withdrawn in the mid-1980s in the face of government policy on the use of local government income, and the proposals to deregulate both municipal and private bus operators nationwide outside London in 1986.[3]

The 1985 preliminary financial appraisal and technical evaluation of the Supertram proposal was complemented by a wider cost benefit analysis, with a view to qualifying for a capital grant from central government under Section 56 of the 1968 Transport Act. Reassurance from the appraisal and the evaluation resulted in a private bill being deposited in Parliament in November 1985. However, the necessary legislation was not passed until 1988, in the face of objections from Sheffield City Council. The approval for a Section 56 grant finally came in December 1990, allowing construction to start in 1991.

It could be argued that the Transport Executive had a professional vested interest in promoting a fixed-track investment, and in opting for light rather than heavy rail. The Executive provides and maintains all fixed public transport infrastructure in the County, except the assets of British Rail. This infrastructure includes stops and interchanges. The policies of the local authorities towards school buses, concessionary fares, etc. are implemented by the Executive, including the support given to social subsidy on the local heavy rail network, but the Executive no longer runs its own bus fleet. It has leased 50% of its buses to private operators. The remainder was sold to its employees on an operating franchise basis in December 1993. The attractions of running an urban light rail system are clear.

In the event, the 1991 construction activity started on a line for Supertram that had not been in the original legislation. The original choice of routes, influenced by the work of consultants, was very political. A second special Act of Parliament had been passed in 1990 to pave the way for a rerouteing of a publically contentious stretch of the original Line 1 out of the large municipal Manor housing estate; but more especially also to allow Line 2 to link the city centre with the large Meadowhall Shopping Centre. This mall-based centre, the largest in the United Kingdom with 1.2

million square feet of retail space, parking for 12,000 cars and 9 million potential customers living within a drive time of 60 minutes, opened in September 1990. The new Line had political support from Rotherham Borough Council which could see the potential for a future extension in its direction. It was also seen as a key transport link for both spectators and competitors for the 1991 World Student Games, between the Ponds Forge swimming pool in the city centre, the athletes' accommodation on Park Hill, and the Don Valley Stadium and the Don Valley Arena, all close to the Line 2 route. However, the 1991 operating deadline was missed comfortably with the legislative and financial delays. Line 2 opened three years later, to run down a corridor (largely on old rail routes) of low residential density, and apparently to support a hugely successful regional shopping centre which has already taken trade from the city centre of Sheffield[4] (figure 12.1). In defence of this, the Line has been seen as offering a contribution to the economic regeneration of the Lower Don Valley.[5] The Sheffield Urban Development Corporation lent its weight in support of the Supertram investment, following an evaluation which claimed a potential contribution of up to 2,000 additional jobs in the Valley along a 400-metre corridor of the track.[6]

The two Acts of Parliament gave the Passenger Transport Executive powers to raise loans as well as to build and operate the Lines. The loans needed to be supported by grant aid from central government under Section 56 of the 1968 Transport Act. This grant aid required that benefits be demonstrated over and above the fare revenues. Consultants were appointed to provide this demonstration (MVA, 1987).[7] The grant has covered half of the total cost of the Supertram investment. The IDOPs Programme of the European Community also contributed 25%, or £13 million, towards Line 2 through the Lower Don Valley. Central government has provided increased financial support to the local authority members of the Passenger Transport Authority to cover the costs of servicing the necessary loan finance.[8] Restrictions on local government capital expenditure in general, however, have made it very difficult for Sheffield City Council to invest in ancillary works and environmental improvements associated with Supertram. In particular, and regrettably, development of park-and-ride sites has come as almost an afterthought, rather than as an integral part of the original investment.

12.3. THE URBAN DEVELOPMENT IMPACTS

In 1989, the criteria for the payment of Section 56 grant aid were changed. Grant is now payable, at varying rates, to reflect external benefits which flow from the transport investment and which are not reflected in the cash revenues. The principal external benefit from an urban public transport

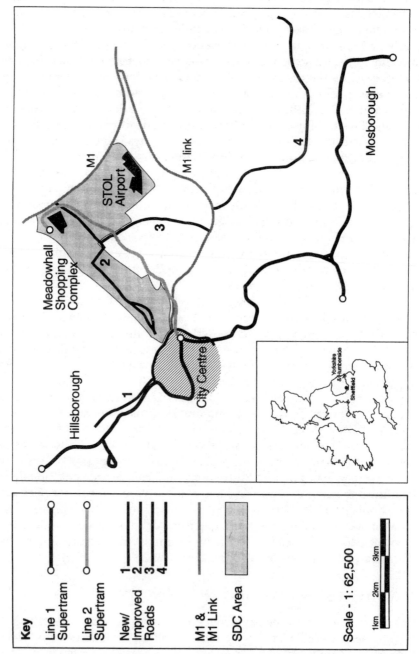

Figure 12.1

investment comes about from the relief of road traffic congestion. In the Sheffield case estimates of patronage levels for the Supertram were derived from a computer model (VIPS) based on passenger movements on the local bus network. These estimates were then used to forecast the gains to be achieved by road users within the city. These estimates are currently being evaluated *ex-post* as the network comes into operation, in a study undertaken for the Department of Transport and the South Yorkshire Passenger Transport Executive by Wootton Jeffries, transport consultants, and the Transport Studies Unit of the University of Oxford.

The transport impacts of urban light rail proposals can be looked at through a cost benefit framework similar to that used for intercity trunk road and motorway schemes. The Department of Transport Standing Advisory Committee on Trunk Road Assessment, which has assisted in the continuous development of the COBA approach to trunk road appraisal, reported in 1986 on the appraisal methodology for urban road improvement schemes (SACTRA, 1986). The Report led to the use of congested trip assignment models for urban road networks. It also recommended allowance be made for the disruption effects during the construction period and linkages to town planning considerations. Both of these two latter aspects have relevance for appraisals of urban light rail systems. It is also appropriate to note that a number of standard criticisms of the COBA approach have a bearing on the assessment of the primary road congestion impacts of a new tramway (Townroe and Dabinett, 1994; and Bateman *et al.*, 1993):

- the focus on vehicles rather than passenger journeys;
- a lack of distinctive adjustment for goods vehicles;
- valuation of pollution effects;
- absence of reference to distributional impacts;
- no counting in of trip generation effects.

The external benefits from a new urban light rail system do not stop, however, at the relief of congestion on the urban road network.[9] There are secondary impact benefits, more often asserted than empirically substantiated, which have to do with wider aspects of urban development. These secondary impacts are frequently put forward as an urban economic regeneration argument for the investment.

New transport infrastructures and transport services will change the accessibility and transport cost profiles within a city. They will do this for both households and for businesses. They will also influence the perceptions held by investors and decision makers of the city overall and of areas within the city. These changes together will be evidenced through the markets for labour, the markets for goods and services and the market for property in the city. And in principle, outcomes can be measured in terms

of physical development and jobs. These secondary impacts are the subject of the Sheffield Supertram Impact Study at Sheffield Hallam University (supported by the Economic and Social Research Council [CRESR,
1993]).

The study is organized around four themes:

- city image;
- land and property;
- business activity;
- labour market patterns.

(a) City Image

Many local governments have come to recognize that the image presented
by the city both to its own citizens and to external opinion formers and
decision makers, can directly influence the confidence with which investment is attracted locally (Kottler *et al.*, 1993). In the past decade, place
marketing has become an additional policy investment for urban regeneration. Cities compete for footloose investment, from both public and
private sectors, while also seeking to offer reassurance to local investors.

A city image is carried on many different shoulders – on the names of
personalities, on the names of companies, on sports clubs and their facilities, on noted cultural amenities, on political reputation, and so forth. A
new transport system may contribute positively to this image. It can
provide:

- an indication of civic pride;
- a message of serious intent in regeneration;
- a marker for the acceptance of modern technology;
- a 'European' flavour;
- a signpost of forward thinking.

These aspects of image in the anticipated overall benefits of the Supertram
investment are particularly important for Sheffield. The recession of the
late 1970s and early 1980s hit the local economy very hard indeed, with a
dramatic loss of jobs in manufacturing, particularly in the Sheffield core
sectors of steel making and metals engineering. The local political response made at that time did not find favour with the United Kingdom
central government. And differences between local councillors and local
businessmen in Sheffield were well publicized. There was a loss of confidence in the city.

However from 1985 onwards a local private/public sector partnership
was built up, institutionalized in the Sheffield Economic Regeneration
Committee, and seen (lack of central government support not withstand-
ing) in the facilities provided for the World Student Games in 1991. The

contribution made by the Games to the local image was perhaps less clear cut than the contribution of the Meadowhall Shopping Centre and the new sporting and civic facilities and the arrival of the Norwich Union and Abbey National as major employers in the city. It was anticipated that the Supertram would be seen as a further endorsement of an upward trend in the Sheffield economy.

(b) Land and Property

The land and property impacts of major transport investments can be very significant. The rise in value of development sites at motorway interchanges is an obvious example. Declines in house prices have also been used to proxy the noise impacts of airports and high-speed trains. Changes in land and property values which result from an urban public transport system are sometimes claimed as benefits which arise from the investment. However, examples of such changes are not well documented, particularly for different types of property and in relation to distances from stops or stations. Such changes have to be isolated from changes occurring elsewhere in the local economy and from changes induced by local land-use planning policies.

The evidence on the property development impact of the Tyne-Wear Metro indicates not only that the impact is relatively small, but that the impact is not simply related to changing accessibility.[10] Urban planning policy changes play a part, and the impact will be dampened by rigidities in the urban property market. These include speculation and the often limited extent of understanding of the changes in the environment by both buyers and sellers. A sluggish local economy will slow down the turnover of land and property. However, park-and-ride facilities and the principal interchanges may provide useful spurs to localized property development.

In terms of social cost-benefit analysis, care has to be taken as to what is being measured, and to whom the benefits accrue when changes in property values occur. Changing property values can be used as a proxy for changes in household welfare (as with aircraft noise). In the present context, they may be taken as a proxy for enhanced accessibility. This can be cross-checked with more direct methods, such as contingent valuation. But changing property values do not constitute a real social resource gain or loss in themselves. They may reflect a redistribution of social welfare, both within the city and from and to beyond (given an assumption of a well working property market). The only real resource gain will come from the stimulus to property construction or upgrading offered by the arrival of the Supertram Line, *over and above what would otherwise have occurred*. This 'marginality' of addition to an existing trend is, of course, extremely difficult to establish.

(c) Business Activity

Any large transport investment in a city will have an impact on the level of business activity in that city overall. The impact on any individual business, however, is likely to be extremely small. Some businesses may suffer significantly from the disruption of the construction period. A few will suffer by virtue of their location relative to the new road or rail line or airport. Others will gain directly, principally from a new level of accessibility offered to their customers. Most will remain unaffected, or will gain more indirectly. Cumulatively across a city this gain could be substantial. Putting a figure on it, however, is a significant research challenge.

There are four principal means by which a rise in overall business activity may be prompted by a large urban transport investment. First, and most obviously, will be the contribution that investment may make to any *relocation decisions*, attracting new industrial and commercial concerns into the local area. This impact is not a full social benefit in a CBA sense, a real resource gain, for it is essentially a transfer (although such transfers are frequently accompanied by incremental investment over and above the non-relocation option for each company concerned, with a rise in the productivity of both labour and capital).

The second contribution is often alluded to in relation to road construction: *a reduction in production costs* achieved by lower transport costs. This is a small gain, even in those sectors where transport costs are a relatively large proportion of total costs (although a larger proportion of the profit margin, clearly). The impact of a public passenger transport investment in this respect will be negligible. The third contribution may be more indirect, through a *reduction in transactions costs*, associated with management, organization, purchasing and marketing. Again, a public passenger transport investment will only offer a marginal benefit here. And the fourth contribution has already been noted above, *an improvement in customer accessibility*; but that gain is mostly just a spatial redistribution of purchasing power within the city, with an element of gain switched into the city from other cities, as local and non-local residents and businesses find local purchasing more attractive (Dabinett *et al.*, 1994).

(d) Labour Market Patterns

The most significant impact upon the local economy of a large public passenger transport investment is likely to come through the contribution made to labour mobility. The local labour market will work at an improved level of efficiency, improving the match of employee to employer.

The gain to the labour market has a supply side and a demand side. On the supply side, the improved degree of accessibility offers gains to:

1. *Existing Employees*, who find easier journey to work trips, either on the tram, or on the now less congested roads. As road congestion builds up in the future, the option of an alternative transport mode may become particularly important.

2. *Job Changers*, who move to more suitable and/or better paid jobs, by virtue of the new transport possibility, replacing out-migrants or retirees in existing firms, or finding positions in new companies or in companies which are expanding.

3. *New Entrants* to the local labour force, who may be existing residents or in-migrants. The existing residents may find that the tram system opens up new opportunities; and, obviously, this will be particularly but not exclusively important to non-car drivers or to secondary workers in a household. In-migrants may well base their choice of residential location in relation to the Supertram, if they know their place of work before they move.

On the demand side the improved accessibility to employees offers advantage to employers:

1. With a *static labour force*, there is always a degree of labour turnover, with job change and retirement. The employer can recruit replacements from a larger labour pool, where that pool includes existing employees of other businesses, workers who have left employment elsewhere, and the new entrants into the labour force.

2. In a *new location*, whether from a local relocation of factory, office or retail outlet or from a move into the city from elsewhere, where there is a need to recruit new employees.

3. With an *expanding labour force*, again recruitment should be both easier and be more appropriate than without the new transport capability.

Over time, the interactions of changing pressures, needs and capabilities on both the supply side and the demand side of a local labour market bring about a changing pattern of the place-of-employment to location-of-residence relationship (Wachs *et al.*, 1993). It is unclear, however, how far changes in urban accessibility result in changes in travel behaviour rather than in changes in workplace or in residential choice. Headicar and Curtis (1993), for example, argue that the former consequence far outweighs the latter. Clearly, the impact of accessibility changes will be different for different types of household. It is also true that individuals vary tremendously in their knowledge of transport routes across a large city, and this limits their job search patterns (Quinn, 1986).

12.4.   A RESEARCH APPROACH

The urban development impact study of the Sheffield Supertram provides an example of an attempt to quantify the impacts referred to above. The new system will bring three sorts of change to the city: in accessibility, in cost structures, and in perceptions. These changes are to be seen in the behaviours and the viewpoints of four groups of local economic agents: individuals in households, employers, investors, and enablers and regulators (to include planners, transport operators etc). Consequential outcomes are to be seen in the labour market, in the markets for goods and services, and in the property market. The outcomes result from changing valuations on both sides of each of these markets. Unambiguously attributable value changes are extremely difficult to identify however. The Sheffield research is tackling values in the property market, but focusing on job changes and on new physical development as the principal overall indicators of impact. These (essentially relative) impacts will provide the most useful lessons for the *ex-ante* appraisals of Section 56 grant applications submitted by other cities.

(a)   Research on City Image

The contribution of the Supertram to the image of Sheffield has been examined by looking at existing literature and analyses (e.g. Peat, Marwick, McLintock, 1988), but also by questioning three groups of people between June and December 1993:

- officials in Sheffield City Council and in Sheffield Development Corporation
- a sample of 10 local developers and agents;
- a sample of 10 national and international relocation advisers.

A follow up complementary survey will be undertaken in 1995. Both surveys focus on the city of Sheffield, rather than on the sub-region (Crocker, 1994).

The interviews involved four lines of questioning:

- asking about knowledge of the Supertram (and of the STOL airport and the new road schemes);
- ranking location factors, which included both internal and external accessibility;
- comparing Sheffield as a location for inward investment for (*a*) manufacturing and distribution and (*b*) offices, with nine other major UK cities;
- asking for opinions on the strengths and weaknesses of Sheffield as an investment location.

Because of its steel and cutlery heritage, Sheffield has a world-wide brand name. Many foreign companies have heard of the city. However, the survey findings demonstrate that this does not translate into a high relative rating as an investment location. This was true in the responses from the national agents, as well as in the answers from the local Sheffield based agents.

The national agents felt that the Supertram would only have a small positive effect on the external image of Sheffield as an investment location. The overall opinion was that it would really only be a factor at the site/ premises evaluation stage in the location choice of an inward investor, and not a factor promoting Sheffield in a league table relative to other cities. This view was taken however before the system became operational, with the attendant launch publicity.[11]

The local agents, as may be expected, were much more bullish about the positive contribution of Supertram to the image of the city. This was despite the strong local adverse publicity generated by the disruption of the construction work. The routes were already influencing retail investment, and were expected to give a much needed boost to office and shopping development in the city centre. The local agents were confident of a significant contribution by Supertram to favourable opinions of inward investors, as well as offering a confidence boost to local investors. This confidence was more to do with image than with the reality of enhanced accessibility however. Local passenger/employee accessibility did not rank highly for either group of agents as a location choice factor.

(b) Research on Land and Property

The impact of the Supertram on the local land and property market was approached in a sub-study that had four components:

1. Gaining a response from local valuers, agents and property developers on their perceptions of value changes and opportunities for property development which will arise (and, later, have arisen) along the track corridors of Supertram.

2. Use of a very detailed data set of property values (and changes therein) related to the physical attributes of buildings close to the lines, and to their locational characteristics.

3. An analysis of planning applications and decisions, before and after the opening of the lines.

4. Monitoring physical development and land use changes along the track corridors.

The monitoring of development is conveniently being undertaken as field work exercises by successive years of urban planning students. A very detailed register of land and property characteristics is being assembled for each of three years (1993, 1994 and 1995), all geocoded for GIS based analysis, for property within 200 m of the track in four locations. The GIS analysis links across to the recording of planning applications and decisions from the records of the City Council, before and after the opening of the lines.

The information on property values is being assembled to provide a number of data sets for hedonic analyses. The Sheffield analyses are going beyond the Manchester (Forrest *et al.*, 1992) and the Tyne and Wear (Pickett and Perrett, 1984) studies, to include industrial, shop and office properties as well as houses. Two value measures are being used: rateable values for commercial properties and published asking prices for residential properties.[12] The date chosen for the 'before' data on these values is 1 April 1988. The rating data are an amalgam of information on the Uniform Business Rates from the Valuation Office in Sheffield, and information on properties available for sale or lease taken from the brochures of local estate agents. The residential price data come from the Sheffield Property File, a compilation of residential property offered for sale by all of the estate agents in Sheffield in one particular month, assembled by CJ Business Services. The commercial and residential value data are digitized and associated with neighbourhood and physical characteristics for each property, together with variables measuring distances to the Supertram line and to the Supertram stations. The initial 'after' data set is for April 1993. A second set will be assembled for April 1995.

Details of the data assembly and the method used to estimate the hedonic equations are given in Antwi (1993*a,b*), together with a review of related literature. Although the impact is likely to be small, the hedonic analyses should allow estimation of the implicit price paid for the advantage (or disadvantage) of proximity of the property to the Supertram line, both before and after the commissioning of the system.

(c)   Research on Business Impacts

The study of the impact of the Supertram investment on businesses in Sheffield has involved four related activities.

The first data collection exercise was a telephone survey in Autumn 1993 of 234 business establishments, in three areas served by the new tram lines (the Upper Don Valley, the Lower Don Valley and Mosborough). Following a pilot survey of 30 firms, businesses for the main survey were identified by postcode and by the industrial categories of manufacturing and producer services. The successful interviews constituted an 18%

sample of the identified population. This survey established a 'before' baseline of information, on which comparisons will be built with a further similar survey in 1995. As a telephone survey, the detail of questioning was necessarily limited, but key findings include:

- 20% of businesses formed within the last three years;
- 33% had relocated from another site, mostly from within Sheffield;
- the most important 'major or decisive' location factors were: suitable land and buildings (72%), general road access (67%) and cost of land and buildings (63%);
- 'access to public transport' was major or decisive to 22%, 'access to rail' to 18%, and 'access to airport' to 3%;
- 50% of businesses used off-site workers;
- approximately 40% of businesses bought and sold mainly in Sheffield, 40% mainly in the rest of the United Kingdom and just 10% or so traded internationally;
- a dominance of small businesses, with only 43% of the sample employing more than 10 people; even though 70% were in manufacturing;
- transport costs were less than 6% of all costs for two-thirds of the businesses;
- asked to allocate £100 million to transport improvements, 26% would spend it on local roads, 48% would spend some on improving trans-Pennine road links, 32% would spend some on improving public transport, 28% on the City airport and 12% only on Midland Mainline Electrification;
- the respondents' perception was that employees lived in Sheffield and used a car for travel to work.

The telephone survey has been complemented by a set of interviews with 19 businesses. All but two of the firms involved employed more than 100 people. They were in services and distribution, metal manufacture, hand tools and the food and drink sector. These firms were asked more detailed questions on attitudes to transport provision, why different methods of transport were used and how transport featured in their strategic plans and investment decisions. This survey will be repeated in 1995.

The retail panel consists of nine high street retail businesses and one bank, totalling 55 outlets in the city. The interviews here have again formed a baseline for future comparisons. The respondents in these businesses, by and large, were unable to discriminate in importance between different forms of transport provision. When asked about spending priorities, opinion from these respondents was split between expenditure on local roads, support for public transport and improvements in car parking. Park-and-ride received a low measure of support. Opinions expressed in relation to the Supertram were very adverse with respect to the disruption caused by the construction work. Opinion on the longer term impacts was divided. On the one hand, there were the city centre retailers with high expectations. On the other hand, the impact on suburban shopping centres along the lines was expected to be negligible or even negative.

The fourth business related activity has been to build up an overall profile of the Sheffield economy from standard secondary data, to provide context for the non-Supertram related changes occurring in the businesses contacted in the various survey exercises.

(d) Research on Labour Market Impacts

Examination of the impact of the Supertram investment on the working of the Sheffield labour market is being undertaken from two directions. The Wootton Jeffries/Transport Studies Unit work on the road traffic impact includes a (larger scale) repeat of a household survey undertaken previously in Sheffield in 1988. This survey will yield standard information on modes and directions of movement of members of the sampled households. The survey has two phases: 1993 and 1995, to yield 'before' and 'after' results (Gore, 1994).

The second direction, from the Sheffield Hallam University team, has four component parts. The first draws upon the personnel records of 18 major employers in or close to the city centre. For each of their employees, a record is made of the full postcode of their home address, their broad job title, the date of their appointment, gender and whether full or part time. This information is imported into the Map Info GIS package to display the geographical distributions, and to undertake spatial analysis in relation to the Supertram routes. The exercise will be repeated in 1995. This research yields a picture of the short run impact of the Supertram on employment catchment areas.

Linked to the analysis of employee records, a second element of the labour market study, with the cooperation of the employers, involves contacting members of staff recruited since the opening of Supertram. They are asked about their job search, their choice of location of residence if relevant, their journey to work and their views on Supertram.

A further study approaches the job search issue in relation to access directly by contacting job seekers via the City Council Careers Service, the Department of Employment Job Centres and appropriate community groups. The thrust of this sub-study will be the impact of Supertram on the job search areas of different categories of potential worker. It is influenced particularly by the work of Quinn (1986) in Birmingham.

The final element of labour market work comes from a review, before and after, of changes in the patterns of unemployment in the 29 Department of Employment wards in Sheffield. This acknowledges the well known limitations of official counts of unemployment. Again, potential linkages of trends and patterns with the Supertram lines can be examined using the GIS software.

12.5. CONCLUSIONS

How is it possible to establish that a major urban transport investment offers 'value for money'? The opportunity cost of the funds involved, in an environment of capped public expenditure, can be made very clear. In principle, a large investment in an urban road scheme or a light rail tramway system competes not only with inter urban and heavy rail investments but also with expenditures elsewhere in the public sector.

Ideally, a comprehensive social cost benefit analysis for such an investment would bring all of the positive and negative consequences of the scheme together, suitably discounted over a projected lifetime. Such an analysis, based on a social rate of return to the capital involved, could: (a) place the scheme in a ranking of other potential public sector transport investments, or (b) (better) set the scheme against all potential public sector investments, in all sectors, or (c) (better still) set the scheme against the social rate of return available to the economy from current private sector investment projects.

Such idealism is impracticable and unrealistic. Public expenditure investment decisions are not taken on this basis; and one of the main reasons, politics aside, why they are not is that the available social cost benefit analyses of schemes are not comprehensive enough or robust enough for adequate comparisons to be made. And yet, decisions have to be made, and rarely on a simple 'go-no-go' basis. The social rate of return at a given point of time on a major urban light rail project will be influenced by:

- overall scale, particularly on suburban extensions;
- corridors of the lines;
- locations of stations;
- time phasing of the investment;
- 'weight' of vehicles;
- developing competition from other modes;
- complementary interchange from other modes;
- planning gains yielded from local land-use policies;
- responses in the local property market and the local labour market.

Each of these facets of a large urban light rail project will not only influence the ridership and the fare income relative to the running costs;

each also influences the pattern and phasing of the secondary benefits. The benefits to road users are fairly easy to establish, on the basis of mode switching. Although in a congested urban road system, the benefits really fall to those who now use the roads and would not have done so without the switch away to the tram by a (broadly equivalent) number of previous road users. The indirect secondary benefits are perhaps more difficult to quantify.

Leaving pollution issues (noise, emissions, visual intrusion) to one side, the indirect secondary benefits of new urban transport infrastructure, of the sort addressed by the Sheffield Supertram Urban Impact Study, are probably small in relation to the overall contribution to the aggregate social welfare of the investment. These elements of return to the body of national taxpayers' contribution to the project, even when applying the standard assumptions of cost benefit compensation principles, will be small relative to the travel benefits. However, to the local community (here, Sheffield), and to elements within that community, these indirect secondary benefits may well be particularly significant. These gains may involve Sheffield benefiting at the expense of other parts of the United Kingdom, as investment is attracted to the city in part induced by the Supertram. (This is a standard cost benefit issue for the evaluation of any urban regeneration policy.) Alternatively, the gain, in the property sector especially, may be to concentrate benefits in one part of Sheffield at the expense of another. Other gains, as in improved 'matching' in the labour market, may be seen as unambiguous overall productivity gains to the national economy.

Whatever the apparent incidence of the costs and benefits of the project, a full assessment requires that they should be identified; and that they should be quantified where possible. The rehearsal in this chapter of the level of research detail required to accomplish this quantification might argue for a complete bypassing of indirect secondary impacts in future *ex-ante* evaluations and appraisals of urban transport infrastructure investments. It would be easier to settle for forecasting and assessment of the transportation impacts alone. But such a limitation would miss much of what is important about such investments to the local communities and the wider urban environment within which they are located – hence the importance of learning in some detail about the secondary impacts of schemes already implemented, to guide the investment planning for schemes in further cities, as well as for local extensions to an existing system.

The key research issues around any effort to establish the secondary benefits to a large transport investment lie in attribution. Impacts on land and property, on business investment and on the labour market of the investment, in a 'before-and after' sense, are always clouded by the impacts of other social and economic pressures present over the same period of time. And there is uncertainty as to what the appropriate period of time should be. Attribution of the contribution of the transport investment alone to the observed shifts in values and behaviours is a major research challenge.

Notes

1.   In 1991 44.9% of households in Sheffield did not have the use of a car, car ownership levels being amongst the lowest in urban Britain.

2.   In the early 1970s Sheffield was also chosen by the Department of the Environment to participate in a concept study for the segregated and automated Minitram system (Robert Matthew et al., 1974). The proposals met with public opposition to the visual intrusion and with trade union fears of destaffing. However, Line 1 of the Supertram uses the appraised route of the Minitram through the Norfolk Park Estate to the south east of the city centre.

3.   Between 1986 and 1993 bus ridership in Sheffield has shown a marked decline, with the number of passengers crossing the central area cordon down by 30%. At the same time the number of bus miles rose by 15%. There are now 70 different private bus operators across South Yorkshire. Bus congestion in the centre of the five main towns (Sheffield, Barnsley, Rotherham, Doncaster and Scunthorpe) is a major traffic management problem (Hill, 1994).

4.   The developer of the Meadowhall Shopping Centre contributed £5 million to the cost of the bus/rail/tram interchange adjacent to the Centre. The loss of retail turnover in the city centre due to Meadowhall has been put at 15% (Lawless and Foley, 1992).

5.   The Lower Don Valley was the centre of Sheffield's steel and heavy engineering industries.

6.   This evaluation focused on the development potential of industrial and commercial land owned by the Corporation.

7.   New appraisal guidelines for the Section 56 grant were introduced in 1989, to reflect an essentially privatized public transport market.

8.   This arrangement, oddly, lowers the ceiling at which expenditure by the local authorities could be capped by Whitehall.

9.   Whether local congestion really will be eased seems unlikely. More likely is a growth in the overall number of journeys on all modes, with those switching from road to rail providing 'space' for additional road trips which would not have otherwise taken place. This is important when environmental gains are claimed for the light rail system.

10.   Unlike the Sheffield Supertram, the Tyne-Wear Metro is a 'heavy rail' system, using largely ex-main rail suburban routes, with no on-street running (Pickett and Perrett, 1984; Robinson and Stokes, 1987).

11.   The national agents made favourable comments about the contribution of light rail investments to the image of Manchester and Newcastle.

12.   Two further possible sources of property value information were rejected for this study either as being unreliable or as being incomplete. These are transaction values (i.e. actual prices paid), and opinions of value from professional valuers.

References

Antwi, A. (1993*a*) The Use of Hedonic Analysis for Assessing the Impact of Transport Investments on Property Values. Urban Transport Investment Studies, Working Paper No. 5, School of Urban and Regional Studies, Sheffield Hallam University.

Antwi, A. (1993*b*) The Impact of New Transport Infrastructure on Land Use and Property Values: Analysis of Theory and Evidence. Urban Transport Investment Studies, Working Paper No. 6, School of Urban and Regional Studies, Sheffield Hallam University.

Bateman, I., Turner, R.K. and Bateman, S. (1993) Extending cost-benefit analysis of UK highway proposals: environmental evaluation and equity. *Project Appraisal*, **8**(4), pp. 213–224.

CRESR (1993) Supertram and Associated Infrastructural Investments: Economic and Physical Impacts. Inception Report for SYPTE and Department of Transport. Centre for Regional Economic and Social Research, Sheffield Hallam University

Crocker, S. (1994) Image Study. Urban Transport Investment Studies. Working Paper No. 13, School of Urban and Regional Studies, Sheffield Hallam University.

Dabinett, G., Morrell, H. and Vigar, G. (1994) Business Operations and Location Impacts of Urban Transport Investment: Baseline and Before Studies 1993. Urban Transport Investment Studies, Working Paper No. 12, School of Urban and Regional Studies, Sheffield Hallam University.

Forrest, D., Glenn, J., Grime, K. and Ward, R. (1992) Railways and House Prices in Greater Manchester, Working Paper No. 8, Department of Geography, University of Salford.

Gore, T. (1994) The Labour Market Impact of Supertram: Components of an Evaluation. Urban Transport Investment Studies, Working Paper No. 11, School of Urban and Regional Studies, Sheffield Hallam University

Headicar, P. and Curtis, C. (1993) The Significance of Strategic Transport Routes in Household Location and Commuting Behaviour. Paper presented to the Regional Science Association Annual Conference, University of Nottingham, September.

Hill, R. (1994) The Toulouse Metro and the South Yorkshire Supertram: A Cross-Cultural Comparison of Light Rapid Transit Developments in France and England (mimeo). School of Urban and Regional Studies, Sheffield Hallam University.

Kottler, P., Haider, D. and Rein, C. (1993) *Selling Places*. London: Macmillan.

Lawless, P. and Foley, P. (1992) *Sheffield City Centre Study*. Sheffield: Sheffield Hallam University and the University of Sheffield.

MVA (1987) *Sheffield Supertram Assessment Study: Phase 1 Final Report*. London: Martin Vorhees Associates.

Peat, Marwick, McLintock (1988) *Sheffield Image*, Report for Sheffield Partnership Ltd, Sheffield.

Pickett, M.W.P. and Perrett, K.E. (1984) The Effect of the Tyne-Wear Metro on Residential Property Values. *Transport and Road Research Laboratory Report*, SR 825, TRRL, Crowthorne,

Quinn, D.J. (1986) Accessibility and job search: A study of unemployed school leavers. *Regional Studies*, **20**(2), pp. 163–173.

Robert Matthew, Johnson-Marshall and Partners (1974) *Minitram in Sheffield*. London: HMSO.

Robinson, F. and Stokes, G. (1987) Rapid transit and land use: the effects of the Tyne-Wear Metro, Centre for Urban and Regional Development Studies, University of Newcastle-upon-Tyne, Discussion Paper 88.

SACTRA (1986) *Urban Road Appraisal.* Report of the Standing Advisory Committee on Trunk Road Assessment. HMSO: London.

SYPTE (1978) *Transport Development Plan.* Sheffield: South Yorkshire Passenger Transport Executive.

SYPTE (1985) *Supertram: A Technical Evaluation of the Hillsborough to Mosborough Light Railway Line.* Sheffield: South Yorkshire Passenger Transport Executive.

Townroe, P.M. and Dabinett, G. (1994) The Evaluation of Public Transport Investment within Cities. Urban Transport Investment Studies, Working Paper No. 9, School of Urban and Regional Studies, Sheffield Hallam University.

Wachs, M., Taylor, B., Levine, N. and Ong, P. (1993) The changing commute: a case study of the jobs-housing relationship over time. *Urban Studies*, **30**(10), pp. 1711–1729.

CHAPTER 13

URBAN RAIL DEVELOPMENT AND THE MEASUREMENT OF IMPACTS

Tom Worsley

Urban policies in Britain and elsewhere have been increasingly concerned with maintaining and enhancing the vitality of the urban area. There are several reasons for these concerns. Some are based on social objectives, aimed at improving the opportunities available to the residents of the inner urban area who, for a number of reasons mainly associated with housing markets and the perceived desirability of less urbanized locations, tend to be among the more socially deprived groups. Other policies are aimed at reducing the environmental costs associated with permitting new developments to be located outside established urban areas. By steering such developments towards often derelict sites in existing urban areas, the economic strength of the conurbation is enhanced and detrimental land-use effects of out of town developments are avoided.

The direct economic impacts of increasing the density with which urban land is used through the effective implementation of such policies are not easily measured. The economies of scale made possible by the closer proximity of households and of firms to each other may be offset to a greater or lesser extent by the costs of congestion and higher land prices.

A range of measures has been adopted with the intention of maintaining the vitality of urban centres. These measures include schemes aimed at providing appropriate skill training and entrepreneurial talents for those living in inner cities so as to enhance their employment prospects. Other measures aimed at eliminating derelict land and other local eyesores are intended to make urban areas a more attractive location for households and firms. Assistance is often provided for local entrepreneurs or other firms to set up within the areas designated as meriting special treatment. Measures aimed at improving the quality of the local labour force and the quality or quantity of local jobs can have a direct and beneficial effect on the local economy by making it more competitive and by reducing or eliminating certain market imperfections. Thus although the strength and hence the cost effectiveness of many of these measures is not well understood, there is general agreement about the overall direction of the effects and hence of their potential benefit to the urban economy.

Measures aimed at improving the transport infrastructure which serves an urban area of policy priority will reduce access costs and generally assist in the efficient operation of the local transport network. But neither economic theorists nor urban geographers can provide any unambiguous guidance as to the nature of the relationship between transport improvements and the vitality of the area in which the improvements take place. Measures which reduce the cost of access to the urban area and make it easier for firms in those areas to serve a wider market contribute to the opening up of local markets to competition from firms located elsewhere. Better transport makes it possible for local residents to work and shop outside the area which the policy is intended to assist. Indeed, our understanding of the relationship between transport and land use is such that we cannot demonstrate from first principles the direction of the contribution of improvements in transport access on the level of activity within the urban area.

The South Yorkshire Supertram project was developed by the Passenger Transport Executive which is responsible for certain aspects of the procurement of public transport in the area. It is being funded through grants paid directly to the relevant local authorities and through giving them consent to borrow, in part against estimates of the future revenues to be earned from passengers carried on the line. The case for grant aiding the project was based on the benefits that the new urban rail system would bring to third parties or 'non users' – in particular to road users on account of the reduction in congestion following the transfer of a proportion of car and bus traffic to Supertram.

Estimates of the extent of such a transfer and of the impact that this has on remaining road traffic can be derived from surveys of potential Supertram users and from the analysis of information from elsewhere on peoples' choice of mode of travel when faced with a ranged of options. The grant awarded for public transport schemes under these arrangements is in general restricted to an amount which does not exceed the relatively easily quantified benefits from the relief of road congestion. This restriction arises because of the difficulty of quantifying and measuring any wider effects. Local regeneration benefits can, however, be taken into account in deciding whether a scheme is worthwhile if it is in an area of regional or inner-city policy priority. An estimate of the value of these benefits was included in South Yorkshire Passenger Transport Executive's application for grant. A separate research study has been set up to analyse the direct effects of Supertram on public transport use and on private car traffic in Sheffield to establish the robustness of the estimates of demand which formed the basis of the central government grant to the scheme.

The decision to proceed with the Supertram scheme also provided an unusual opportunity to analyse the wider effects of the scheme on the local economy. The absence of any very clear theoretical model of the nature of these effects precludes the direct approach of establishing certain hypotheses and testing these using data collected expressly for the purpose. So initially the study is concerned with the collection of a wide range of data and setting this up in a form which makes it possible to test a variety of explanations of the possible effect of the scheme on urban development patterns.

There are three aspects of the analysis. The first relates to measuring the changes that take place in the urban area as a whole and in establishing whether such changes are more pronounced or are following different patterns in those corridors served by the scheme. There are a number of dimensions to the changes that might take place and these are being addressed under four themes:

1.   the image of the city;
2.   the land use and property market;
3.   business activity;
4.   labour markets.

Extensive surveys are being carried out to provide data on these themes. For all data with a spatial dimension, the information is identified according to proximity to a Supertram stopping place. Analysis of these data will make it possible to identify the effect, if any, of Supertram on the various themes and hence on the pattern of urban development in Sheffield.

The identification of the changes associated with Supertram will be followed in a second stage of the study by analysis aimed at establishing the causal link between improved public transport and the specific effect identified. Surveys need to be analysed so that a model of the impact of the Supertram can be built. This would allow the particular results of this study to be applied more widely. This part of the study will deal with such questions as the relationship between improved accessibility to jobs and changes in the functioning of the local labour market. It will examine whether the relatively small changes in the comfort, convenience and speed of travel that Supertram can bring about have an influence on the decisions which firms make on their choice of location.

Some of the changes identified in this analysis might be no more than a redistribution of activities within the urban area. For many firms and households, decisions to relocate are taken within a narrow set of choices and within a specific locality. Better public transport in one corridor might make that corridor more attractive relative to another location but it may do little to change the attractiveness of the urban area relative to its competitors. To the extent that better public transport has certain beneficial supply side effects on the local economy and enables it to function more efficiently, local increases in the number of jobs, in value added and in the level of employment are less likely to be offset by corresponding reductions elsewhere. But where such offsets do occur, the overall effect of the scheme will be predominantly redistributional rather than providing a net addition to national income. This is not to deny the significance of redistributional effects which can be a worthwhile objective in themselves and are a factor which influences the policies of government in the UK and elsewhere.

This stage of the analysis will examine whether any correlation can be established between, for example, trends in local unemployment levels and the changes in journey time or other measures of the cost of travel which follow from the introduction of Supertram. The use of control corridors – data on trends in the relevant variables in parts of Sheffield which are unaffected by Supertram – will help to attribute any effects observed in those locations served by Supertram to the improvements in the public transport network. Some factors, such as the effect of Supertram on the image of the city and its ability to present a positive impression of Sheffield as a place in which industry will prosper, cannot be quantified and identified rigorously.

The final stage in the process of analysing the wider effects of Supertram on the urban economy is concerned with valuing, where possible, the consequences of these impacts. In some cases valuation is straightforward. Indeed, where land is concerned there is no intermediate measure and an estimate of the increase in the value of sites served by Supertram provides an immediate first round estimate of its benefit. There is no such straightforward measure of the value to be placed on jobs brought into the corridor served by Supertram or on the previously unemployed who enter the labour market following the introduction of the scheme. But other government programmes have established a range of estimates of the costs of bringing jobs into areas of policy priority and of making it possible for the residents of such areas to enter the labour market. These cost per job figures provide a yardstick against which any Supertram employment benefits might be assessed.

Conventional transport appraisal techniques provide a measure of the benefits of a transport scheme in terms of users' willingness to pay for the timesavings and other improvements in journey quality, the additional revenue earned by the operator and the benefits to other users of the transport network in terms of congestion relief and accident savings. These techniques are often complemented by an environmental assessment of the scheme. The economic theory underlying these appraisal techniques gives no guidance as to whether these conventional benefits can be added to any wider benefits that might be derived from this study of the impact of urban rail in Sheffield. Alternatively, the benefits assessed in the course of the study might be seen as an alternative means of assessing the value of the scheme. We do not know to what extent user benefits, measured in terms of the value of time savings are captured by landlords in terms of higher land prices. Better access to jobs and increases in local employment levels as a result of the scheme might make it possible for employers to pay lower wage rates and hence capture part or all of the benefit recorded in the transport appraisal as accruing to those travelling to work.

The Supertram scheme provides the rare opportunity for a before and after study of a range of possible consequences of a transport scheme. Although these wider effects may not be very great – Supertram cannot be compared in its impact on travel patterns with the M25 London orbital motorway – the local nature of the scheme makes it possible to collect an extensive range of data and to investigate a large number of possible consequences of the scheme. The challenge lies in the unambiguous attribution of any observed secondary effects to the scheme and thereby in advancing our understanding of the nature of the urban economy.

CHAPTER 14

DEVELOPMENT EFFECTS AT AIRPORTS: A CASE STUDY OF MANCHESTER AIRPORT

Jim Twomey and Judith Tomkins

14.1. INTRODUCTION

As an essential part of the operational infrastructure in the aviation industry, airports are commercial organizations with a capacity to create significant income and employment. The location of airports within regional and national economies, particularly in relation to other transport networks, the predominance of tourism over business and freight customers, and operation as an international hub or as a maintenance centre for airlines collectively determine the nature and extent of employment directly created within the airport site.

The economic significance of airports is, however, potentially far greater than their role as a purely commercial establishment. An airport is a strategic asset to a regional and national economy, both facilitating and promoting economic growth. The movement of goods and people within the exchange process can create significant frictional costs, and the aviation industry is a major force in minimizing the impact of the latter, creating more efficient market exchange and contributing to the competitiveness of business (Commission of the European Communities, 1993; Ernst & Young, 1990). The emerging borderless economic landscape is, to some extent, the outcome of the enhanced linkages between regional, national and international markets which have been forged by the aviation industry. As the focal point of high-value import and export activity, airports play a key role in this process.

Airports may be viewed, therefore, as a national economic asset, providing a gateway to international markets. In addition, however, it is now well established that there is often present a general tendency towards centralization of economic activity, as evidenced in the growth of commercial centres, particularly in capital cities. An airport, located close to such a centre, thus takes on a national significance, and becomes an integral part of this virtuous circle of growth, reinforcing and benefiting from this trend. An adverse consequence of centralization can be, however, spatial disparities in income and employment. In this regard, a regional airport can be a positive influence in terms of distributing economic development away from national centres, for example, by allowing companies to divide their activities between regional production centres and more centrally located headquarters without incurring excessive costs from such separations.[1] The airport may not only be a direct generator of employment, but a magnet for further growth. It is this latter characteristic which encapsulates the development potential of an airport to an area.

Substantial off-site employment may be created within a locality from sources such as hotels, other visitor expenditure, air-freight users and transport or tour operators, and together with the direct on-site employment, further induced or multiplier effects will follow. The total of these income and employment effects arising from the airport operation, the contributions to local public finances and any further capital investments to expand the facility collectively can make a considerable contribution to local economies. Furthermore, as a provider of high value communication and distribution links, an airport can become a significant factor in determining inward investment. Not only are existing businesses supported by airport facilities, but new business is attracted. This may consist of complementary activities (such as tour operators) which have, in a sense, already been included in the 'indirect' or 'off-site' category. The type of business attracted as consumer of the airport's services, however, will be that which requires effective national and international links for its employees and/or the movement of goods. In this respect, air links are often most valued by companies which are strategically alert, dynamic and seeking to maximize market opportunities wherever they arise (AACI, 1992). A wide range of industries might fall into this category, so that airport access routes become desirable industrial locations, which expand and develop as agglomeration economies emerge (McMillen and McDonald, 1990). There is the potential for an international business district to develop in the proximity of the airport, alongside expansion in the traditional services of existing central business areas.

In the context of mobile investment, surveys have revealed that proximity to an airport is frequently cited as a critical or important factor in the location decisions of firms (Commission of the European Communities, 1993; Ernst & Young, 1990). Table 14.1 summarizes some of this evidence relating to transport infrastructure and shows the significance

Table 14.1. Critical and important factors in location decisions.

	Nation		Region		Nation		Region	
	Crit¹	Impt²	Crit	Impt	Crit	Impt	Crit	Impt
Infrastructure	Manufacturing %				Offices %			
Proximity to airport	9	14	6	31	23	15	46	15
Quality of road/rail	23	20	15	32	8	31	46	15
Telecommunications	5	12	2	11	15	15	39	15
Proximity to port	8	11	6	15	–	–	–	–
	Distribution %				Services %			
Proximity to airport	25	20	25	25	7	13	7	40
Quality of road/rail	45	20	35	15	7	0	27	7
Telecommunications	20	15	10	10	27	7	27	7

1. *Crit* = Critical.
2. *Impt* = Important.
Source: Commission of the European Communities, 1993.

placed upon airport access, both in a national *and* regional context. In the case of manufacturing, for example, proximity to an airport was rated at the regional level as equivalent to proximity to markets, and only slightly behind availability of labour and good access to road and rail (both scoring the highest at 32% of responses). For offices, airport access is seen to be critical for many firms in a regional context, and for the category of services, airport access was the most commonly cited important feature in location decisions, alongside market proximity (both at 40%). With regard to futher developments, for a wide range of companies including high-tech, European headquarters, distribution and services, airport proximity is viewed as an *increasingly* critical factor in location decisions. Even traditional manufacturing establishments considered this to be important for the future.

Thus, in terms of the positive development effects of airports, there are two key components. As commercial bodies, they are a source of growth in their own right, providing a service which contributes to the efficiency of other enterprises. Arguably more important, however, is their capacity to draw in additional key economic activities, be they complementary endeavours, supporting services or direct consumers of airport services.

In terms of negative development impacts, these fall generally under the heading of adverse environmental effects associated with land-use and noise (for example, Uyeno, Hamilton and Biggs, 1993; Pennington,

Topham and Ward, 1990). Journeys by air generate connecting journeys by other modes of transport; airports as effective terminals must be linked to the wider land transport networks of road and rail. Pressure on land use arises both for the airport facility itself through the demand for terminal space, parking and so forth, and for the road and rail access routes. Aircraft noise, road traffic noise, air pollution and congestion are classic externality problems arising from transport expansion. Such effects are relatively local, falling on the more immediate vicinity of the airport terminal, in contrast to the benefits which are much more widely distributed throughout the region and nation. The market pressures for development to meet the increasingly sophisticated and voluminous level of demand raise issues which need to be considered in the context of land-use planning and regional economic development. Nevertheless, it seems likely that airport growth will continue to be a prominent factor in economic development strategies at all levels of government.

This chapter is a case study of development at Manchester International Airport in the north-west of England. Manchester Airport is an interesting case for analysis since it is one of the very few large international airports outside South East England and has experienced extensive growth throughout most of the last decade. Such growth has, accordingly, placed significant pressures on the existing transport infrastructure in the local environment of the area and has raised a number of land-use issues which still exist today. The principal focus of this chapter is, however, the role of the Airport in regional and local economic development.

14.2. MANCHESTER AIRPORT – BACKGROUND

Manchester Airport is the third largest airport in the UK handling 12.4 million passengers (including transits) in 1992, compared to 45.2 million at Heathrow and 20 million at Gatwick, and freight volumes of 80.6 thousand tonnes, compared to 834.9 and 200.6 thousand tonnes at Heathrow and Gatwick respectively. In terms of *international* passengers, Manchester Airport is amongst the 20 largest airports in the world, some 1 per cent lower in 1992 international passenger travel than Paris Orly, 7 per cent lower than Toronto and 17 per cent lower than Miami. These numbers still fall significantly short of throughput at major European airports such as London Heathrow, Frankfurt, Paris Charles De Gaulle, London Gatwick and Schiphol, but the 1980s did see substantial development at the airport with growth rates which were, at times, among the fastest in Europe.

Progress towards this current position began in 1929 when the city of Manchester became the first municipality in the UK to have its own licensed aerodrome on a temporary site in south Manchester. Although a permanent site was established the following year next to the Manchester Ship Canal, it was not long before the Barton site, which is still in use today, was perceived to be inadequate. Land was acquired by the City Council in 1934, leading to the airport development at Ringway where operations began in 1938.

After the Second World War, significant growth in passenger traffic took place, both in the immediate post-war years and subsequently. Passenger throughput quickly reached 93,000 by 1949, rising to 6 million by 1985, and finally attaining the rate of 13.3 million passengers per annum (mppa) by 1993. Air cargo throughput has also grown rapidly, particularly in the 1980s, from a base of 27,659 tonnes handled in 1980 to 81,000 tonnes in 1990. Continual expansion in terminal facilities and runway capacity has therefore been necessary. New terminal buildings were opened in 1949 and 1962, the latter to accommodate 2.5 million passengers per annum, and a new departure hall and check-in facilities were opened in 1973, followed by a dedicated domestic terminal in 1989. Phase 1 of a second international terminal became operational in 1993, with Phase 2 to follow in line with demand, and each designed to cope with 6 million passengers. Runway capacity has naturally followed a similar path of expansion, with regular runway extensions to accommodate new generations of aircraft and to facilitate its activities as the sole Gateway International Airport outside London.

The strict categorization of airports by role, and Manchester's position as Gateway International Airport, was ultimately abandoned by government in the 1980s, in line with the move towards a more liberalized and competitive market environment. It was felt that the role and development of airports should reflect the strength of demand for their services. The implications of this for Manchester's position as the leading regional airport outside the South East were not, in practice, of great significance. It appeared that the demand for long haul services in the regions was unlikely to be sufficient to allow the growth of an alternative regional airport in the foreseeable future. The nature of demand by major international airlines is also such that significant benefits exist in the concentration of services at particular key airports, increasing efficiency and allowing the development of complementary networks. Thus, the gateway position remained implicit and has been strengthened by the gradual move to more liberal agreements. For example, within agreements allowing any UK regional point to be served, Cathay Pacific chose to serve Manchester from Hong Kong and all US airline applications (ten in total) for the two additional route rights negotiated in 1990 to UK regional points were for Manchester.

It is clear that the position of Manchester Airport has changed dramatically over the post-war period, from a small regional airport predominantly reliant upon holiday charter traffic to its present role as a major hub with a growing range of inter-line opportunities. In 1990, over 80 airlines were operating services from Manchester to over 160 destinations, and by 1992, scheduled international traffic accounted for 25% of all passenger movements, with a further 16% related to domestic scheduled services. The remaining share (at approximately 60%) consists of charter traffic, and is such that Manchester is now second only to London Gatwick in terms of passengers and destinations offered.

The history of the development of the airport is therefore one of rapid growth in demand, placing constant pressure upon the airport infrastructure which, to date, has been accommodated through expansion within the existing operational area.

14.3. FUTURE GROWTH

Manchester Airport expects to remain the dominant airport in North West England, serving a catchment area which extends as far as the Midlands and the Scottish borders for some long haul intercontinental services. Long term traffic forecasts to 2005 for both passenger throughput and air traffic movements (ATMs), prepared in 1990,[2] are shown in tables 14.2 and 14.3.

Passenger forecasts are shown separately for international scheduled,[3] international charter,[4] domestic and hub traffic. A key feature of the passenger traffic forecasts is the division between scheduled and charter services. Previous estimates produced in 1987 had expected similar total passenger movements of 16 million by 1995 and 23 million in 2000, but charter traffic was still expected to dominate at 66% of the total. The 1990 forecasts, on the other hand, predict a much smaller share for international charter traffic of 38% in 1995 declining to 33% in 2005, with a corresponding rise in the share of scheduled services. This has significant

Table 14.2. Forecast passenger throughput (mppa) 1995–2000.

	1995		2000		2005	
	mppa[1]	%	mppa	%	mppa	%
Domestic	2.70	16.8	3.60	16.3	4.82	16.1
International scheduled	5.70	35.4	8.41	38.1	12.23	40.8
International charter	6.16	38.3	7.86	35.6	10.03	33.4
Total	14.56	90.5	19.87	90.0	27.08	90.3
Hub effect	1.52	9.5	2.20	10.0	2.92	9.7
Total	16.08	100	22.07	100	30.00	100

1. *mppa* = millions of passengers per annum.

Source: Manchester Airport.

Table 14.3.   Forecast air transport movements 1995–2005.

	1995	(ppatm)[1]	2000	(ppatm)	2005	(ppatm)
Domestic	52,104	(51.8)	56,520	(63.7)	75,456	(63.9)
International scheduled	84,200	(67.5)	113,800	(69.3)	171,900	(71.1)
International charter	36,341	(169.0)	33,823	(232.0)	52,960	(189.5)
Total	172,645	(93.1)	204,143	(108.1)	300,316	(99.9)

1. *ppatm* = passengers per air traffic movement.
Source: Manchester Airport.

implications for the expected volume and pattern of air traffic movements.

The shift in the composition of international traffic predicted by the 1990 forecast stems, in particular, from the recognition of three important features of the industry at this time – the slower growth in international *charter* traffic, the stronger growth in international *scheduled* traffic and the creation of the Manchester *hub*. In the first case, a number of features emerged in the 1980s which affected the UK inclusive tour (charter) market. Strong price competition between tour operators for market share in the mid to late 1980s produced large volumes of business, but a reduction in profit margins. The desire to consolidate profitability in turn led to a restructuring of fleets and a reduction in capacity.[5] In contrast, scheduled services in the 1980s experienced strong demand which was expected to continue generally, and at Manchester in particular. In the course of the 1980s, Manchester became increasingly competitive as an alternative to the London airports, extending its regular long haul services, so that by 1990, 36 airlines were operating to 61 international destinations. The frequency and range of operations was increased, both to major airports and to smaller regional/provincial destinations, and new operations established, particularly to the USA and the Far East. Finally, there was the anticipated growth in domestic travel derived from the establishment of the Manchester hub, with operations to 16 UK airports and enhanced inter-line transfer opportunities, together with an expansion in traffic on the trunk routes to London.

Passenger forecasts therefore present an unambiguous picture of growth, and this is also the case for freight traffic.[6] However, the changing composition of projected passenger traffic has major implications for the volume of air traffic movements (ATMs).

During the 1980s, average aircraft size increased so that the average annual rate of growth in ATMs was somewhat lower than the growth in passenger numbers. However, the anticipated switch in traffic mix to scheduled services suggests a reduction in the average number of passengers per ATM, since the high load factors achieved by charter airlines (95%) are typically not observed in scheduled operations (at 65% to 70%). Similarly, seating densities are higher for charter travel. As table 14.3 shows, the volume of passengers per ATM for scheduled services is significantly less than half that for charter flights, so that a given number of scheduled passengers would generate at least twice the number of ATMs as charter passengers. The timing of ATMs is also of importance, in addition to the quantity, and it is in this context that the hubbing strategy is of relevance. The development of Manchester as an effective hub requires an efficient interchange of passengers, requiring synchronization of flights. *Waves* of departures and arrivals generate a peak load problem, especially if the main hubbing activity is concentrated into the scheduled traffic peaks. The implication of the ATM forecasts in conjunction with the peaking problem is that the demand for runway capacity could potentially exceed the supply even by 1995.[7]

These forecasts of future growth naturally have great significance in terms of local land-use and regional economic development.

14.4. Land Use – Airport Operations

The Operational Area at Manchester Airport, which lies principally although not exclusively within the City of Manchester's boundaries, has remained effectively constant since 1974, despite the extensive traffic growth experienced so far and described above. By European standards, a relatively efficient use of space in terms of passengers per hectare has therefore been achieved. A number of factors have contributed to this phenomenon, not least of which was the inclusion, in 1961, of the airport site within the Green Belt, which would typically have restricted most other forms of development. However, the City Council acknowledged the importance of the airport to the region at an early stage, and hence recognized the need to accommodate airport development as a special exception. Similarly, local plans allow for development deemed necessary for the efficient operation of the airport facility. It is also the case that the Airport has refrained from providing land for developments (such as an industrial estate or business park) which might reasonably be located elsewhere, on the grounds that the future expansion by the Airport itself within the Operational Area would then be ruled out. It has therefore been possible to construct a second terminal and cargo centre without extension of this Area to date. The Green Belt policy has also prevented any concentration of development on the boundaries of the Airport which has helped to restrain potential local congestion.

However, in the light of the expected growth in demand outlined above, pressures for further expansion of the Operational Area are accumulating. This will particularly be the case if permission is granted for a second runway, and also due to the fact that the forecast traffic levels to 2005 tend to suggest a potential requirement for a third terminal to handle some 10 to 15 million passengers, notwithstanding any projected increase in freight shipments.

The most significant and most controversial aspect of this possible expansion in terms of land use is the requirement for a second runway. Apart from the case put forward by Manchester Airport, another source of support for such a view stems from recent consideration of additional runway capacity in South East England.[8] In July 1990, the Civil Aviation Authority produced a report, CAP 570: *Traffic Distribution Policy and Airport and Airspace Capacity: The Next 15 Years*. This report was produced in response to a request for advice from the Secretary of State for Transport covering strategic options for the long-term airport capacity needs, primarily in the London area. Following earlier consultations during 1989, CAP 570 presented the CAA's conclusions that additional runway capacity would be needed in the South East prior to 2005 with options at Heathrow, Gatwick and Stansted being preferred, in that order, in terms of passenger convenience. The report also outlined future traffic projections for regional airports in the UK. The figures for Manchester terminal passengers were not, in fact, too dissimilar to those of the company. Based on these projections, the CAA concluded that within the time frame of the requirement for additional runway capacity in the South East, there would also emerge a need for a new runway and terminal capacity to serve demand in the North West.[9]

In addition to possible new runway and additional passenger terminal facilities, further land requirements stem from a number of other sources associated with the growth in traffic. At present, significant volumes of cargo are trucked into and out of the airport, but the latest Company forecasts indicate that by 2005 only 13 per cent of cargo will be transhipped by road rather than by air. Following the completion of the Phase 3 Cargo Terminal in 1991, about 25,000 m^2 of transit shed space is now provided, but in the light of the cargo forecasts, it is proposed to reserve a further 5 hectares of land for additional transit sheds. In line with volumes, demand for freight agent units has also grown throughout the 1980s, and over 8,000 m^2 of space has so far been provided. On the basis of the current forecasts, additional units will be required in a relatively short space of time.

The lack of a major airline based at Manchester has inhibited the development of large-scale maintenance activities for a long period of time,[10] and for many years, facilities were restricted to wartime hangars. Maintenance facilities at the airport are still viewed as relatively outdated, requiring substantial improvement to handle the future expected maintenance requirements associated with volume forecasts. The Airport is therefore proposing an extended maintenance area which does come very near to a designated Site of Special Scientific Interest and which therefore would require suitable landscape proposals.

The number of staff working at the airport site across a wide range of services is forecast to increase from nearly 10,000 in 1990 to approximately 30,000 by the year 2005, assuming anticipated growth in passenger numbers is realized. An increase in staff numbers on this scale will have a major impact on the demand for additional office space in terms of quantity, quality and category. Apart from Airport Company staff, accommodation will be required for airlines, handling agents, commercial tenants, statutory and control authorities, and airport related ancillary services. Finally, the estimated demand for hotel accommodation by the year 2005 is 2150 bedrooms, in contrast to the 829 available at the end of 1993. Further hotel facilities are therefore necessary, and planned over the next 10 years.

14.5. LAND USE – TRANSPORT LINKS

It is apparent that growth in passenger traffic has significant land-use implications for the efficiency of airport operations. There are, however, major implications for the ground transportation infrastructure linking the airport to its catchment area. Such infrastructure usage originates from passengers, the airport's working population, visitors, airport support services, freight and mail. In 1990, the main mode of transport linkage for passengers was the private car (table 14.4), and this is expected to remain the preferred choice for the future, although the establishment of an Airport rail link in 1993, serving parts of Lancashire and West Yorkshire is forecast to capture 7% of passenger journeys by 1995. The Airport Company also believes that an effective marketing strategy could double this rail usage. In addition, plans exist to establish a southern rail spur carrying passengers south on a direct link to Crewe and points in the East Midlands, West Midlands and Wales.

Although the development of the rail link will divert some traffic away from the road network,[11] car dependence is expected to continue.

Table 14.4. Transport mode choice 1990.

Private Car	Taxi/Minicab	Hire Car	Bus/Coach	Hotel Courtesy Coach
66.0%	19.0%	3.0%	10.0%	2.0%

Source: Manchester Airport.

Manchester Airport is reasonably well-placed in this context, having direct access to the national motorway grid and with its expansion built into local infrastructure programmes for road and rail, although the anticipated growth in traffic must inevitably create greater congestion and hence further demands for improved access, with attendant environmental implications. For the Airport itself, however, one particular problem to be addressed arising from road traffic expansion is the provision of adequate parking space. In 1990, bus and coach access to the airport accounted for 10% of all trips, and increase here will require improved parking and related facilities. Similarly, hire cars, used in the main by business travellers on domestic or European scheduled services (where demand is expected to grow) have land-use implications for the Airport since a convenient location is vital in terms of customer service, as are the backup services of maintenance, vehicle storage and adminstration.

By far the largest land requirement in the Airport's immediate vicinity, however, stems from the demand for private car parking space. Many forms of parking are generated by the Airport – from business users, the leisure market, spectators and staff. Sites for parking are provided both within the Operational Area and at 'off Airport' car parks which are independently owned and operated. Demand for short stay parking spaces consists of two elements; parking for less than 24 hours generated in the main by motorists who are meeting or dropping off air passengers, and parking for one to four days generated by business travellers using scheduled flights. The estimated rate of growth for this type of parking is greater than for parking overall and reflects the forecast growth in scheduled air services. The majority of long stay parking is currently met at sites run by independent operators outside the Operational Area. In 1990 an estimated 10,500 spaces were provided off airport, and within the operational area a further 5,500 public parking spaces were provided. As the provision of off-Airport parking lies outside the control of the Airport Company, and the development of such sites faces severe constraints, it is intended to accommodate all additional long-stay demand within the Operational Area. This is estimated to mean an additional 20,000 spaces by 2005. The extension of the Operational Area will therefore need to include an allowance for this development.

14.6. THE ECONOMIC IMPACT OF MANCHESTER AIRPORT

National, regional and local economies are complex phenomena with a vast range and variety of production, exchange and trading relationships. Such relationships reflect not only historical patterns of development but change continually with the everyday dynamics which combine to alter the nature and direction of transactions between producers and consumers. The development of transport infrastructure is a primary factor which contributes to change in such dynamics.

There is a wide range of benefits that accrue to a regional economy from having a regional airport, in terms of the employment and income generated both directly and indirectly by the airport. There are individual benefits to leisure and business travellers due to reduced overall travel time and reduced travel costs, and the efficiency of industry is improved where individual companies benefit from reduced costs and transit times for goods exported from and imported to the region.

On the other hand, the costs of airport development are largely environmental, in terms of loss of land for other uses (principally rural/ recreational), noise, road traffic congestion and pollution associated with airport links to the ground transportation network. Where an airport is already established, the land-use issue arises only when an expansion in the operational area is proposed, and when significant expansion is experienced such that road traffic poses a problem for the locality. On a continuing basis, however, the single most important environmental issue associated directly with the aviation industry is that of aircraft noise.

Significant progress has been made over the last ten years in the development of quieter jet engines for civil aircraft and more effective noise abatement procedures.[12] Although noise disturbance is a subjective issue related to perception and a range of social factors, there are methods of identifying the areas most affected by aircraft noise and the nature of the impact. Sophisticated methods are also available to forecast future noise impact. Indeed it is the time of the event and type of aircraft which has the most impact on the noise nuisance created. Chapter 2 aircraft (older aircraft fitted with low bypass turbofan engines) give rise to 95% of noise complaints despite the fact that these aircraft comprise only about 50% of jet movements. It is clear that a phase out of these aircraft would have the most significant impact on reducing aircraft noise, and considerations by the European Commission point to a phase out of chapter 2 aircraft operations at European airports early in the next century.

The environmental costs outlined above are difficult to express in monetary terms, involving as they do non-traded environmental commodities such as clean air, peace and tranquillity, although techniques do exist to provide estimates.[13] Furthermore, such costs are relatively narrowly dispersed within the local community, as opposed to the benefits of airport development which are much more widely distributed. A comparison of cost and benefits involves, therefore, significant distributional issues and hence cannot be a simple quantitative exercise. Extensive public debate is usually aroused. It is not the purpose of this chapter, however, to engage in a distributional debate, and in terms of economic impact, therefore, the remainder of the chapter will be concerned with the issue of the benefits of development at Manchester Airport.

The measurement of benefits is not a particularly straightforward task and can take a number of forms (Benell and Prentice, 1993; Batey, Madden and Scholefield, 1993; Parsons, 1984; Higgins, 1971; Nwaneri, 1970). Foremost among these is the use of standard multiplier analysis to assess the direct, indirect and induced impact of airport activities (ACI, 1993). Although these techniques are fairly straightforward in concept, they are often complex in application.[14]

Research by the Ecole Nationale de l'Aviation Civile shows that something in the order of 1,000 new jobs are created on-site at an airport for every additional million passengers. With a throughput of just over 10 million passengers in 1990 and a workforce around the 10,000 mark, Manchester Airport appears fairly typical. If this relationship were to remain constant, the passenger forecasts outlined above would indicate employment rising to around 30,000 by 2005.

Although the Airport Company is the largest employer, with approximately 20% of on-site employees, there are over 150 other companies based at the airport. These range in size from the very large to companies employing one or two people and vary in activity from airline companies and tour operators, shops, hotels, air freight businesses, to those providing passenger services and handling, maintenance and support activities. Also of major importance is the wide range of jobs and skills that are required.

The Centre for Local Economic Strategies (CLES, 1988) in Manchester was commissioned in 1988 to analyse the role played by the airport in the wider economic development of the region. This showed that in addition to the 8,400 staff employed on-site at the time, another 12,000 were sustained in the region through the airport, making 20,400 in total. Projecting these estimates forward to 1990, Airport publicity material claimed that an additional 15,000 jobs within the region were dependent on the airport. This CLES research also highlighted the Airport as the single most important factor in the attraction of inward commercial and industrial investment. Between 1983 and 1988 nearly 150 inward investments were made in the North West, providing over 13,000 jobs.

In 1991, York Consulting were also commissioned to investigate the economic development potential of the Airport. This produced different conclusions as outlined in table 14.5. Here, the direct on-site jobs match the Airport estimate of 10,000. The York report (York Consulting, 1991) quotes local research by 'local authorities and others' for the estimated 5,000 off-site jobs, similarly quotes 'local research' to suggest 5,000 indirect jobs and estimates a multiplier effect from the direct and indirect jobs of a further 3,000 jobs. This sums to 23,000 in total, which is reasonably close to that of the CLES study, although the processes by which each set of estimates is derived are not particularly transparent.

The York study also attempted to quantify what it referred to as the

Table 14.5.   Estimated regional impact of Manchester
Airport.

Direct employment – On site	10,000
Direct employment – Off site	5,000
Indirect employment	5,000
Induced employment	3,000
Transportation impact	15,000–25,000
Total	38,000–48,000

Source: York Consulting Ltd, 1991.

'transportation impact' of the Airport. This is not defined rigorously but appears to represent the intangible benefits of the infrastructure, the employment effects of which are said to 'overlap with, but are also additional to, those from the direct and indirect economic impact'. The report relates evidence of this effect from around the world and quotes the Airports Association of America which estimates the job effect as two times on-site employment or some 5% of US GDP. Work at Los Angeles International Airport sets the size of this effect at 2.9 times on-site employment, but this is double the figure estimated from some French studies. In the end, a range between 15,000 and 25,000 jobs is suggested in the York study.[15]

Such analyses are rather aggregate in nature and do not, generally, consider the impact of airport activities in terms of those industry sectors which the airport supports directly, or indeed those sectors which likewise can be viewed as important customers of the airport and which go some way to sustaining its operations. Yet the linkages between airports and industry infrastructure are important to our understanding of the way in which this form of transport facility interfaces with other elements of the business community and of the potential role played by such facilities in regional economic development as an inward investment catalyst.

The background to our analysis of Manchester Airport's economic role within the region lies in recent research (Twomey and Tomkins, 1995) intended to establish a broad methodology to examine the economic development potential of UK regions. The task is complicated by the fact that neither appropriate tools nor information for the assignment are technically available. This chapter thus represents an early outing for this methodology in a setting which is far narrower than that in which it is designed to operate. Nevertheless, it does provide a useful basis for a preliminary discussion of linkage between airports and industry.

The importance of economic linkage to regional development has been implicit in the variety of approaches that have been taken to analysing the development process. Whether couched in terms of agglomeration and localization economies, growth poles, or cumulative causation, the ability of an area to develop successfully depends to a large extent on either developing or strengthening the intensity or scale of mutually advantageous trading which we denote by the term economic linkage.

There have been two broad means of investigating the changing nature of economic linkages in sub-national space. One approach has been to undertake a series of specific area surveys regarding the sourcing of supply requirements (Phelps, 1993; Turok, 1993) and the other approach has been to utilize area-specific input-output tables to indicate levels of economic connectedness (Szyrmer, 1985, 1986). The approach used in this section of the chapter is the latter.

The methodology in question is not complex, indeed it could not be so in the information vacuum that is regional economics in the UK. The objective of the exercise is to establish an average reference pattern of linkage between industry sectors at a broad spatial level and then to examine the extent of divergence from that average at a smaller spatial scale, the region. The outcome of the process as a whole is that an estimate is produced of the number of jobs in any one sector supported by demand from another identified sector. In this present study, the principal sectors of relevance are air transport and air transport support services in the North West region, with a view to establishing the linkage between these sectors and the rest of the local/regional economy.

The application of the methodology to the case of Manchester Airport is a little complicated for a number of reasons. For example, the analysis is based on Census of Employment data which do identify both employees in employment in air transport (SIC 7500) and support services for air transport (SIC 7640), but aggregate all miscellaneous transport services and storage jobs together into SIC 7700. In addition, a number of on-site jobs at the airport are probably classified according to function[16] rather than location, placing some downward bias on the estimates produced. It is also the case that the analysis uses aggregate North West data which include Liverpool as well as Manchester Airport. While the latter is far bigger than the former, the indivisibility of data does introduce another difficulty of interpretation and will overstate the estimated linkage impact.

Finally, the nature of the linkage data which underpin the analysis combines support services for air transport with support services for both

inland transport (SIC 7610) and sea transport (SIC 7630) and miscellaneous transport services. Some apportionment is thus required to establish a linkage magnitude for air support services, a process which again
introduces some degree of inaccuracy, the magnitude of which cannot be
quantified without more detailed scrutiny. In the absence of any indication of the extent to which air related activities are included in miscellaneous transport services, this sector is excluded from the analysis and
will add to downward bias in estimates.

In a wider context, there are a number of implicit assumptions in the
approach which may require future modification. Most important among
these is an assumption that there is no spatial variation in either the
productivity with which air transport services are provided to industry or
the *unit intensity* with which the latter purchase goods and services from
industry.

It must also be stressed that this approach is very different from typical
impact analysis since it is concerned only to examine the nature of the
linkages between what is effectively *direct* on-site employment (as expressed in the employment of the air service sectors) and the local/
regional economy. It is *not* providing an estimate of the total employment
attributable to the airport in terms of the number of direct, indirect and

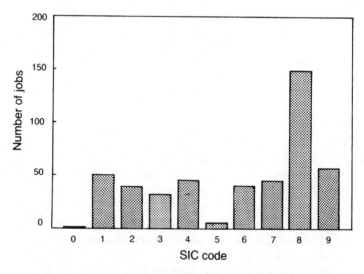

Figure 14.1   Air transport jobs sustained by North West industry.

Key
0 Agriculture
1 Energy   4 Other manufacturing 7 Transport/communication
2 Metals   5 Construction   8 Business services
3 Engineering   6 Hotels, catering, etc 9 Public services

induced jobs created, as is the case in the previous two impact studies outlined above.

Figures 14.1 to 14.4 illustrate the results from the application of the methodology outlined above. In the 1991 Employment Census, some 2,257 full-time and 59 part-time jobs were classified as belonging to air

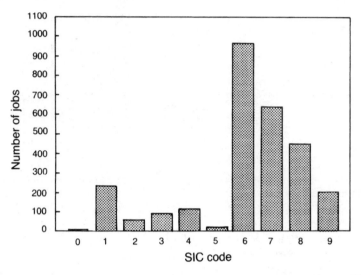

Figure 14.2 Support service jobs sustained by North West industry. (Key as in Figure 14.1).

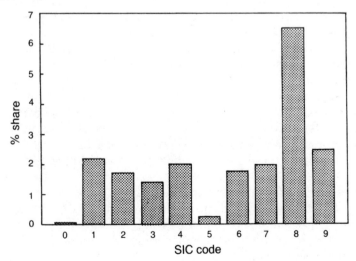

Figure 14.3   Share of air transport jobs sustained by North West industry. (Key as in Figure 14.1).

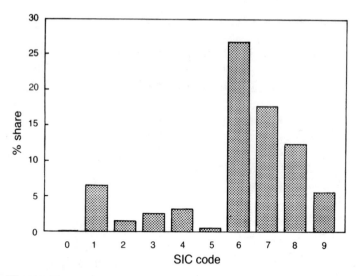

Figure 14.4   Share of support service jobs sustained by North West industry. (Key as in Figure 14.1).

transport, and some 3,685 full-time and 123 jobs were classified as belonging to air transport support.[17] The first figure concentrates on the jobs sustained by North West industry through their purchases from the air transport sector; that is, the number of air transport jobs directly supported by linkage with North West industry. It is seen from figure 14.1 that the service sector accounts for the majority of such jobs and that business services account for by far the largest number. Altogether, some 464 jobs are identified by this process. This represents approximately 20% of the total air transport complement in the 1991 Census and demonstrates the importance of *charter* traffic in this period (i.e. purchase by individual consumers rather than business) to airport activity in the North West.

Figure 14.2 shows the results relating to the air transport support services sector. Overall, the linkage with North West industry is greater than in the case of air transport, but once again it is the service sectors that tend to dominate the picture. The analysis indicates that 2,778 support jobs, or some 75% of the regional total, can be attributed to the linkage between North West industry and the Airport, as reflected in the purchases of the former. By far the largest share of this total (35%) stems from division 6, distribution, hotels and catering, with other significant contributions from divisions 7 and 8, transport and communication (23%) and business services (16%).

Figures 14.3 and 14.4, finally, show the proportions of actual regional air transport and support service jobs which are identified from the 1991

Census and which are directly linked to North West industry. Both present a picture in accordance with that outlined in the earlier figures.

This set of results provides a profile of the sectoral composition of the purchases of air transport and support services by North West industry, and in this way indicates those areas of the economy which are, and would be in the future, attracted to an airport location as customers. In the light of anticipated relative growth in scheduled traffic compared to holiday charters, there is thus some evidence with which to identify likely sources of such growth.

Figures 14.5 to 14.8 now consider the reverse case; that is, the impact of Manchester Airport in terms of North West industry jobs that are *directly* supported by the existence of the airport infrastructure. Figure 14.5, for example, details the sectoral profile of jobs in the region directly sustained by the air transport activity. Altogether the analysis suggests that some 5,487 jobs are supported in this manner with a distribution not far removed from expectations. The jobs in division 1 (energy) are essentially related to fuel inputs, for airlines which dominate the total, as well as electricity, gas and water supply. The relatively large number of jobs in division 3 (engineering and allied industries) is overwhelmingly related to aerospace and is presumably a reflection of technical and maintenance support for airlines. The final manufacturing sector, division 4 (food and other manufacturing) consists of jobs in the food and drink and paper and printing industries with smaller numbers in the clothing and fabric sectors.

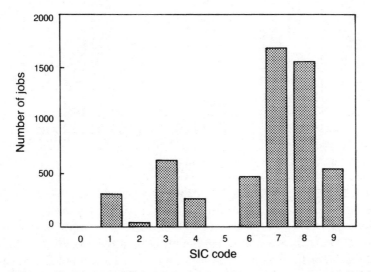

Figure 14.5   North West industry jobs sustained by air transport activity. (Key as in Figure 14.1).

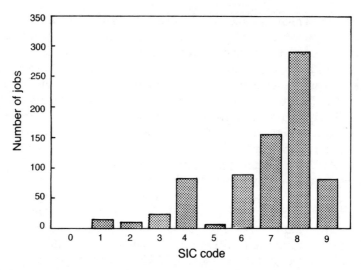

Figure 14.6   North West industry jobs sustained by air services. (Key as in Figure 14.1).

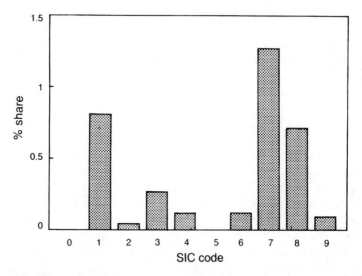

Figure 14.7   Share of industry sector jobs sustained by air transport activity. (Key as in Figure 14.1).

The 470 jobs in division 6 are mostly accounted for by distribution companies, which presumably reflect freight traffic, and hotels and catering. Eighty-four per cent of estimated division 7 (transport and communication) jobs are allocated to transport support services with the bulk of the

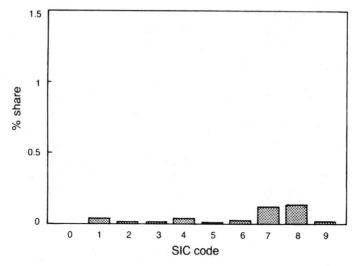

Figure 14.8   Share of industry sector jobs sustained by air services. (Key as in Figure 14.1).

remainder assigned to postal services (mail freight) and telecommunications. The 1,500 or so business service jobs identified by this process are spread across the whole range of such services but with particular concentrations in insurance and computing.

The latter could, of course, reflect the wide variety of hardware and software configurations that go to support air transport operations but the insurance linkage is a little more complex to explain and indicates another difficulty of interpretation. Insurance is clearly of paramount importance to an airport. This analysis suggests that, on average, the scale of the insurance required by Manchester Airport should be sufficient to support a reasonable number of insurance jobs. There is, of course, no reason to expect that all such jobs will be located in the North West and indicates that particular care should be taken in interpreting the linkage from the Airport to business services in the region. If anything, the business service estimates should be considered as containing a probable upward bias.

Figure 14.6 considers the profile of linkage between air transport services and industry in the North West. Generally speaking, the numbers involved are relatively low compared with air transport itself (754 in total) but still tend to show a relative services bias.

Figures 14.7 and 14.8, finally, demonstrate the magnitude of the estimates in the context of actual 1991 North West Census employment, showing the percentage of jobs in each division directly supported by air transport and support services. Only in division 7 (transport and communication) does the estimate exceed 1% of the total, for the case of air transport. The estimated linkage effect of support transport services is negligible in terms of total employment.

This final set of results illustrates the direction in which the expansion in activity at Manchester Airport, predicted for the next 10 to 15 years, will be transmitted to other sectors. The analysis is preliminary and exploratory, as already stated, and confined to the economic linkages which stem from *direct* on-site employment. The analysis does not include the full multiplier effects of airport activity, nor their corresponding linkages. However, it does present a different perspective on the economic impact of an airport, to complement the more usual aggregate impact analysis, which could fruitfully be extended.

14.7. CONCLUSION

The issues which are raised when considering the impact of an airport are wide ranging indeed. Questions of appropriate land-use planning, environment effects and local or regional economic development are fundamental to the debate, as are the distributional concerns of who actually bears the costs or receives the benefits from airport development.

In terms of the specific issue of economic development, apart from standard multiplier techniques, we have few tools with which to assess the development impact of airports, and more generally, transport infrastructure. The contribution of the latter to regional development has always been taken for granted but has proved enormously difficult to quantify. The major difficulty is the very same that always plagued early evaluations of UK regional policy itself, which is the specification of a counter-factual position, or an analysis of the likely process of development in the absence of the infrastructure. We are still unable to crack this problem but the key to an effective evaluation of transport infrastructure on spatial development must lie in the emergence of a methodology which can accommodate this complex issue.

We can take a view on the income and employment effects of airport development in North West England. In this chapter we have attempted to provide a little more detail on the direct linkage effects between the airport and the wider regional economy but we need to set our sights higher and to begin addressing issues such as the contribution of Manchester Airport to the growth rate of the North West region. In this area our methodology is weak and we, instead, turn to survey evidence of the role of infrastructure in location choices. This evidence is important and does confirm that transport infrastructure is a major determinant of choice, especially to potential inward investors, but at the end of the day the evidence is insufficient to aid quantification. There is still much to be done.

Notes

1.   The potential risk in this scenario, of course, is the development of a 'branch plant' and hence less self-contained regional economy, because of easy access between the region and central headquarters elsewhere.

2.   The forecasts are based on an econometric forecasting model prepared in 1985 by transport consultants for the Airport, using economic data on UK personal disposable income and GDP, GDP in the EU, USA and the remainder of the world economy, the £/$ exchange rate and indices of air fares. In total, six scenarios were generated, using different assumptions about rates of economic growth and the changes in the international charter market. The forecasts shown are those used by the Airport in future planning. Forecasts are presently under review in the light of the public inquiry regarding the second runway application.

3.   The forecasting model is used to predict total UK international scheduled air service demand. Manchester's share of this estimated traffic is calculated on the basis of access times, fares and frequencies, allowing for the input of new services from the airport and derived from the known intentions of carriers.

4.   The demand for international charter services was produced separately, with an expected growth rate for total UK charter traffic derived from the judgement of the airport company in conjunction with leading tour operators and charter air-lines. This growth rate was entered into the forcasting model and traffic once again allocated to individual airports.

5.   Wide bodied capacity has been replaced by smaller aircraft; for example, DC-10 aircraft replaced by Boeing 757.

6.   Since the opening of the first phase of the World Freight Terminal facility in 1985, cargo throughput has grown from 34,000 tonnes to over 80,000 tonnes. Cargo throughput is estimated to increase by 11% per annum, reaching 247,000 tonnes by 2005.

7.   An unconstrained morning peak demand of some 60 ATMs per hour contrasts with the existing capacity limit of 41 per hour, although different pricing policies and schedules changes could conceivably go some way towards dealing with this capacity constraint in the short term. Bishop and Thompson (1992), Oum and Zhang (1990) and Carlin and Park (1970), for example, examine the use of the price mechanism to resolve the problem of the allocation of peak capacity.

8.   More recently, within the Department of the Environment's guidance note PPG 13 on Transport, there is also a recognition of the benefits of development at regional airports to achieve higher utilization, economies of scale, and reduce long surface journeys, whilst also contributing to local/regional economic development (Department of the Environment, 1994).

9.   The report states that, *prima facie*, a site in the Manchester area may be war-ranted. More recently, North West England has witnessed a second airport stake a claim for a share in the future of air transport in the region. Liverpool Airport has outlined expansion plans which claim to reduce the necessity for construction of additional runway capacity at Manchester. It is not the intention of this chapter, however, to debate the relative merits of the two locations in terms of accommo-dating future air transport growth in the region.

10.   In 1989 Qualitair (later to become FFV Aerotech) built a new jumbo hangar providing full maintenance and repair capability for all sizes of aircraft.

11.   Pressure on the road access routes will also be alleviated to a degree by the construction of a fuel pipeline which will minimize external tanker traffic and

accommodate planned fuel requirements, moving away from the situation where all aviation fuel is delivered by road tanker.

12.   At Manchester, for example, a number of measures in excess of statutory requirements have also been taken, including an agreed night quota, a system of fines and operational penalties on noisy aircraft, a comprehensive Noise Insulation Grant scheme and the operation of 24 hour noise and track monitoring systems.

13.   Cropper and Oates (1992) provide a comprehensive survey of techniques, such as hedonic pricing or contingent valuation. For particular studies of the impact of aircraft noise, examples are Pennington, Topham and Ward (1990) and O'Byrne, Nelson and Seneca (1985).

14.   Karyd and Brobeck (1992) provide a critique of the way in which this technique has been applied within aviation.

15.   Interestingly, in a Manchester Airport response to Liverpool Airport publicity material, this range of jobs is described as the inward investment catalyst and is projected forward to form part of a preliminary view that the second runway could make the Airport responsible for between 78,000 and 104,000 jobs.

16.   For example, airport catering included in the category of catering rather than airport activity.

17.   This compares with the data cited above of just under 2,000 Manchester Airport Company employees in 1990 and just under 10,000 employees at the airport as a whole.

References

AACI Europe (1992) *Airports – Partners in Vital Economies*. Brussels: AACI.

ACI Europe (1993) *The Economic Impact Study Kit*. Brussels: ACI.

Batey, P.W.J., Madden, M. and Scholefield, G. (1993) Socio-economic impact assessment of large-scale projects using input-output analysis: A case study of an airport. *Regional Studies*, **27**(3), pp. 179–191.

Benell, D.W. and Prentice, B.E. (1993) A regression model for predicting the economic impacts of Canadian airports. *Logistics and Transportation Review*, **29**(2), pp. 139–158.

Bishop, M. and Thompson, D. (1992) Peak-load pricing in aviation: The case of charter air fares. *Journal of Transport Economics and Policy*, **26**(1), pp. 71–82.

Carlin, A. and Park, R.E.(1970) Marginal cost pricing of airport runway capacity. *American Economic Review*, **60**(3), pp. 310–319.

Centre for Local Economic Strategies (1988) *The Impact on the Local Economy of Past and Likely Future Development at Manchester Airport*. Manchester: Centre for Local Economic Strategies.

Civil Aviation Authority (1990) *Traffic Distribution Policy and Airport and Airspace Capacity: The Next 15 Years*, CAP 570. London: CAA.

Commission of the European Communities (1993) *New Location Factors for Mobile Investment in Europe*. Brussels: CEC.

Cropper, M.L. and Oates, W.E. (1992) Environmental economics: A survey. *Journal of Economic Literature*, **30**, June, pp. 675–740.

Department of Environment (1993) *Transport*, PPG 13. London: HMSO.

Ernst & Young and Corporate Location Europe (1990) *The Regions of Europe: A*

Comparative Review of their Attractiveness to International Corporate Investors. Milton Keynes: Ernst & Young.

Higgins, B. (1971) The Montreal Airport site: The spatial multiplier and other factors affecting its selection. *Growth and Change,* **2**(1), pp. 14–22.

Karyd, A. and Brobeck, H. (1992) The delusion of social benefits. *The Avmark Aviation Economist,* January, pp. 16–17.

McMillen, D.P. and McDonald, J.F. (1990) A two-limit Tobit model of suburban land-use zoning. *Land Economics,* **66**(3), pp. 272–282.

Nwaneri, V.C. (1970) Equity in cost-benefit analysis: A case study of the Third London Airport. *Journal of Transport Economics and Policy,* **4**(3), pp. 235–254.

O'Byrne, P.H., Nelson, J.P. and Seneca, J.J. (1985) Housing values, census estimates, disequilibrium and the environmental cost of airport noise: A case study of Atlanta. *Journal of Environmental Economics and Management,* **12**(2), pp. 169–178.

Oum, T.H. and Zhang, Y. (1990) Airport pricing: Congestion tolls, lumpy investment and cost recovery. *Journal of Public Economics,* **43**(3), pp. 353–374.

Parsons, D. (1984) Employment stimulation and the local labour market: A case study of airport growth. *Regional Studies,* **18**(5), pp. 423–428.

Pennington, G., Topham, N. and Ward, R. (1990) Aircraft noise and residential property values adjacent to Manchester International Airport. *Journal of Transport Economics and Policy,* **24**(1), pp. 49–59.

Phelps, N. (1993) Branch plants and the evolving spatial division of labour: A study of material linkage change in the northern region of England. *Regional Studies,* **27**(2), pp. 87–101.

Szyrmer, J.M. (1985) Measuring connectedness of input-output models: 1. Survey of the measures. *Environment and Planning A,* **17**, 1591–1612.

Szyrmer, J.M. (1986) Measuring connectedness of input-output models: 2. Total flow concept. *Environment and Planning A,* **18**, pp. 107–121.

Twomey, J. and Tomkins, J. (1995) The Economic Development Potential of UK Regions. Department of Economic and Economic History Discussion Paper, Manchester Metropolitan University.

Turok, I. (1993) Inward investment and local linkages: How deeply embedded is 'silicon glen'? *Regional Studies,* **27**(5), pp. 401–417.

Uyeno, D., Hamilton, S.W. and Biggs, A.J.G. (1993) Density of residential land use and the impact of airport noise. *Journal of Transport Economics and Policy,* **27**(1), pp. 3–18.

York Consulting Ltd (1991) *Economic Development Potential of Manchester Airport.* York: York Consulting Ltd.

Chapter 15

Development Effects at Airports

Sean Barrett

15.1 Introduction

In their chapter Twomey and Tomkins cover the history of the impact of Manchester Airport, investment policy at airports and the evaluation of the impact of airports on the overall economy. In their conclusion they note that the contribution of transport infrastructure to regional development

> has always been taken for granted but has proved enormously difficult to quantify. The major difficulty is the very same that always plagued early evaluations of UK regional policy itself, that is the specification of a counter-factual position, or an analysis of the likely process of development in the absence of the infrastructure.

There are many difficulties in assessing the economic impact of airports on their hinterland. Table 14.5 indicates that the regional employment impact of Manchester airport becomes more difficult to estimate as one seeks to measure ripple effects further away from the direct employment at the airport itself. The highest claim made for employment impacts is the cited 'preliminary view that the second runway could make the airport responsible for between 78,000 and 104,000 jobs.' Such estimates depend on the assumptions made and these should be clearly specified. While they find that the York Consulting estimate of jobs dependent on Manchester Airport 'is reasonably close to that of the CLES (Centre for Local Economic Strategies) study . . . the process of calculation is just as unclear.' Some of the definitions are difficult to interpret. For example, in the York study, the transportation impact of the airport 'is not defined rigorously but appears to represent the intangible benefits of the infra-structure the employment effects of which are said to overlap with, but are additional to, those from the direct and indirect economic impact.'

Twomey and Tomkins' own research from the Census of Employment data shows that in the linkage between air transport services and industry in the North West the numbers involved are relatively low compared with air transport itself and that the estimated linkage effect of support transport services is negligible in terms of total employment.

15.2. The Nature of Infrastructure

The task of 'the specification of a counter-factual position, or an analysis of the likely process of development in the absence of the infrastructure' requires the discussant to consider issues such as the nature of infrastructure, its financing and its development effects. An example of the classical treatment of these issues is given in Hirschman (1958) where the following characteristics are said to distinguish infrastructure investments from directly productive activties:

1.   They are an input to directly productive activities.

2.   They are typically provided by public agencies or by private agencies under public control.

3.   The products supplied are either free or at regulated prices.

4.   The products are not subject to competing imports.

5.   Production is characterized by 'lumpiness' (technical indivisibilities) and a high capital output ratio.

6.   Output may not be measurable.

Economic and technological changes since Hirschman defined infrastructure in the above terms have eroded each of the above distinctions between infrastructure and directly productive activity. The changes concerned are:

1.   Pricing mechanisms are available for roads, seaports and airports. The exclusion principle can be applied.

2.   Capital intensity and lumpiness are less a barrier to investment now than when Hirschman wrote. In the immediate postwar period the development of airports coincided with a belief that only the state had the resources to undertake such large projects. By contrast, at the present time many governments are experiencing problems in the public finances whereas private sector financial institutions have experienced a large increase in the funds available for investment.

3.   Administrative reforms have been instituted to establish agencies charged with devising pricing rules for privatized utilities such as gas, water, electricity, telecommunications and airports.

4. International interconnectors for gas and electricity and reverse charges for international phone calls have made these products internationally traded goods.

5. Output measures have been developed through research in subjects such as programme budgeting, cost benefit analysis, cost effectiveness analysis, and research on factor productivity.

6. The successful privatization of many transport companies, including transport infrastructure companies such as Associated British Ports (1983) and British Airports Authority (1987), indicates that any distinction between social overhead capital and directly productive investment is no longer a deterrent to capital markets.

15.3.   THE NEW ECONOMIC ENVIRONMENT FOR AIRPORTS

The new economic environment for airports has been created by the reinterpretation of the economic characteristics of infrastructure as noted above; the financing of airports through the private rather than the public sector; and the increasing contestability of aviation which is quickly replacing the regulatory regime of non-competing airlines and airports by deregulation of the markets for airlines, airports and the services provided at airports. These fundamental changes are likely to change considerably the operation of airports and their investment planning. The old system of planning airports as described by Twomey and Tomkins was based on administrative decisions such as the designation of airports like Manchester as gateways and provision of extra capacity at Stansted rather than Heathrow. The preferred choice of the airlines is different.

In the world of price collusion among airlines, airport charges were simply passed on to the passenger by non-competing airlines. Competing airlines on the other hand are forced to review every cost both external and internal to the airline. Economic rents built up under airline price collusion, market sharing and output control will be eroded.

Airports and related services account for about a quarter of costs of intra-European flights (EEC, 1984). The proportion is higher the shorter the journey and stage length. As airlines enter into competition there will be pressures by airlines on airports to reduce passenger and landing fees. Airports where passenger and baggage handling is operated on a monopolistic basis will face competitive pressures to deregulate the service. Just as airlines facing price competition will bring competitive pressures on airport managements, so will the airports in turn put pressures on suppliers of services such as air traffic control with a system of competitive tendering likely to develop. The system of grandfather rights which allocates scarce capacity at busy airports to airlines in order of seniority is likely to be replaced by a non-discriminatory system. Demand at airports in a competitive environment will depend on the commercial decisions of airlines and passengers who are the customers of airports; the efficiency of airport managements and their profit record; and their ability to attract investors.

We already have some examples of how airline and airport competition might influence resource allocation. The United Kingdom/Ireland deregulation of 1986 produced a doubling of passenger numbers in under three years and fare reductions of over one-third in real terms. It is Europe's most dramatic airline deregulation to date. The London-Dublin route is the second busiest international route in Europe and its record under deregulation has implications for both airports and airlines. Since slots at Heathrow were not available to new entrants in 1986 that airport could not play a major innovative role in deregulation Initially, Luton served as the London airport for the expanded market under deregulation. Stansted and London City have since entered the London-Dublin airport market and Ryanair, the new entrant airline in 1986, is now the largest carrier at Stansted. In the North West competition between airports and new airlines produced a similar result after 1990, when the presence of low cost airlines at Liverpool increased Liverpool's share of all traffic to the North West from Dublin from 27% to 43%. Currently there is competition between the Dublin-Glasgow and Dublin-Prestwick routes. In Belfast, the City or Harbour airport, has taken a market share of about a quarter of the traffic from the total Belfast market previously controlled by and served by Belfast International airport.

15.4. AIRPORT INVESTMENT APPRAISAL – A MARKET MODEL

In the old world of adminstrative decisions determining airport investment one might specify a model with the alternative to investing at Manchester, as the loss of traffic to Amsterdam or further afield, or further congestion at Heathrow. In the deregulated world of airline and airport competition a failure to invest would cause the airport to reach capacity. Airlines would then seek alternative airports, bringing with them the prospect of extra revenues. The alternative airports would conduct an investment appraisal of the costs and revenues arising from the additional traffic. In the Manchester case airlines at the margin would seek to accommodate extra passengers at airports such as Liverpool, Leeds-Bradford, Blackpool, East Midlands and others. The deregulated UK charter airline sector is a major user of regional airports in such a competitive way. Airports with an attractive product and price will attract business and generate extra profitability. Manchester would seek to attract investors on the basis of its strong growth performance. Airports in competition are likely to be imperfect substitutes for one another. It is unlikely that all the combination of services at Manchester could be replicated elsewhere but, as the examples reviewed above indicate, substantial competition between airports can be generated in a deregulated market by airlines willing to 'shop around'. The greater the number of potential competing airports the less likely are significant differences in costs to airlines from investment at airport A rather than airport B.

15.5. AIRPORT INFRASTRUCTURE AND ECONOMIC GROWTH

In a competitive airport market it is unlikely that large numbers of jobs could be shown to depend on a particular runway investment. Such job estimates are based on the historic allocation of airport investments by administrative decisions. The system of market prevention in aviation is coming to an end.

A case made for administrative rather than market allocation of investments in airports is market failure to recognize the developmental role of airports in a region. The case made is that, left to itself, the market would underinvest in airports. For example, private time preference might be claimed to discount the future benefits of airports too heavily compared to social time preference. The case might also be made that the state has greater forecasting abilities than the market. On the other hand it could be pointed out that under public sector ownership many airports in Europe have underinvested and that, combined with state underinvestment in air traffic control, this has caused severe bottlenecks in air transport. Faced with the many competing demands for public expenditure governments have underinvested in airports and related infrastructure. Most OECD countries are experiencing deficits in their public finances which will continue to restrict state investment in the air transport sector.

A further aspect of the market failure argument is that only the public sector can invest well ahead of forecast demand. Since the supply of infrastructure is likely to generate demand the argument is that only the public sector will stimulate the development benefits that inevitably follow from infrastructure investments. Such a belief underlies the substantial EU transfers for infrastructure in low-income regions.

I am extremely sceptical of such a case. Subsidies to infrastructure may simply result in underused airports, railways, seaports and motorways. The availability of such subsidies promotes rent-seeking in the recipient economies. Capital intensity is increased since this is invariably the subsidized factor and the attention of infrastructure managers is diverted from matters such as serving the market, pricing policy and resource allocation, to subsidy seeking (Barrett, 1984).

In drawing these remarks to a conclusion the question posed by Jim

Twomey and Judith Tomkins remains vital. How do we specify 'a counter-factual position, or an analysis of the likely process of development in the absence of the infrastructure'? The traditional non-market system of resource allocation in aviation produced answers to this question as high as 104,000 jobs depending on Manchester Airport as cited in the paper. In the modern market-let model on the other hand competing airports have to meet the test of the marketplace. If they fail the efficiency tests set for them by airlines, passengers and freight forwarders, airports will fail the market test for investment and competing airports will benefit.

References

Barrett, Sean D. (1984) *Airports for Sale, The Case for Competition*, London. Adam Smith Institute.
European Economic Community (1984) Civil Aviation Memorandum No. 2.
Hirschman, A. (1958) *The Strategy of Economic Development*. New Haven: Yale University Press.

CHAPTER 16

SEA PORTS, LAND USE AND COMPETITIVENESS: HOW IMPORTANT ARE ECONOMIC AND SPATIAL STRUCTURES?

Eddy Van de Voorde

16.1. INTRODUCTION

Ports are an important link in the total transportation chain. A large part of international trade is transferred in sea ports. It needs to be understood that in terms of total costs ports are a more important link than the actual maritime transport.

Hence there is a need to measure and evaluate a port's performance. The link between port performance and investment policy is a typical example. It has too often been assumed that port investment is a catalyst for regional development plans. In most cases, this has merely resulted in a tremendous over-capacity, while other ports have suffered from an important under-capacity, which has led to expensive waiting times for arriving ships. Both cases result in substantial economic losses.

Another important problem related to ports is the often inadequate pricing policy. Port tariffs are often obscure, mostly because they include so many types of taxes. Moreover, the structure of these costs does not bear a clear relation to the economic reality.

The scientific literature pays increasing attention to the relationship between development in the transport sector on the one hand, and land use on the other (Button, 1993, p. 18). This is a relationship that works both ways. Developments within the transport sector in general have a distinct effect on the land use and the economic development of a region. Conversely, the effect of land use on the transport sector has also been recognized. Button (1993, p. 19) writes: 'From a pragmatic standpoint one has to make a rather careful judgement whether to treat land use as influenced by transport or vice versa.'

This chapter goes into various aspects of the relationship between port development and land use. The relationship is mainly seen *within* a port, and not so much between port and city, or between localization, mobility and accessibility (e.g. Van de Voorde and Witlox, 1992). Another aspect dealt with in this chapter is the link between port investments on the one hand, and prosperity effects on the other. The port is approached as a case study, and the aim is to provide (quantitative and empirical) material in order to understand that relationship. The concept of port competitiveness appears to be a key element here.

This chapter is intended to be a *tour d'horizon* in order to define new research directions. The chapter is subdivided in the following sections. A first part defines what a port actually is or can be/has to be. Then we go into the relationship between a port and land use: a screening is made of the link between port organization, port technology and land use; then we deal with the link between port area and port capacity. We also look into the contribution of port investments to the economy and prosperity. After that, we discuss a number of future research themes.

16.2.   THE CONCEPT OF A PORT

How do we define a Port?

Before we further go into the (double) relationship between port development and land use it is necessary to understand the most salient characteristics of the production (and organization!) of port services.

The most important function of a port is to ensure the transfer of goods from inland transport to maritime transport and vice versa. Jansson and Shneerson (1982, p. 9) give a schematic subdivision of the entire process in a port into 7 major partial processes:

- the ship's approach via river or canal, and its mooring at the quay;
- the unloading of the cargo from the ship's holds to the quay;
- the transportation of the cargo from the quay to the transit storage;
- transit storage;
- the transportation of the cargo from its transit storage to loading platforms;
- the loading of the cargo to inland transport modes;
- the departure of an inland transport vehicle from the port.

In addition there are a number of other functions such as customs clearance, storage in the port area, preparation of the cargo (pre-slung, container stuffing, and so on). These are supplementary functions rather than straightforward water-bound functions. Yet here we find important consequences for the relationship with land use.

What needs to be understood is that a chain is only as strong as its weakest link, which is certainly true for the production of port services. More precisely, in the subdivision mentioned above, the capacity of each link needs to be adapted to that of each other link. When the potential capacity of one link relatively increases because of innovation, the other links in the chain should also be adapted. Only then can the complete potential of the original innovation be realized.

In particular, this means that technological developments should be channelled in such a way that the increased capacity of each link in the chain should be the same on average. Of course, in the short term imbalances cannot be avoided, especially for important innovations. The containerization process is a typical example, which has led to the phenomenon that the loading and unloading of general cargo ships is now almost as speedy as for bulk ships.

A Port Management's Aims

The *output* of a port is usually defined in terms of the number of tonnes that is transferred per unit of time (year/month/day), or the throughput. We will come back to this later. Reference is also made to other important elements such as the contribution to the national product, employment etc.

By way of illustration we will give a number of indicators for Rotterdam for the year 1991 (Evers *et al.*, 1994, p. 29). For a sea-bound throughput of about 290 million tonnes, Rotterdam's contribution to the gross national product was about 50 billion guilders, of which about 12 billion was contributed directly and about 38 billion indirectly. Direct employment amounted to more than 70,000 persons, while the total port-related employment numbered nearly 300,000 persons.

It needs to be established what the ultimate aim of a port management is or should be (Suykens and Van de Voorde, 1992, pp. 478–486). Is it the maximization of *tonnage*? But tonnage does not say everything as ports are incomparable in terms of the composition of their commodity package. A port like Marseille, where in 1991 71.3% of the total tonnage was related to oil, appears to be tremendously vulnerable on account of this oil-dependency. Also here diversification is imperative to reasonably long-term prospects.

Could it be a port management's aim to maximize *added value*? Here the port of Antwerp is undoubtedly in a strong position, for two reasons. From the composition of the goods package it is apparent that general cargo has a relatively large share. Compared to bulk goods, general cargo creates a higher added value. This is a result of more labour intensive throughput techniques, but also because of the storage and distribution operations related to these commodities. At the same time and during a number of years, important industrial activities have been concentrated within the port of Antwerp. The petrochemical sector is the best example here.

A port management may also have the maximization of *companies' profits* as its aim. Yet one might wonder to what extent a port management has direct control over this objective. It is probably better to think in terms of optimizing the environmental factors, such as pricing and improved accessibility of the port infrastructure. One could go much further and take measures preventing congestion problems from disrupting the just-in-time supplies to port companies.

Ultimately, of course, there is a link between these three possible aims. It is in a port management's interest to maximize tonnage, if only because more tonnage results in more ship movements, and thus also in increasing port duties. It is assumed that the added value, employment and the company profits will evolve in a similar way.

The aims of a port, or rather the combination of the above-mentioned aims, have direct repercussions on land use. This could be fully illustrated with the example of Antwerp.

Revenues received by the Antwerp port management can be roughly divided into two categories: revenues from the leasing out of port land and revenues from port duties. The revenues from the leasing out of land can be considered as insensitive to economic climate, since they are based on long-term contracts linked to the index of the cost of living. Port duties, in contrast, are a direct function of transferred tonnage, and hence sensitive to economic climate, albeit with a certain time lag (cf. stock fluctuations).

The policy of the Antwerp port management has always been aimed at leasing out the maximal amount of land, assuming that throughput would follow suit. And in any case this policy meant some guaranteed income. At the same time it was a stimulus to industrialization, with all its positive derived effects for employment and tonnage.

Some other European ports have followed entirely different policies, often under the pressure of shortage of available land. Land has been exclusively destined for straightforward port and water-bound activities. Yet a possible consequence could be that certain activities, such as the stuffing and stripping of containers, has to be relocated to terminals outside the port, with for instance negative results for the number of dock workers, port revenues and indirectly also the potential for port investments.

16.3.   PORT ORGANIZATION, PORT TECHNOLOGY AND LAND USE

The study of the relationship between port development and the effect on land use starts from a thorough understanding of the port organization. That organization appears to be led by maritime developments, but at the same time also by developments in the area of port technology.

Historically there has always been a continual struggle among and within ports to increase throughput. Jansson and Shneerson (1982, p. 10) conceive of the total port throughput as a function of the expected capacity utilization of the berths, the number of berths (usually measured by means of the total quay length), and the expected throughput capacity per berth.

How could each of those variables be influenced to realize the aim of an increased throughput?

In the *short term* this is clear. An increased demand is met by an increased capacity utilization. There is of course a limit to this, in the sense that a 100% capacity utilization cannot be realized. Before it is ever realized it will lead to unacceptable waiting times.

In the *longer term* a rising demand will be met by an expansion of capacity. This may be realized by increasing the number of berths, or by increasing the throughput per berth. If the port's goods package is rather heterogeneous, one could also work towards specialization, i.e. separate port sections for different types of cargo (bulk, unit loads, . . .).

If one looks at the historical development of many ports, it becomes clear that such a development goes through a double process:

- a fairly long period of capacity expansion through an increase in the number of berths;
- that development is limited physically, mostly because of land shortage; that is why in the next phase the emphasis is on the improvement of berth capacity.

Starting from this scheme, ports can be positioned. For example, ports in developing countries are in a different stage of development than north-western European ports. Yet there is a mutual impact. The fact that a further 'jumbofication' of bulk transport is being slowed down is connected to the fact that certain supply ports in the Third World have not kept up with the most recent port developments.

In the next section we will further go into a number of elements that are important for the development and expansion of a port, always with our attention focused on the consequences for land use (see also Jansson and Shneerson, 1982).

Expanding through increasing the Number of Berths

This form of development is best illustrated by an example. When we take a look at the development of the port of Antwerp, we see that originally the port was situated right in the city, so to speak (the old port). The expansion was carried through towards the north, until an obstacle halted that development (in this case, the Dutch border), and until the internal transport costs within the port also became too high. Many other ports have gone through the same type of development.

When the port size did not allow any further expansion, the capacity was extended by increasing the number of berths within a given port size, by means of the so-called finger pier configuration (cf. Hamburg and Bremen). This was related to the fact that formerly the transfer from sea vessel to hinterland modes was done immediately, for instance from the ship straight on to the trainwagon.

Yet this gave rise to a number of problems. On the one hand there was regularly congestion on the land side, among other reasons because the back-up area on land was too limited (say, when there was a city) and because of congestion in the hinterland. A port like Lisbon (14.1 million tonnes of throughput in 1991) is even today confronted with those two phenomena. In addition there were also often co-ordination problems. In both cases this meant time loss for the ships.

The continuous increase of the ship size meant a stronger growth for sea vessels than for hinterland modes. That is how *transit-storage* became necessary. As a result, the speed of the handling operations has been boosted for sea ships as well as for inland transport. As these operations are independent of one another in the short run, rotation times have also been minimized (cf. the value of the time factor; see also Blauwens and Van de Voorde, 1988*a*, *b*; 1991).

Expanding through improving the Berth Capacity

The use of storage as a buffer meant an important growth for the expected transfer capacity per berth. Yet there were still problems, for reasons such as the limited backup area for storage and transport. Indeed, given the average time shipments are stored, the intake capacity of storage facilities has to be proportional to the throughput.

The pressure to limit even more the transit time in a port became stronger. For that reason pre-slung and the use of pallets became more frequent, so that small shipments were turned into larger ones. This lowers transit time and also handling costs in the port itself. A consequence is that larger units cannot be handled on the basis of manual labour anymore, and that tools like the so-called forklift truck became indispensable. However, this again required more space, because, in order to avoid ship delays, the cargo was left ready on the quay. This has led to a new configuration, with larger strips alongside the quay to allow for a further mechanization.

This development has also brought along a few problems: more danger during the operations and greater damage liability (due to goods being left on the quay exposed to every kind of weather). The logical result was containerization and the trend for larger units. The standardization of container sizes allowed for the productive use of expensive container cranes with a very large capacity. It is worth noting that simultaneously a number of other technological developments has led to an equally effective capacity improvement (e.g. roll-on/roll-off, bulk cargo handling).

Expanding through increasing the Handling Capacity

It could be asked why the handling capacity of a crane in a container system is so much higher than the capacity per crane in a traditional break-bulk system. Studies designed to trace and eliminate bottlenecks have pointed to problems with stowage in the ship's hold. The stevedores' productivity has risen, but the process remains more expensive, unless a higher added valued can be realized.

In this connection it is interesting to examine the present productivity figures for containers. Port productivity is determined by an interplay of factors, quantitative (terminal area, loading and unloading infrastructure capacity, storing capacity, . . .) as well as qualitative ones (speed, professional know-how, punctuality, . . .).

The available empirical material on productivity is scant. However, a study by Marconsult (1991) deals with productivity and handling costs for containers for the most important European ports. The empirical material relates to the first four months of 1990. The cost figures have to be interpreted from the perspective of the port users, in other words these are prices charged by the terminal operators.

From table 16.1 it is apparent that there is a high productivity of ports in the Hamburg-Le Havre range compared to ports in the Mediterranean. A different productivity is immediately translated in different handling costs, albeit in interplay with other influencing factors. Table 16.2 gives for the same ports, in ascending order, the total cost index (ship costs + handling costs, for each voyage and container).

It is clear from table 16.2 that ports from the same range are not so far apart in terms of pricing. Antwerp is the most productive and hence the least expensive, Hamburg on the other hand is relatively expensive. Yet there are marked differences between the ranges.

In spite of its partial nature, (one type of goods flow: containers) the

Table 16.1. Productivity for handling containers (first quarter of 1990).

| Port | Number of Containers Handled per Portainer Crane | | | | Duration of a Shift |
| | Per Hour | | Per Shift | | |
	average	maximum	average	maximum	
Antwerp	30	35	210	228	7.3
Rotterdam	25	30	180	220	7.8
Hamburg	25	30	175	205	7.6
Le Havre	25	30	150	180	6.0
Marseille	22	28	150	280	7.0
Venice	20	25	100	175	7.0
Genova	15	25	100	160	6.5
Trieste	14	28	90	180	6.5
Naples	14	20	80	100	6.5
Piraeus	12	20	90	120	7.1

Source: Marconsult (1991).

Table 16.2. Handling costs for containers.

Port	Total Cost Index
Antwerp	125
Rotterdam	155
Le Havre	173
Piraeus (export)	187
Marseille	188
Hamburg	188
Naples	225
Venice	249
Trieste	263
Genova	270

Source: Marconsult (1991).

above empirical material gives an indication of the differences in produc-tivity and handling costs between the different ports. These differences are partially due to differences in land use.

The Growing Need for Backup Land

Compared to the traditional break-bulk berths, the need for back-up land is much bigger for container berths, for roll-on/roll-off berths etc. At the same time the berth throughput is many times higher. That is why it may be worthwhile examining the amount of back-up land used per trans-ferred tonne.

Jansson and Shneerson (1982, p. 18) give figures (estimations) for the throughput for different types of cargo handling techniques and land requirements (see table 16.3).

Why are larger container berths needed? The new container ships have become bigger, and as a result the loads have become bigger as well. In fact the back-up land needed should at least be proportional to the size of the ship load. This is often coupled to an organization with a double location for containers: one close to the quay, and the other some way further away. It is necessary that the land available is sufficient for a safe and speedy movement of the containers within.

By way of illustration we give in table 16.4 the order of magnitude of the loading capacity of deep-sea container ships on the North Europe/Far

Table 16.3.   Estimations of land needed per berth and per transferred tonne.

Cargo-handling Technique	Land per Berth (hectares)	Throughput per Berth per Year	Throughput per Hectare per Year
Conventional break-bulk	1–2	100,000	75,000
Palletized cargo	3–4	200,000	60,000
Containers	7–10	500,000	60,000

Source: Jansson and Shneerson, 1982.

Table 16.4.   Loading capacity of a number of deep-sea container ships (North Europe/Far East Trade).

Operator/Service	Number of Ships plus Capacity
Conference	
OOCL/'K' Line	8 (1,950–2,800 TEU)
Hapag-Lloyd/NYK/MOL	9 (3,600–4,400 TEU)
Maersk	9 (3,000 TEU)
Nedlloyd/CGM/MISC	9 (2,950–4,400 TEU)
Non-Conference	
COSCO/BR Line	15 (1,200–2,100 TEU)
Evergreen	12 (11 × 2,728 TEU, 1 × 1,810 TEU)
Norasia/Sea-Land	13 (1,900–2,200 TEU)
ABC Containerline	5 (1,500–1,900 TEU)

Notes:
1. Conference: Any type of formal or informal agreement between shipping companies, usually in the liner trades, that restricts competition and is designed to secure regularity and frequency of service and stability of rates (Stopford, 1988, p. 17).
2. Non-conference (outsider): Liner service that is not a member of the conference on the route and does not conform to its rules (Stopford, 1988, p. 17).

Source: Lloyd's Shipping Economist (October, 1992, p. 9).

East Trade. Of course, it seldom happens that a complete ship load of containers is unloaded in one port (cf. the mainport concept, linked to feedering from smaller ports). Yet it may be reasonably assumed that the scale increase in container ships will sharpen port competition: a shipping company with a ship of, say, 4,000 TEU (twenty foot equivalent unit) will only aim at ports where a sufficient load is offered (e.g. 1,000 TEU, incoming and outgoing loads taken together).

The above figures mean that the use of containers requires a much larger back-up area. Suppose that it is our goal to design the lay-out of the container berth in such a manner that the cost of the port infrastructure (quay length and paved back-up area) is minimized. The optimization might consist of making the berth equal in length to one ship, linked to an inland size of the back-up area proportional to the throughput of that berth. But in such a berth the costs of internal handling and transport will rise fast.

Research has shown that the actual optimum is that the length and inland size of the berth are roughly equal. This may give a (mistaken) impression of overcapacity in terms of quay length, as the total quay length is much greater than the sum of the ship lengths that can be serviced simultaneously given, for instance, the cranes on that quay. Yet the quay length should no longer be a binding limitation to the throughput at a container terminal.

How is the required back-up area calculated? The necessary back-up area is mostly determined by the ship size. Thus second generation container berths needed a paved back-up area twice as large as for first generation ships (16 instead of 8 hectares). The planned capacity was twice as high, so that the throughput per hectare remained unchanged.

A potential new bottleneck for containerization lies in the fact that the loading and unloading capacity for container transport is not followed by the capacity of the other links, which are still largely conceived for traditional break-bulk handling. That is why most of the required land serves to store containers in transit, and to keep them moving in a way that the container cranes are perfectly fed.

This whole development is partially connected to the move of larger ports away from the city, towards a cheaper location and deeper water. In the older port the draught is often insufficient to receive the new ships, and there are land shortage problems as well. Typical European examples of such developments are Lisbon and Antwerp.

16.4. PORT AREA AND PORT CAPACITY

Port developments, and their derived effects on land use, are direct functions of the port capacity. Before going into the question of capacity, it

Table 16.5.   Infra- and superstructure in Belgian sea ports (1990).

Ports	Area of Berths (ha)	Length of Quays (km)	Number of Cranes	
			Port	Private
Antwerp	1,788	125.0	141	339
Ghent	525	20.2	53	45
Zeebrugge	981	8.9	19	24
Ostend	130	8.0	16	–

Source: Ministry of Transport and Infrastructure.

seems necessary to consider the port area. What do ports have to offer in terms of infrastructure and superstructure?

The port infrastructure and superstructure have a direct influence on the handling of the shipping, and hence also on the costs. Table 16.5 illustrates this with an overview of the present infrastructure and superstructure present in the most important Belgian sea ports in 1990. The scale differences speak for themselves.

For their infrastructure and superstructure, ports continually have to adapt to the new developments in the shipping world. One of those developments is, among other things, the explosive growth of container transport. Within the port of Antwerp, the first Scheldt container terminal (beyond the sluices, hence with an important time saving) appeared to be immediately successful. A second container terminal on the river Scheldt was only recently allocated.

Capacity: An Attempt at a Definition

We first have to make a distinction between the global port capacity and the capacity of the various parts of the transit process. One should also take into account here that there may be fluctuations in each of these elements.

The literature gives several different definitions of the concept of port capacity. In any case it is a concept difficult to grasp. First of all, there is theoretical capacity, which is never fully realized in practice because it leads to bottlenecks before that point is reached. A further refinement teaches us that the capacity of a terminal will also equal the maximal capacity of the smallest of the different terminal activities (transfer from the ship to the quay, transport from quay to storage, storage facilities, . . .).

The transition from a theoretical to a practicable capacity norm comes down to this: there needs to be a certain (necessary) overcapacity, if only to allow for an optimal organization of labour and equipment.

In practice this means that a distinction should be made between intrinsic or optimal capacity on the one hand, and the effective or economic activity on the other. The difference between these two is the reserve capacity which can be used on certain days, but only for a very limited period (the so-called slack capacity).

Many of the port decisions are to be seen in the context of port expansion plans. In the past it was mostly argued that capacity was to be extended proportionally to the predicted growth of traffic (Nonneman 1979, p. 333). Yet this is only economically sensible when the starting point is a reasonable (or optimal) capacity utilization. Yet when the starting point is an overcapacity, this overcapacity will only be perpetuated.

Port capacity and capacity utilization are closely linked to each other. In the preceding sections we have presented a static overview of the available port area. Yet this is not indicative of the actual (albeit theoretical) processing capacity, and even less about the utilization of that capacity.

Port throughput consists of different links, which do not necessarily have the same processing capacity (e.g. storage room). Where then is the capacity utilization measured? This problem explains why there has been quite some opposition to the possibly premature conclusion that the existing capacity utilization might be considerably improved without planning new port expansion. In the past the position was extreme to the point of proposing so-called target capacity utilization degrees; for some goods this was 0.80 and 0.90.

Excessively high target utilization degrees which also become effective degrees create the risk of waiting times for the loading and unloading of ships. That is why there is an urgent need for a calculation of the maximal capacity utilization degree which can be realized without exaggerated waiting times for the ships. For American ports this has been estimated at 40% (Suykens 1989, p. 3). A trade-off has to be made between the loss of time resulting from ships waiting to berth and the costs of additional capacity. However, for western European ports and under normal circumstances, waiting times for obtaining a berth are unacceptable.

Relationship between Capacity and Price

There is a clear relationship between capacity and price. Overcapacity as well as a lack of capacity is translated in the price of the goods handled as well as the port manager. This is clearly not just a matter of transferred tonnes, but also of financial returns. A port terminal with overcapacity will have higher average costs than a port terminal with a more favourable utilization degree.

How could a manager of a less competitive terminal react? On the one hand he could accept lower returns, because the tariffs are too low a function of the costs. Yet when, on the other hand, the higher costs are charged, it will mean a further tainting of the competitive position.

To a certain extent, a port with the lowest overcapacity is the cheapest. A port with the highest utilization degree will get the greatest advantage from a capacity extension. In the short run, a capacity increase of the port installations will be achieved by overtime, night and weekend labour, and using more shifts. Yet all this has a price-increasing effect.

We can now take this a step further by looking at the cost for the ship owner. Those costs will also be a function of the port capacity. At the berth itself a larger tonnage leads to specialization and a limited lowering of the loading and unloading times. At the same time, a greater volume at a given capacity will lead to waiting times. The total time of the ship in the port increases, which is translated into a higher cost.

The Capacity of Various Port Elements

When a ship calls at a port, this process has to be split up into the links of the transport chain. We have to focus special attention on the *aspect of capacity*, particularly in combination with the question of land use. Investigating capacity problems when a ship calls at a port, requires taking into account the capacity problem in a horizontal or vertical sense at each of the distinct segments.

Maritime Access

To what extent is the draught within the maritime access way important for the competitive position of a port? We need to look at the *division* of the calling ships into size categories, and also at the *hour intensity*. Indeed, ships do not arrive at random. There are peaks in port traffic (departures: peaks during the evening hours; arrivals: peaks during the morning hours).

In sea transport more and more importance is attached to *speed* (meaning: the minimization of the duration of the stay of a ship in the port). This has consequences for the priority given to, for example, ships sailing out (cf. the tides). Moreover, liners want to sail at regular hours, independent of the tide, and do not want to accept delays caused by other ships. All this sometimes results in an intensification of the existing peaks.

A port management might then have the following aims:

- raising the tonnage of ships that can reach the port (cf. bulk goods);
- making the regular liners independent of the tides.

Such aims have of course a great influence on the capacity of the waterway. Thus the use of larger ships, at equal tonnage, will lead to fewer ship movements. Practically, this means a lowering of the frequency and intensity, and an increase in tide-dependency (cf. the limited duration of high tide); at the same time a larger share of tide-independent ships (liners) means a larger sailing slot, and hence a better distribution.

We will not go further into a number of other physical characteristics that are important for the waterway, for example the waterway width (cf. overtaking and crossing moves). We should also consider the fact that the capacity of the maritime access way is equally influenced by ancillary services (pilots in foggy weather, at unusually busy times, . . .) and the use of guidance systems (cf. radar).

The Sea Locks

The accessibility of a sea port is chiefly determined by the capacity of the sea locks. It is precisely at these locks that bottlenecks often occur.

The lock capacity of a lock (i.e. the total volume of tonnes that can be processed within a given time) is a function of a number of factors that can be divided in two major classes (Suykens, 1989, p. 22):

• the characteristics of the lock itself; these are fixed, like the lock size, the mechanical characteristics, . . .
• the nautical-technical circumstances; these are variable elements such as the regularity or irregularity of traffic flows as a result of atmospheric circumstances, the tide-dependency, seasonal influences, defects, . . .

A good lock management requires the maintenance of a certain reserve capacity, to deal with peak situations for instance. Table 16.6 illustrates this with the global commercial and the maximum lock capacity. This shows that the operation of the Berendrecht sluice raised the existing commercial lock capacity by more than 60%.

The Docks

Also docks can cause problems in terms of capacity, and equally in terms of draught and width. Then there is the additional problem of the bridge channels, which may be rather narrow for certain ships.

The Terminals

We have already pointed to the large number of partial markets, often with a limited substitution potential. Most often a distinction is made between the following groups:

• fluids: with a distinction between loading and unloading terminals for refineries and/or chemicals companies, storage companies for mineral oils or chemical products;

Table 16.6.   Global commercial and maximum lock capacity of the Antwerp sea locks.

Global Commercial Lock Capacity

Lock	Area (m²)	Commercial Capacity (in GRT/m², with 20% reserve)	Yearly Commercial Lock Capacity
Van Cauwelaert	9,450	3,000	28,350,000
Boudewijn	16,200	3,000	48,600,000
Zandvliet	28,500	3,150	89,775,000
Berendrecht	34,000	3,150	107,100,000
			273,825,000

Maximum Lock Capacity

Lock	Area (m²)	Maximum Utilization Coefficient (in GRT/m²)	Maximum Yearly Lock Capacity
Van Cauwelaert	9,450	4,287 (88)	40,512,000
Boudewijn	16,200	4,694 (88)	76,042,000
Zandvliet	28,500	5,466 (88)	155,781,000
Berendrecht	34,000	5,466	185,844,000
			458,179,000

GRT: 1 tonne = 100 cubic feet of internal space.
Source: Antwerp Port Authority.

- bulk goods, with a usual distinction among three groups: throughput for coal and ore; throughput for non-ferrous ore, phosphates, sand, . . . ; throughput of grain, fodder, . . .
- general cargo, with a further subdivision in:
    break-bulk general cargo or conventional general cargo;
    neo-bulk loads like iron and steel, wood, cars, etc;
    container traffic;
    ro-ro traffic.

We can also concentrate on the capacity of the installations of the *goods handler*, a group that thinks in terms of HEAT (highest efficient attainable throughput) (Suykens, 1989, p. 30). This concept stands for the traffic that can be handled efficiently under normal circumstances, even if a higher tonnage could be realized by additional tasks, by night and Sunday labour, by the use of additional material etc.

The goods handler will focus his attention on three factors: the quay length, the number of cranes, the number of foremen and storage managers they can have at their disposal. We shall go into each of these three elements in further detail.

Quay Length.   To give a quantitative outline: for conventional general cargo the estimate is 1,250 tonnes per running metre of quay wall per year, for a terminal with a land measure of about 100 m between the quay wall and the road, plus a piece of spare land of about 50 m at the other side of the road. This amounts to a return of about 8.3 tonnes per square metre of leased land area. In practice, of course, everything is more complicated, for instance because ships with more than one deck are used, or because of re-stowage when the ship is not calling at its first port etc.

Number of Cranes.   Again, we shall give an idea of the order of magnitude of operations: at an average use of 250 jobs per year, and an average production in conventional general cargo of about 300 tonnes per day, this gives a general average of about 75,000 tonnes per crane per year.

Suykens (1989, p. 32) gives complementary data here. Suppose that there are 5 cranes spread over 2 subsequent berths of 150 m each, i.e. a crane every 60 m. This gives a yearly throughput of 300 tonnes per day per crane and this multiplied by 250 jobs is 375,000 tonnes, to be divided by 300 m of quay. The result is 1250 tons per running metre of quay.

However, these are only indicative figures. Loading and unloading steel in packages or steel plates with a higher unit weight, means a rise in capacity. The same is true for pallets. Goods in cardboard, with a lower unit weight, will lower the capacity.

Number of Foremen and Storage Managers.   For a goods handler the aspect of port labour is very important. That is why a lot of importance is attached to the productivity of the shifts, for instance for bagged goods, which is a specialist's job.

By way of illustration table 16.7 shows for a number of Antwerp docks the average return per used unit of area. In any case, productivity in throughput requires an understanding of the lay-out of the quay, the back-up area at the handler's disposal etc.

We can take this a step further and examine how many cranes with

Table 16.7.   Return per used unit of area.

Place	Average Return (per running metre/year)	Area Depth	Return
Scheldt quays	500 tonnes	60 m	8.3 t/m²
North-quay Albertdock	800 tonnes	100 m	8 t/m²
south 5th + 6th dock	1,250 tonnes	100 m road-quay 50 m other side	8.3 t/m²
Churchill dock	3,000 tonnes	360 m	8.3 t/m²

Source: Suykens, 1989.

which lifting capacity can be used. At this moment container cranes with a lifting power of 40 tonnes are frequently used. The throughput per running metre of quay is thus not only influenced by the area, but also by the technical equipment.

Hinterland Connections

It may suffice to mention here that there are also often bottlenecks in the hinterland transport to or away from the port (cf. the congestion phenomena). We illustrate this with a number of forecasts for goods transport which are relevant for the Antwerp port and region (Meersman and Van de Voorde, 1991, pp. 49–52):

1.   For international transport (excluding transit) between Germany and Antwerp and with reference to the year 1988, a growth of 27.4% is expected in 1995, 52.2% in 2000, 108.6% in 2010.

2.   For the transit transport to and from the Netherlands and with reference to the same year 1988, 2010 shows a growth rate of 94.3% from the Netherlands, and 70.4% to the Netherlands.

For the period 1993–94 a large-scale research project investigates goods and passenger transport in the region of Antwerp, and includes the making of a disaggregated forecasting model.

16.5.   THE CONTRIBUTION OF PORT INVESTMENTS TO PROSPERITY

Cheshire (1990) and Bruinsma and Rietveld (1993, p. 292) both claim that the dependency of the local economy on ports has a magnifying effect on urban problems. One of the major causes for this would be the introduction of the container, which has resulted in a sharp decline of employment in ports. We will not pursue this matter any further.

Yet every analysis of the consequences of land use within a port will automatically end up with a screening of the port investments. Which projects should be carried through? When and with which priority? What are the consequences for the goods flows, the goods throughput, employment etc?

Government Investment and Economic Effects

Investing in infrastructure gives an important impetus to the economy and employment. Hence the recent European primary goal to realize economic recovery by means of an accelerated development of the European transport network. National authorities link up with this, and opt for an accelerated investment programme for infrastructure and hope to get European support.

The European Union's policy (cf. summit meeting of 11 December 1993) posits that building large European infrastructure networks (for transport, communications and energy) is the key to a better competitiveness. The emphasis here lies on an integrated approach for multimodal transport infrastructures, and aims at efficient accessibility to all European regions. In the approved White Paper 'Growth, Competitiveness and Employment', financial support of 800 billion Belgian francs per year during 6 years is planned (1994–1999) for the above-mentioned investment programmes. Within this framework three more indicative plans will be proposed, one of which is for sea ports.

Within that economic and social structure, port development mainly fits into a strategy aimed at reinforcing its position as a distribution region. Conditions are created for an attractive investment climate and for employment growth. In respect to the latter, there is an important employment effect because of and during the realization of the projects. On the other hand, there is a structurally derived employment effect, as a consequence of the multiplier effect of the transport sector on other economic sectors.

By way of illustration we will give a few figures for the Belgian context (Kelchtermans, 1994, p. 21). Studies indicate that 2.1 million Belgian francs investments in transport facilities lead to one person-year of employment. For public works, every invested billion BEF means about 420 units of employment (300 direct and 120 indirect units of employment). Moreover, the structurally derived effect can be estimated as follows: every 40 million Belgian francs in transport infrastructure will in due course lead to three permanent jobs.

Port Investment and Returns

A government investment cannot be judged like a private investment. In Belgium port investments have been systematically subjected to a cost-benefit analysis since 1986, whereby the international as well as the national viewpoint is taken. On the benefit side there are port income, economies for port users, employment and unpaid supplies to related projects. On the cost side we find the investment and maintenance expenditure, environmental cost and sometimes the low utilization of existing port capacity (Blauwens, 1993, p. 55).

Additional costs and benefits can only be counted when the market mechanism is deficient in accounting for additional effects. In the case of the Belgian port projects, this is true for the four following effects: employment; environmental effects, causing under-utilization in other ports; unpaid supplies to other projects (for instance dredgings).

A typical example of a possible double counting is the development of the national industry, because a well-developed port attracts multinational companies (relocation) or makes national companies more competitive in markets abroad. Port investments have a favourable influence, but it should not be counted in a cost-benefit analysis because re-localization cannot be considered as an additional activity. Moreover, it needs to be said that support given to the industry is not different from economies for the port users.

In table 16.8 we will give a comparative overview of the results of five recent investment projects in Belgian ports. The results are expressed in the form of a benefit ratio, which is the net return per invested franc. At the same time a sensitivity analysis was carried out, based on a low traffic forecast.

What can be concluded from table 16.8? The benefit count is usually lower from a Belgian point of view than from an international one. Striking is the differing sensitivity of the projects for the sensitivity analysis. Each project is clearly yielding some returns, such that we could classify them in terms of the benefit ratio.

Table 16.8.   Benefit ratios for five Belgian port projects.

Project	Benefit Ratio International	Benefit Ratio for Belgium
First container quay on river Scheldt in Antwerp		
– standard calculation	3.33	1.12
– low traffic forecast	2.85	0.91
Container quay in outer port of Zeebrugge		
– standard calculation	4.88	1.56
– low traffic forecast	0.18	−0.59
Renovation Amerika dock- 3rd dock in Antwerp		
– standard calculation	1.41	1.45
– low traffic forecast	1.15	1.21
Verrebroek dock (Antwerp, left bank)		
– standard calculation	5.53	3.23
– low traffic forecast	5.06	2.75
Renovation of the port of Ostend		
– standard calculation	1.27	0.91
– low traffic forecast	0.77	0.61

Source: Blauwens, 1993, p. 69.

16.6. CONCLUSION: THERE IS A NEED FOR MORE PORT RELATED RESEARCH

The aim of this chapter was to go into the relation between transport and land use, with an application to sea ports. The literature is relatively poor, and the same is true for empirical results. It thus goes without saying that from a research point of view there is still a great deal to be done.

It was impossible to treat all possible relations in this chapter, so that we had to make a choice. Studying the relationship between transport and land use is for sea ports usually part of a larger picture – the improvement, or at least maintenance of the competitive position.

First of all, the growth of many ports is spatially limited (cf. the shortage of free land). At the same time there is a continual pressure for scale increase. If ports do not grow along with the world-wide port developments, it means a declining competitiveness, with negative consequences for a number of derived effects like employment and added value. On the other hand, infrastructure development also creates consequences for competitiveness. Each port has its hinterland, on the condition that the competing port does not operate more cheaply. Formerly the competitive struggle was fought at the borders of the natural hinterland, now the competition is much sharper.

In what follows we will briefly examine a number of research topics which deserve attention in the short term. These concern methodological as well as empirical research, with the emphasis on internationally comparative and interdisciplinary research.

Spatial Re-orientation of Port-Related Activities

To what extent should weakening ties to the port location of activities such as storage, distribution, and the processing of goods be accounted for? Indeed, recently a re-location towards the hinterland has been observed.

With the help of empirical studies economic and spatial change processes in the relationship between sea ports and the European hinterland have to be looked into. What also needs to be considered here is the changed composition of maritime goods flows, logistic developments, and a changed division of labour. In practice such investigation comes down to answering the following questions. Is part of the presently port-related activity relocating elsewhere? What is the geographical effect of this process (e.g. re-localization, infrastructure, economies of scale, . . .). What is the effect on the competitive position of sea ports (e.g. specialization)?

Changes in the Spatial Structure of Sea Ports

Until now, little attention has been paid to a quantitative and qualitative comparison of sea ports. Key policy questions would include how are ports structured spatially? Is there land shortage or is expansion potentially unlimited, and how is this dealt with? What is the need for renovation of old port sites? Extremely important is also the question of the port authorities' policies on infrastructure provision, industrialization and leasing/selling of port land.

The Consequences of Infrastructure Provision

A good (port) infrastructure is indispensable for the competitive battle at an international level. The attractiveness of locations for the establishment of economic activity depends on the accessibility, and as such on the quantity and quality of the transport infrastructure (Bruinsma and Rietveld, 1993, p. 279).

Port investments, on land as well as on the waterfront, should be aimed at keeping or reinforcing the competitive power. This again requires a swift reaction to changes in the market, and a consideration of the potential pressure from companies already located in the port (for instance their requests for renovation of older port sites). If this does not happen, there is the threat of traffic loss, with indirect effects for employment. Understanding these effects requires the necessary tools (cf. goods flows in Rotterdam). These kinds of tools will be needed for a clear view on the relation between European sea ports, the spatial-economic development in European regions and the construction of European (transport) networks.

The Effect of Changing Market Developments

One may reasonably expect a further liberalization of the European and international trade. Coupled to a further opening up of eastern Europe and a further spreading of a rising prosperity, this should lead to a strong growth in international goods flows. Yet a number of questions again come to mind here: will this growing international transport go through the existing ports? Will there be geographical moves of port hierarchies, for instance between the port ranges? Will there not be capacity problems within certain ports? To illustrate this: it has been calculated for Rotterdam that for an equal competitive position, container transport through the mainport will be multiplied by three in the coming 15 to 20 years and reach 6 million TEU per year (Evers et al., 1994, p. 30).

An important theme to be investigated is the possible economies of scale. Indeed, a scale increase generates several consequences. First of all it can be assumed that starting from an acceptable capacity utilization, the capacity will expand in such a way that the rising demand can be met. Yet the question arises then to what extent this capacity extension leads to a cost increase or lowering, and what the consequences are for the port competitiveness. This requires an understanding of the cost structure, for the global transport chain as well as for the separate transport links.

Economic Structures and the Effect on Land Use

An important theme to be investigated is the relation between the economic (or competitive) structures and land use. If we apply this to the port of Antwerp, it leads us to the following detailed questions. To what extent are there any monopolistic or oligopolistic (sub)markets (say, for the allocation to Hessenatie of the first container terminal beyond the sluices)? Is there an increase in vertical integration? What is the relationship between the allocation of port land and port competitiveness, and the example of CAST relocating from Antwerp to Zeebrugge comes to mind here (land free of charge)?

References

Blauwens, G. (1993) Kosten-batenanalyse van haveninvesteringen in België, in Blauwens, G., De Brabander, G. and Van de Voorde, E. *De dynamiek van een haven*, Uitgeverij Pelckmans, Kapellen, pp. 55–72.

Blauwens, G. and Van de Voorde, E. (1988a) The impact of port choice on inland transportation. *Maritime Policy and Management*, **16**(2), pp. 127–140.

Blauwens, G. and Van de Voorde, E. (1988b) The valuation of time savings in commodity transport. *International Journal of Transport Economics*, **6**(1), pp. 77–87.

Blauwens, G. and Van de Voorde, E. (1991) Port renovation and optimal ship size: The case of bulk transport, in Winkelmans, W. (ed.) *Shipping and Ports in the National Economy – Economic Relations and Models*. Antwerp.

Bruinsma, F.R. and Rietveld, P. (1993) De structurerende werking van transportinfrastructuur: een survey betreffende de invloed van infrastructuur en bereikbaarheid op de ruimtelijke spreiding van activiteiten. *Tijdschrift Vervoerswetenschap*, pp. 279–302.

Button, K. (1993) *Transport Economics*, 2nd ed. Aldershot: Edward Elgar.

Cheshire, P. (1990) Explaining the recent performance of the European Community major urban regions. *Urban Studies*, **27**(3), pp. 311–333.

Couper, A.D. (1992) Environmental port management. *Maritime Policy and Management*, **20**(2), pp. 165–170.

Evers, J.J.M., Bovy, P.H.L., de Kroes, J.L., Sommerhalder, R. and Thissen, W.A.H. (1994) Transport, infrastructuur en logistiek: een proeve van een integrerend onderzoeksprogramma. TRAIL onderzoekschool, Delft.

Farrell, S. (1986) The subsidization of seaports: An alternative approach. *Maritime Policy and Management*, **14**(2), pp. 177–184.

Hoyle, B.S. (1992), Waterfront redevelopment in Canadian port cities: Some viewpoints on issues involved. *Maritime Policy and Management*, **20**(3), pp. 279–295.

Goss, R.O. (1982) National port policies, in Van de Voorde, E. (ed.) *Haven en Vervoer in de Hedendaagse Economie*, pp. 9–21.

Heaver, T.D. (1993) Shipping and the market for port services, in Blauwens, G., De Brabander, G. and Van de Voorde, E. (eds.) *De dynamiek van een haven*, pp. 227–248.

Jansson, J.O. and Shneerson, D. (1982) *Port Economics*. Cambridge, Mass: MIT Press.

Japanese Maritime Institute (1991) Medium to Long-Term Analysis of the Shipping Market (1995–2005). JAMRI, Tokyo.

Kelchtermans, T. (1994) *Het Vlaams InfrastructuurPlan: een geïntegreerd voorstel, Vlaams Ministerie van Openbare Werken*. Brussel: Ruimtelijke Ordening en Binnenlandse Aangelegenheden.

Marconsult (1991) *Container Handling Costs and Organization at the Main European Ports*. Naples: Marconsult.

Meersman, H. and Van de Voorde, E. (1991) De vraag naar personenen goederenvervoer, in *Verkeer in België in 2000: mobiliteit of chaos?* referatenboek twintigste Vlaams Wetenschappelijk Economisch Congres, pp. 3–63.

Nonneman, W. (1979) Prognose van het Belgisch maritiem vervoer. *Gewestelijke Economische Raad voor Vlaanderen, Elementen voor een havenbeleid*, Berichten 22, pp. 243–283.

Parlement Européen (1993) *Politique Européenne des ports maritimes*. Luxembourg: Direction Générale des Etudes.

Stopford, M. (1988) *Maritime Economics*.

Suykens, F. (1986) Ports should be efficient (even when this means that some of them are subsidized). *Maritime Policy and Management*, **14**(2), pp. 105–126.

Suykens, F. (1989) Havencapaciteit, een relatief begrip. Mimeo. Havenbedrijf, Antwerpen.

Suykens, F. and Van de Voorde, E. (1992) Het belang van de haven voor de uitstraling van Antwerpen. Of: een continu gevecht voor competitiviteit en marktaandelen. *Economisch en Sociaal Tijdschrift*, pp. 447–499.

Van de Voorde, E. and Witlox, F. (1992) De bedrijfslokalisatie vanuit een transporteconomisch oogpunt. *Economisch en Sociaal Tijdschrift*, pp. 255–282.

Acknowledgement

We are very grateful to G. Bleuwens, K. Dickele and H. Meersman for helpful comments on earlier drafts.

CHAPTER 17

TRANSPORT TERMINALS, INTERCHANGES AND ECONOMIC DEVELOPMENT

Kenneth Button

17.1. INTRODUCTION

Transport terminals are often neglected in debates surrounding the influence that transport infrastructure may exert over economic location and development. For example, in the recent up-surge of interest in the activities of high-technology firms, the vocabulary inevitably gravitates to the notion of transport links – the M4 Corridor and Route 128. Any consideration of the role of sea ports, train terminals or bus stations is rather pushed aside, although some consideration is given to airports. In practice, of course, economic activity is often clustered and these clusters tend to be around interchange and terminal sites. This concentration is particularly pronounced where fixed track transport is involved (such as high-speed rail transport), or where common resources (such as the sea or air) are used in the actual movement.

Our general understanding of the exact link between transport and economic development is far from complete and is even less precise when it comes to considering the roles of specific pieces of infrastructure such as major terminals or interchanges. Despite this there is continual competition at the national and local levels to attract such facilities to specific sites in the belief that positive economic effects will follow.

The aim of this chapter is to consider the importance of air and sea ports as focal points for industrial and commercial development. More specifically, it is to review the insights offered by Twomey and Tomkins and Van de Voorde on this topic. In many ways these studies provide interesting complementary insights into the specific issues associated with the role of terminals and interchanges in economic development: one looking primarily at the external considerations while the other focuses more on internal economic factors.

17.2. IMPORTANCE OF TERMINALS

Initially it is useful to isolate the particular common features that make transport terminals and interchanges worth considering in their own right and independently of the links in the transport network. One can break the main features of terminals down into:

1.   Terminals tend to be located near concentrations of population and, therefore, are often responsible for generating a range of local negative environmental effects.

2.   Terminals involve, almost without exception, multi-modal activities.

3.   A combination of developments in electronic data interchange (EDI) technology, deregulation of transport markets, yield management techniques and just-in-time (JIT) management has lead to increased use of hub-and-spoke operations in transport and an increased emphasis on the role of hubs.

4.   Terminals usually have a long physical life once completed.

5.   Transport terminals and interchanges involve very large, often indivisible investments which make marginal changes in capacity difficult.

6.   Terminals and interchanges seldom have any alternative practical use.

7.   Terminals, because of the above physical features, are often characterized by decreasing costs.

8.   There has traditionally, although this is now declining, been a substantial public sector role in the provision and operation of infrastructure.

These features make it particularly wasteful if inappropriate investment decisions are made which lead to problems of pricing and management once the facility becomes operational. In particular, once constructed, the low marginal cost of use makes it particularly attractive for policy makers to keep charges low and subsidize other costs.[1] This raises not only issues of the internal managerial efficiency of the infrastructure, but also whether the ultimate outcome is simply one of politicians using the supposed economic characteristics of terminals and interchanges to play 'beggar-thy-neighbour' games with each other, with a consequential over-capacity problem. The Manchester and Liverpool Airport example cited by Twomey and Tomkins offers a possible example of this as does the situation regarding port subsidies in a large part of the European Union. From a spatial development perspective, it means that even if infrastructure can attract economic activity to an area, the impact is neutral because all terminal charges are excessively low.

17.3. PROBLEMS OF ASSESSING DEVELOPMENT IMPACTS

There are a number of problems in assessing the development impacts of any form of transport infrastructure investments and these would seem to apply in particular to terminals. Perhaps the most cited is that of defining the relevant counter-factual for the assessment (Botham, 1980). The approach suggested with regard to Manchester Airport, for example, is to develop a simple industrial linkage model and to explore what would happen as the result of further airport capacity coming on-line. There are two limitations with such an approach. First, from a predictive standpoint, a Leontief technology is assumed. This is a rather rigid assumption to make when looking at a piece of long-lived infrastructure. Second, it is assumed that no policy efforts aside from the airport development would be made to improve the area's economic efficiency. These or similar assumptions are not unusual, and should be seen as reflective of general weaknesses in our understanding of dynamic processes rather than a specific criticism of this work.

Remaining with this study, there is also relatively little said about alternatives to developing Manchester, in terms either of possible technical developments that could reduce the need for additional capacity, or of alternative scenarios regarding developments of airports elsewhere, including those on Continental Europe. Again, this is standard practice in most studies of this kind where a relatively limited range of options is reviewed, and this is often a reflection of institutional intervention failures brought about by inadequate geographical divisions of responsibility or sectoral myopia.[2]

The spatial impact multiplier, usually expressed in terms of employment creation, is the work-horse in assessment of the effect that transport terminal or interchange development can have on any area. The difficulty is that both the estimates of the multiplicand and the multiplier pose serious problems. This may not be immediately transparent when looking at studies dealing with this topic – they all utilize what appear to be fairly standard parameters. The problem is often that this apparent robustness hides the weakness of the ground it is built on. There are, in fact, few empirically derived estimates of employment impact multipliers let alone secondary and tertiary multipliers.[3]

Figure 17.1 offers a fairly standard diagram depicting the employment impacts of any major transport investment over time. There are the direct

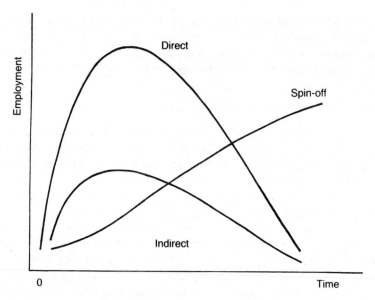

Figure 17.1

jobs created in association with the construction of the terminal or interchange, the indirect effects of the construction on local industries and the
longer term spill-over effects from new activities moving to the area. The
evidence that we have to date provides very little insight into either
the magnitude or exact profile of these employment effects.[4] A good
example of these types of problem, albeit only partly related to terminals
and interchanges, has been the difficulty of predicting even the immediate
effects of the Channel Tunnel on the local construction industries in Kent,
let alone the longer term effects of the facility on firm locations and
expansions (Button, 1994).

17.4. INTERNAL EFFICIENCY

While Twomey and Tomkins are primarily concerned with the possible
implications for the region's economy of expanding an air terminal, Van
de Voorde in his chapter puts far more emphasis on the internal efficiency of transport investments. The standard attitude of advocates of
transport infrastructure as an instrument of spatial economic policy is to
ignore questions of management. The new facility is assumed to be operated effectively, although the exact nature of the management is left as
something of a black box in most studies. There is also a tendency to
assume that managerial choices are very restricted, mainly for technical
reasons. But, as is shown in the case of ports, this need not be so and

managerial flexibility, and thus the development implications, can in fact be quite considerable.

In practice, and for a variety of reasons including fear of local monopoly exploitation, 'beggar-thy-neighbour' strategies and the perceived decreasing costs of terminal services supply, economic regulation and subsidies are common in many countries. Indeed, in many instances, the extreme form of regulation, namely public ownership, is deployed. Van de Voorde carefully sets out the nature of the problems that this can pose for managing such facilities and the potential for resource wastage that can result from an inappropriate response.[5] In particular, his chapter highlights the political nature of many of the actions taken, especially in terms of attempting to circumvent market mechanisms through the use of subsidies to attract traffic away from competing facilities.[6]

17.5. FULL COSTS

Even if one can circumvent the problems of setting up a realistic framework for the way a terminal will be managed and make acceptable predictions concerning employment (or income) generating effects, there still remains the problem of specifying the true costs of an investment. The risks of financial cost over-runs are considerable in the context of major transport investments as has been borne out by the experiences of the Channel Tunnel. This in itself raises questions of the opportunity costs involved in such ventures as well as more pragmatic questions concerning the role of risk sharing between the public and private sectors.

There are, however, other important elements concerning costs. Transport infrastructure in all forms poses serious external costs in the form of localized congestion and environmental intrusion if adequate counter measures are ignored.[7] In practice such measures are seldom adequately implemented and the true opportunity costs of any economic development are underplayed. When such costs are considered, it is often in terms of the primary mode concerned (for example air movements at airports), but in fact it is often access to the facility by secondary modes (such as cars to airports) which poses the major external costs. These costs not only adversely impact on local residents in the area of the terminal but can influence the specific locations of undertakings that may elect to locate themselves in the general area of the terminal. This makes predicting the detailed spatial implications of a terminal difficult.

There is a further dimension to the environmental cost issue. The physical scale and longevity of terminals mean that at the end of their useful life there is an adverse legacy effect. Many of the poorer regions and parts of inner-city areas are encumbered by derelict transport infrastructure (such as docks or rail marshalling yards) which makes them unattractive to new investors. Ideally, these costs should be embraced in any assessment of the development benefits of terminal or interchange investments and part of the cash flow set aside for the ultimate restitution of the site (Button and Pearce, 1989). In practice, of course, this is seldom if ever done and the notion is absent from most of the discussion of the subject.

17.6. CONCLUSIONS

Terminals and interchanges are both important as key elements in modern transport networks. Their role as catalysts for local economic development is often stated in planning strategies but in fact detailed knowledge of the interactions involved or of the scale of the development effects of specific schemes is still far from adequate. It is quite clear that in some cases investment in this form of infrastructure is highly desirable from an economic and social perspective, but picking winners is still extremely difficult and being made increasingly so with the globalization of trade. What the two chapters by Twomey and Tomkins and by Van de Voorde demonstrate, besides offering insightful case studies, is the degree to which our understanding is limited and the extent to which the political processes that surround decision-making are often dominant over economic rationality.

Notes

1.   This is a point clearly in the mind of Van de Voorde when he states that 'Port tariffs are often obscure . . . the structure of these costs do not bear a clear relation to the economic reality.'

2.   See Button (1992) for a discussion of forms of intervention failure found in transport.

3.   Twomey and Tomkins also quite correctly hint at the degree of subjectivity which can go into the choice of multiplier value to adopt producing what Americans often refer to as political forecasts. Some indication of the degree to which this politicization can extend in transport forecasting, albeit in the context of US urban transit systems, is provided by Pickrell (1989).

4.   The profile is particularly important given the proclivity of politically based decisions to attach high discount rates to the stream of jobs associated with major investments.

5.   Very little rigorous econometric research has been conducted on the relative importance of economic regulation of prices and of public ownership in the transport sector. Evidence from the energy field (Button and Weyman-Jones, 1994) indicates that changing regulatory regimes can significantly influence X-efficiency but that privatization *per se* has very little effect.

6.   The evidence which is available is that deregulated and non-subsidized ports in Europe, such as those in the UK, can compete with some success with the

subsidized ports because of their greater internal efficiency (Brooks and Button, 1991).

7.   Of course the ideal measure is the allocation of property rights *à la* Coase, but more pragmatic devices such as pollution and congestion charges or command-and-control instruments are possibly more realistic.

References

Botham, R.W. (1980) The regional development effects of road investment. *Transportation Planning and Technology*, **6**, pp. 97–108.

Brooks, M. and Button, K.J. (1991) *Europe '92: Impact on the Provision of Maritime Transport Services*, Ottawa: Transport Canada.

Button, K.J. (1992) *Market and Government Failures in Environmental Policy: The Case of Transport*. Paris: OECD.

Button, K.J. (1994) The Channel Tunnel and the economy of South East England. *Applied Geography*, **14**, pp. 107–121.

Button, K.J. and Pearce, D.W. (1989) Improving the urban environment: how to adjust national and local government policy instruments for economic and environment gain. *Progress in Planning*, **32**, pp. 135–184.

Button, K.J. and Weyman-Jones, T. (1994) The impacts of privatisation policy in Europe. *Contemporary Economic Policy*.

Pickrell, D.H. (1989) *Urban Rail Transit Projects: Forecast versus Actual Ridership and Costs*. Cambridge, Mass: U.S. Department of Transportation.

CHAPTER 18

PRIVATE TOLL ROADS IN THE UNITED STATES: RECENT EXPERIENCES AND PROSPECTS

Jose A. Gomez-Ibanez and John R. Meyer

18.1 INTRODUCTION

Interest in toll roads has increased in the United States since the mid-1980s as state and federal governments realized that highway needs have grown faster than traditional highway revenue sources, most notably the gas tax.[1] This revival has even extended to the possibility of private toll roads: roads to be built and operated by private companies under state franchises or concessions. By early 1994 eight states and the Commonwealth of Puerto Rico had enacted legislation permitting private toll roads, and the US Congress had passed a law relaxing prohibitions on tolling roads built with federal aid and even allowing states to use federal highway grants to help build private toll roads. One private toll bridge had opened in Puerto Rico, two private toll roads were under construction (one in California and the other in Virginia), and perhaps a dozen other projects had received state franchises and were in various stages of feasibility study or environmental permitting, although it was clear that some of these would never be built.

In this chapter we examine the recent experience of US toll road proposals to assess whether and where private toll roads might be built in the United States and what their advantages and disadvantages might be. The United States has been experimenting with modern private toll roads for less than a decade, and thus has less experience than some European countries, particularly Spain and France.[2] The US experience is in some respects richer than that of Europe, however, because the federal system allows the states to pursue different strategies for privatization so that different approaches can be compared.

To foreshadow the results somewhat, we argue that toll roads are unlikely to be a very promising area for privatization, although still one worth pursuing. One basic problem is that there are probably not very many opportunities for financially viable new toll roads, largely because most roads that might be profitable from tolls alone have already been built, and because supplementing tolls with contributions from land-owners or state and local governments usually creates serious com-plications. This problem is compounded, moreover, because private developers appear to offer few obvious advantages in construction or operating cost savings or in overcoming the environmental or other ob-stacles facing public highway agencies. The principal advantage of private operators is that they appear to be a valuable source of innovative ideas on highway design and operations. For this reason alone, however, they seem worth promoting, even though they may never become a major part of the highway system.

18.2.   THE US EXPERIENCE IN OVERVIEW

The Revival of Private Toll Roads

The revival of private toll roads is a sharp departure from recent practice, since most of the US highway system is presently publicly owned and operated and financed from fuel and other taxes rather than tolls. This has not always been the case, however. Between 1790 and 1850 perhaps as many as 20,000 miles of private toll roads were built in the United States, although these roads all but disappeared with the arrival of canal and railroad competition in the middle of the nineteenth century. Toll roads reappeared in the late 1930s as many northeastern states used toll financ-ing to begin building their high performance expressway systems. These toll roads were public rather than private and their construction virtually stopped after 1956, when the US Congress funded the Interstate and Defense Highway System. Under the Interstate Program, the federal government assumed 90% of the cost of building a 42,000 mile network of high performance highways, with the federal share financed largely out of a federal tax on gasoline of 4 cents per gallon. The Interstate Program reflected a decision that an integrated national high-performance high-way system could be more readily financed through fuel taxes rather than the continued state-by-state development of toll roads. Tolls would not be permitted on roads built with federal highway aid, although approxi-mately 2,500 miles of then existing public toll roads were grandfathered into the Interstate System.

Interest in toll roads did not re-emerge until the late 1970s and early 1980s, after the Interstate System had been largely completed and high-way traffic was continuing to grow steadily. At that point it became clear to many states that further increases in the high-performance expressway system were needed either to augment existing capacity in certain highly congested urban corridors or to extend the system to areas that had developed (or were showing signs of development) in the years since the Interstate System map had been drawn. Maintaining the now extensive highway system was absorbing most of federal and state gasoline tax receipts, moreover, leaving little funding for system expansion. Although the federal government increased gas taxes twice in the 1980s and most states raised theirs as well, by the mid-1980s the shortfall between perceived highway needs and highway revenues led Texas, Florida, Oklahoma and several other states to begin building or planning new public toll roads.

The toll road revival of the mid-1980s included proposals for private as well as public toll roads. The decade had been marked by increasing scepticism about the capabilities and effectiveness of government. The staggering cost of many of the needed additions may also have fuelled an openness to private as well as public sector solutions Finally, there had been some apparently successful experiments with privatizing other forms of infrastructure in the United States in the early 1980s, most notably solid waste disposal, power cogeneration, wastewater and drinking water plants (Donahue, 1989).

Early Models: Virginia, California and Puerto Rico

The first three major private toll road programmes developed almost entirely independently of one another in Virginia, California, and Puerto Rico. The earliest dates from 1986, when a group of private entrepreneurs, later organized as the Toll Road Corporation of Virginia (TRCV), proposed building a 15 mile toll road connecting Dulles International Airport with Leesburg, Virginia. The private road, now known as the Dulles Greenway, would connect with an existing state-owned toll road at Dulles Airport and extend into the rapidly developing western outskirts of the Washington, DC metropolitan area. By 1988 the Greenway's backers had convinced the Virginia Assembly to pass the legislation needed to authorize 35-year concessions for private toll roads in the state; by 1991 they had secured all needed state and local government environmental and zoning permissions; and in the fall of 1993 they completed financing and began construction.[3]

California's programme emerged in 1989 largely as the initiative of state government rather than private entrepreneurs. In that year the state legislature passed Assembly Bill (AB) 680 authorizing the California Department of Transportation (Caltrans) to enter into agreements with private companies to build and operate four private transportation facilities (rail lines were eligible as well as toll roads). Caltrans announced a competition for private proposals anywhere in the state and established an elaborate judging scheme to avoid complaints of favouritism or political influence.[4] The competition drew eight entries and Caltrans signed franchise concession agreements with the four selected winners in January 1991. By early 1994 only one had begun construction while the other three were still trying, in some cases half-heartedly, to secure environmental permits and financial backing.

The most successful California franchise to date is for a 10-mile, four-lane toll road built completely within the median of the existing State Route 91 (SR-91) freeway in Orange County to the south of Los Angeles. Orange County had originally planned to build high-occupancy-vehicle (HOV) lanes in the median in order to relieve congestion on SR-91, which connects rapidly growing residential areas of western Riverside County with the jobs of central Orange County. A private consortium initially led by a large design and engineering firm proposed to Caltrans that the lanes be privately built instead and financed by opening them to toll-paying single occupant vehicles (SOVs). HOVs would still be allowed to use the lanes, and those with three or more persons would travel free or at reduced rates.[5] Tolls would be collected electronically and vary by time of day and, with an expected rate of 20 cents per vehicle mile during rush hours, would be sufficient to pay back the expected $88 million construction costs. The private company began construction in the fall of 1993 and expects to open the project in 1995.

Of the remaining three California franchises, the most viable is the proposal by a consortium led by Parsons Brinkerhoff (a large transportation and environmental planning firm) to extend SR-125 in eastern San Diego County. The SR-125 toll road would run north-south approximately 10 miles to the Mexican border, and would serve growing residential communities in the eastern end of the County as well as the increasing truck traffic to and from the Mexican maquiladora plants just the other side of the border. The $400 million project was initially delayed by disputes over environmental issues and concessions requested by local governments; by the time these issues were largely resolved, the weakening of the California housing market threatened the financial viability of the project by reducing traffic and toll projections and the prospects that local real estate developers would contribute needed land or cash. The SR-125 consortium is hopeful, however, that a combination of the North American Free Trade Agreement and a recovery of the San Diego housing market will soon allow it to begin construction.

Far less likely to be built, at least in the near term, is the proposal by a consortium led by the Parsons Corporation (another larger construction engineering company) for a new 85-mile 'Midstate' toll road from I-680 at

Sunol in the South San Francisco Bay area to I-80 near Vacaville. The first 40-mile section from Sunol to SR-4 near Antioch would cost $600 million and provide a high performance alternative to congested local roads for the developing areas of eastern Contra Costa County and northern Alameda County. The second section, also costing around $600 million, would be a 35-mile extension from Antioch to Vacaville that would open up areas of largely agricultural central Solano County and provide an alternate route between the Sacramento area and South San Francisco Bay. This project was to have been financed by a combination of tolls and land or cash donations from the 70 odd communities along the route. Although some communities are supportive, opposition from environmentalists and others concerned about urban sprawl has forced the consortium to abandon the second section and has seriously delayed the first section.

The least active of the California franchises is that of a consortium organized by H. Ross Perot, Jr., the Dallas real estate developer. The Perot group proposed building an 11-mile toll extension of the SR-57 freeway from Interstate 5 (I-5) near Anaheim stadium, through central Orange County, to I-405. The road would complete a long needed north-south link in the County's freeway network and, to mollify neighbouring communities, would be built over a channel of the Santa Ana River, a partially concrete-lined river that is usually dry and serves primarily for flood control. The Perot group planned to reduce construction costs to $700 million by adopting innovative building techniques and restricting the four-lane viaduct to passenger cars only. Tolls would vary by time of day ranging from $5 per car in the rush hours to $1 per car in the evening. The consortium has been slow to finish environmental and other studies in the four years since it was awarded the franchise, probably because it now has serious doubts about the project's financial viability.

Puerto Rico's programme was also an initiative of state government but in Puerto Rico's case the government, not the private sector, identified the specific projects to be franchised. In September 1989, the same year California passed its AB 680 legislation, the Commonwealth of Puerto Rico announced a competition to award franchises to build and operate two private toll facilities: a bridge across the San Jose Lagoon and an extension of the government-owned SR-66 expressway, both near San Juan. The franchises were awarded in 1990 to a consortium composed of Dragados, Spain's largest contractor and a major stockholder in Spanish private toll road concession companies, and Rexach, a Puerto Rican construction firm.

The Puerto Rican government and Dragados decided to build the bridge first, since it was the simpler of the two projects. Detailed negotiations for the bridge franchise were completed in early 1991 and the $134 million facility opened for service in February 1994, with the distinction of not only being on budget and ahead of schedule but also the first major private toll facility in the United States in many decades. The 2.1 kilometre bridge connects San Juan's international airport with major residential areas and provides an alternative to congested arterial streets that go around the San Jose Lagoon. Tolls were set initially at $1.50 and traffic in the first few weeks was about 10% higher than projected.

Negotiations for the SR-66 franchise have gone slowly, however, largely because a different party won the gubernatorial elections of 1992. Although the new administration has been somewhat suspicious of the private toll road programme begun by its predecessor, Dragados is hopeful that its success with the San Jose Lagoon bridge will lead to a final agreement on SR-66.

ISTEA, Arizona, and Washington

The pioneering efforts of Virginia, California and Puerto Rico soon stimulated supportive federal legislation and new privatization programmes in other states. The US Congress made several changes intended to encourage tolling and private toll roads when it reauthorized and reformed the federal highway aid programmes in 1991. The Intermodal Surface Transportation Efficiency Act of 1991 (known as ISTEA and pronunced 'ice tea') allowed states for the first time to charge tolls on highways built with federal aid, although still not on the Interstate Highway System.[6] ISTEA also permitted states to use their federal highway funds to help support private toll road franchises.

Six additional states passed laws authorizing private toll road projects but there has been little activity so far in four. Florida enacted a law allowing private toll roads in 1991, for example, but no serious private proposals resulted in part because the requirement in the law that each franchise agreement be reviewed by the state legislature raised fears of last-minute demands. In Texas, a number of private firms applied for concessions under a long-forgotten nineteenth century Texas toll road law; the state legislature repealed the old law and replaced it with a more modern version in 1991 but disputes among the implementing agencies have discourgaged its application.[7] Laws in Missouri (1990) and Minnesota (1993) also have not resulted in much activity in those states yet.

Much more interesting and important are the experiences of Arizona and Washington. Both states established programmes modelled on California's competition soliciting private projects anywhere in the state. Under the Arizona law, enacted in 1991, up to four projects could be selected. The Washington law, enacted in 1993, allows up to six projects.

Arizona's competition drew strong interest from the private sector but was largely abandoned due to strong political opposition to the projects proposed. Ten proposals were submitted in May 1992, including nine for roads in the Pheonix metropolitan area.[8] Three proposals were to build various sections of Squaw Peak Parkway, a main commuting artery to the downtown; three others were for parts of the Pima Highway, a planned beltway; and another was for a Pheonix area bridge. Two projects drew the most attention and controversy, however. One was a proposal, inspired by the SR-91 project in California, to allow toll-paying SOVs to use the existing median HOV lanes on Pheonix's I-10 freeway and to use the proceeds to build similar facilities in the medians of other Pheonix expressways. The other was an ambitious proposal to complete the entire Pheonix area expressway plan whose delay had been an important impetus to the private road programme. In 1985 metropolitan area voters had passed a special half cent metropolitan sales tax to build a 231-mile system over 20 years; by the early 1990s it had become clear that the funding would be sufficient for only 70 miles. The private consortium proposed to use a combination of the tax proceeds and tolls on the entire system, including the already built portions, to complete the $3.5 billion plan.

Even before the four winners were selected, the proposals generated a firestorm of complaints about various alleged inequities of tolling, disadvantages to local businesses or communities not served by proposed projects, and provisions overly generous to the private consortia. Some observers argue that the intensity of the opposition was due largely to the failure of the Arizona Department of Transportation to consult with local governments and other state agencies beforehand. In any event, the backers of the winning projects, all less controversial individual freeway segments, withdrew after it became apparent that the governor would no longer support the programme. In 1993 the state began negotiating with the only consortium still active, that proposing to complete the entire expressway system. A final agreement appears unlikely, however, even though the consortium has revised its proposal to eliminate tolls on existing expressway segments and other controversial provisions.

Washington's programme differs from its predecessors in that for the first time a state has indicated its willingness to consider proposals that mix public with private funds. The Washington Department of Transportation announced that it would consider, for example, taking an equity position in a project or providing junior long-term debt. The possibility of leveraging private monies with public stimulated 14 proposals by 11 private consortia by the May 1994 deadline. The variety of projects proposed is startling, including five toll bridges, two new toll highways, a large network of toll HOV lanes inspired by California's SR-91, toll tunnels near Seattle's downtown, two schemes for park-and-ride lots, an automated transit system for Seattle's airport and a high speed ferry system for Puget Sound.

The extent to which the proposed Washington projects rely on public monies is unclear since the Department of Transportation and the consortia regard the details as proprietary until the selection process is completed. The few details available suggest that the consortia are proposing a variety of forms of public support including unsecured loans for preparation of environmental impact statements, outright grants, and the right to collect tolls on existing roads. Whether these schemes will prove politically acceptable is still unclear.[9]

In short, the US experience, though brief, is highly varied. It includes programmes where the private sector identifies projects, for example, as well as programmes where the public sector does. A variety of types of highways have been nominated; most of the projects – such as the Dulles Greenway, SR-125 and the Midstate in California, and many of the Pheonix expressway segments – are development roads serving areas that are still largely undeveloped but are expected to grow rapidly in the next decade. The others – including the SR-57 viaduct and the SR-91 HOV lanes in California, the San Jose Lagoon Bridge, the median HOV lanes in Pheonix, and most of the roads and bridges in Washington – are designed to relieve congestion in already built up areas. There have been failures as well as successes.

18.3.   KEY BARRIERS TO PRIVATE ROADS

The Importance of Financial Self Sufficiency

By far the most important barrier to private toll roads in the United States is the difficulty of finding a new road or bridge project where toll revenues will cover most, if not all, construction and operating costs. Tolls can be combined with other sources of support or revenue, of course, the most common being cash or in-kind contributions from government or local land developers. To the extent the project can rely primarily on toll revenues, however, its chances for success are greatly improved.

Finding a self-financing project is difficult largely because the United States already has built 54,000 miles of high performance expressways, including many (or even most) of those with sufficiently high traffic volumes to be supported from toll revenues. Advocates of new toll roads must therefore search out those remaining unserved opportunities where tolls might cover all or most of costs.

Congestion-relieving roads appear to face very different tolling and financial problems from roads that service or anticipate development. The congestion-relieving road has the advantage of strong traffic volumes in the early years, but it usually has the disadvantage of high construction costs because of high land prices and expensive amenities designed to ameliorate the objections of the built-up communities through which it passes. The congestion-relieving road is more likely to face competition from the existing expressway network as well. The most obvious and least-cost alignments through these built-up areas are likely to have already been exploited by public authorities, leaving private developers only the most difficult and costly alternatives (e.g. tunnels, cut-and-cover, or viaducts). The existence of free alternatives may also mean that the congestion reliever road can count on heavy traffic volumes only during the peak hours, when the untolled alternatives are congested. By contrast, the development road may enjoy relatively low construction costs per mile, especially where it travels through open country, and is less likely to suffer from free-road competition. A development road generally suffers the disadvantage, however, of facing a slow and uncertain traffic build up.

None of the projects proposed or under construction is financed entirely from tolls, although the congestion-relievers come closer than the development roads. In the case of the congestion relievers, the non-toll contributions are generally in kind rather than cash and not very visible to the public. All of the construction costs of the SR-91 median lanes and the SR-57 viaduct are to be financed from tolls, for example, although state authorities are to provide much of the right-of-way at no cost (in the expressway median for SR-91 and over the Santa Ana flood control channel for SR-57). The $134 million construction cost of the San Jose Lagoon bridge is to be financed entirely by toll receipts but the Puerto Rican highway authority invested around $10 million in approach roads and paid for the studies needed to secure environmental permits.

In the case of the development roads, the non-toll contributions typically take the form of donations of cash or right-of-way by local real estate developers or governments along the route. The Dulles Greenway received right-of-way donations worth an estimated $60 million from local land developers, although these are relatively modest compared to the $360 million in development costs that are to be toll financed.[10]

Many of the delays experienced by projects are partly attributable to the difficulties of securing needed non-toll contributions. For example, SR-125's backers suggested that donations of $30 million in right-of-way from land developers and $15 million in cash from local government would be sufficient to make their $300 million project viable; these projections were probably optimistic and, in any event, they have been unable to secure them yet. Midstate's backers have been more vulnerable to local environmental opposition in part because they have been counting on local government contributions of $150 million to $200 million to the cost of their $600-million first phase.

The basic problem, of course, is that negotiating contributions from local government or landowners can greatly complicate franchise negotiations and leave the project vulnerable to the demands of an increasing number of outside parties. Significant contributions from property developers, for example, are only really feasible where a handful of large landowners control most of the right-of-way. Indeed, it is striking that Dulles Greenway and SR-125, which rely primarily on land donations, are routed through property mostly controlled by a few large landowners while the Midstate, which passes through land held by many owners, relies on local government contributions instead. Even then, landowner donations often come at a cost of added interchanges, more circuitous routeing, or complex three-way negotiations with local governments for permits or other concessions the developers seek in return. The Dulles Greenway was only able to secure its right-of-way contributions after several years of negotiations in which it allegedly changed its alignment to serve the interest of a major property owner and brokered a deal to secure from local government certain development permissions another key property owner had long wanted.

State and local governments also can be induced to contribute if they have a stake in the proposed road and are convinced that contributions are necessary. Governments often face budgetary problems of their own, however, and the contributions will compete with other social service or infrastructure needs. Moreover, public officials and citizens may condition the contributions on design changes and other modifications that add to road costs. Finally, financial contributions to a private enterprise seem to make US state and local officials somewhat nervous, perhaps of charges that they have spent public funds unwisely. These anxieties might be alleviated by the traditional practice of tendering specific franchises, with negative bids accepted. Such schemes are harder to implement when the private sector identifies the project rather than the public sector. It is striking that none of the roads under construction have received cash contributions from government, although SR-91 and the San Jose Lagoon bridge received contributions in kind. It also remains to be seen whether the state of Washington will be able to manage the potential controversies involved in investing in or subsidizing private franchises.

Profitability usually not only simplifies negotiations but also provides the private concessionaire with the wherewithal to buy its way out of other problems or objections. A road profitable from tolls alone is obviously better able to finance amenities to placate environmentalists or communities along the route. Of course this can backfire – demands may escalate if the concession is perceived to be highly profitable. The most favourable situation is probably a project just profitable enough to eliminate the need for landowner or government contributions but not so profitable as to incite their greed.

None of the private toll roads franchised so far rely on federal aid since federal law prohibited charging tolls on roads built with federal assistance (except under special and limited circumstances) at the time the projects were developed. However, ISTEA now allows states to use federal funds to pay 50% of the cost of building a toll road, public or private, provided that the facility is new or substantially improved and not part of the Interstate System. A 50% subsidy obviously would increase the number of situations where toll roads are financially viable, perhaps significantly. Such federal aid could eliminate the need for landowner or local government assistance required by the three development roads studied, for example, or reduce the required tolls on SR-57 to more plausible levels.

The prospects of capturing federal aid for toll roads are uncertain. Congress left the decision to use federal aid for toll roads to the states, and provided no special toll road funds above and beyond each state's normal apportionment of federal highway funds. The use of federal aid for a toll road (public or private) therefore will come at the expense of its use for other state road projects. Although Congress increased the level of funding for highway programmes under ISTEA, most states have a backlog of unfunded non-toll road projects large enough to absorb easily the federal aid available. Toll road proponents might argue that their projects would make federal aid go farther, but this argument would be particularly compelling only in states that did not already have enough state or local tax receipts to match federal aid.

Political Acceptance of Tolls

Political controversies over tolling also have been a barrier to private toll roads, although not as much as one might expect given that tolls are the exception rather than the norm for financing roads in the United States. The history of the US public toll road movement in the 1940s and 1950s, as well as its revival in the 1980s, suggests that the American public will accept tolling when they perceive that public budgets are constrained and new roads are badly needed. Many states (Virginia, California, Arizona and Washington, for example) adopted highway privatization programmes only after studies revealed a large backlog of needed projects that could not be financed from existing revenue sources.

A state budget shortfall alone is not enough, however, to convince local communities and their elected officials that their particular road should be among the minority financed from tolls. Two general rules seem to apply. Tolls will be accepted only if local residents and officials feel (1) that there was little prospect that their road would be built as a free road; and (2) that the process for determining state or local road funding priorities is fair. This fairness doctrine can be undermined, for example, if one community feels that it is being called on to pay tolls when a neighbouring community with no apparent greater need is receiving an untolled road.

Virginia's Dulles Greenway and California's SR-57 are examples of projects where there have been few objections to tolling *per se* because it was clear from the outset that the road would never be built without toll financing. The original Dulles Toll Road was built as a public toll highway a decade earlier, when shortages of state funds made it obvious to local officials that tolls were the only realistic source of finance. Perhaps as a result, the possibility that the extension would be a free road was never seriously raised; the debate focused instead on whether the tolls should be collected by a public agency or a private developer. Similarly, SR-57 had been deleted from California state highway plans in the 1970s largely because the only alignment potentially acceptable to neighbouring communities – on a viaduct over the Santa Ana River channel – was widely viewed as prohibitively expensive. Some additional source of revenues, such as tolls, would be needed to offset the high costs if SR-57 was ever to be built.

Tolling sometimes can be more acceptable if it is done by a private enterprise rather than a public agency, as illustrated by the case of Puerto Rico. Puerto Rico created a public toll road authority to build many of the Commonwealth's high performance highways, probably because the Interstate System was never extended to the island. Politics has kept the public authority's toll rates so low, however, that it could not make many needed investments in the 1980s. Given this history, Puerto Rican authorities thought it would be politically more acceptable for a separate and private company to charge the higher tolls needed to finance the San Jose Lagoon bridge.

Tolling a project that had once been promised as an untolled facility can provoke intense disputes, as illustrated by California's SR-91 median lanes. Orange and Riverside Counties originally had planned to build free HOV lanes in the median of SR-91. Riverside County actually had begun construction of its portion at the time that the private consortium proposed to build the Orange County segment as a tolled facility. As a consequence, Riverside County argued that HOVs should be allowed free access to the tolled Orange County median lanes, in keeping with the plan the two counties had originally accepted. A guarantee of free access for HOVs threatened the viability of the private proposal in Orange County, as HOVs eventually might so seriously congest the toll facility as to make it unattractive to toll-paying SOVs. Riverside officials eventually compromised and accepted that HOVs with only two persons might be tolled, but only after polls revealed that Riverside residents were more concerned that the lanes be built quickly than whether they were tolled.[11]

Controversies can also arise if the procedures used to determine which

roads would be funded by gas taxes and which by tolls are poorly understood or perceived as unfair. This happened in Arizona's debacle, for
example, in part because many local officials and citizens felt they had not
been warned that the newly-passed half cent regional sales tax might
prove insufficient to fund the whole highway plan, and that priority
setting was therefore a critical exercise.

Environmental and Anti-Growth Controversies

All new roads, public or private, face potential objections concerning their
environmental impacts, the growth they might induce, or the land takings
they require. Private road proposals have proven fairly vulnerable to such
controversies, although probably no more so than public roads.

Private entrepreneurs usually seek out those road projects where the
environmental and related objections are more manageable, but it is usually impossible to avoid controversy altogether. The private proposals for
congestion-relieving roads are typically designed to minimize land takings, for example, since takings are particularly sensitive in built up areas.
(They do so in a variety of ingenious ways: by crossing a lagoon, using a
freeway median, or building over a flood control channel.) Even so, the
California congestion-relievers, SR-91 and SR-57, face difficult air-quality
issues since air quality in the Los Angeles area is so bad. SR-91's backers
secured environmental permits by arguing that the project would improve air quality because it promotes HOVs and provides only a small
increment in capacity for SOVs. SR-57's backers will have a harder time
arguing that it improves air quality, and they are also likely to face
objections over the noise and unsightliness created by the elevated structure. The apparently agreed upon and 'politically acceptable' alignment
may be less acceptable when the public has a closer look at preliminary
models.

The development roads vary greatly in the intensity of the environmental and anti-growth objections they raise. Environmental concerns seem
surprisingly manageable for the Dulles Greenway or San Diego's SR-125,
for example. The Dulles Greenway's sponsors won over environmental
opponents by replacing, two for one, the acreage of wetlands they filled
and by redesigning a bridge so that it was less obtrusive. SR-125 faces
objections over the disturbance of the nesting areas of some endangered
bird species. These can probably be met by relocation of the right-of-way,
since the road passes through largely open and undeveloped country so
that right-of-way options are not too restricted.

Concerns about growth management are potentially more serious for
the development roads, although attitudes vary from case to case. For
example, the Greenway faced few problems because the local government

whose permissions were needed, Loudoun County, felt that growth was desirable, or at least inevitable, and wanted to avoid the local traffic congestion that had accompanied the unplanned growth in a neighbouring county. To Loudoun County, the toll road seemed like a possible compromise, providing the extra highway capacity needed to accommodate growth without adding to congestion. Even so, Loudoun County conditioned its approval of the Greenway on some costly design changes, aimed primarily at insuring that the road would not become congested in the future.

SR-125 represents an intermediate case. Again, relatively few local governments are involved. Although local communities, especially Chula Vista, are having second thoughts, they have historically been in favour of growth. Moreover, growth seems beyond Chula Vista's control since it is occurring in considerable part in unincorporated areas of the County and nearby in San Diego City's industrial zone at the Otay Mesa border crossing. Furthermore, in the context of Southern California's growth trends, the road will almost certainly be needed and could be available earlier with private than with public development. Nevertheless, Chula Vista, like Loudoun County before it, has argued for costly changes in the timing and design of intersections and improvements to access roads to insure that SR-125 does not worsen congestion on local highways.

Midstate faces the biggest growth-management problems. Some 70 local governments can be found along the route, including three counties. Some communities in the middle of the route want growth. On the other hand, at either end of the proposed project there is either outright opposition to growth (as at Livermore), or at least considerable scepticism (rural Solano County). The Greenbelt Alliance and the Sierra Club, both influential environmental groups, have also joined forces to oppose the Midstate on the grounds that it will promote the sprawling development of the San Francisco metropolitan area.

The histories of these projects suggest that private roads have both advantages and disadvantages in overcoming potential environmental, growth management, and land assembly objections. The primary advantages are the private sector's great sensitivity to the cost of delays and their greater flexibility in finding compromise solutions. The Dulles Greenway's backers sought out environmental groups and were quick to offer generous solutions to the concerns they raised. Since time was money for the backers, speedy and generous compromises were much more sensible than protracted litigation. Similarly, a private firm may be able to avoid forced land takings by right of eminent domain where a public agency could not. California's right-of-way acquisition laws limit the state to paying fair market value for a parcel, for example; private firms are not so bound and may pay more if it is worthwhile to avoid protracted eminent domain proceedings.

Private developers also face disadvantages as well. In the first place, their greater sensitivity to delays can be a disadvantage as well as an advantage. The backers of each private road typically estimate that preparing the environmental analyses and detailed designs necessary to secure environmental and other permits will cost them several years and at least $10 million or more – the Greenway's backers spent three years and about $20 million to secure permits for a road with comparatively few objections. Raising venture capital for this effort is extraordinarily difficult since the risks are perceived to be high; the Greenway's backers were lucky to find a wealthy individual with faith in their project while the others have had to rely primarily on contributions of 'sweat equity' from the planning, design and financial firms in their consortia. In short, while the high cost of added delay may make these private backers more ready to compromise than litigate, obstinate delays and objections can also easily become deal breakers by frightening away investors at the development stage.

Private developers may also generate more suspicions than a public agency might, particularly where growth management or land assembly is an issue. In matters of growth management, for example, a private toll road may raise the spectre of collusion with real estate developers. This suspicion is reinforced when, as in many of the development roads, the project backers seek contributions from developers who own large adjacent parcels of land.

Finally, the perception of flexibility may sometimes work to the disadvantage of private road developers by raising issues that might not have occurred with a public highway authority. The fact that private road developers are not constrained to pay fair market value by state compensation statutes may encourage land owners to hold out for more, for example. And in some cases local communities along a private route insist on assistance for their feeder road systems that private developers doubt would ever be asked of a state highway agency.

18.4. POTENTIAL PROBLEMS OF MONOPOLY AND REGULATION

Surprisingly little controversy has arisen so far over the potential problems of monopoly or excessive competition that might arise with private toll roads. The difficulty, of course, is to strike a balance between protecting the private operator from 'excessive' free-road competition (so as to achieve sufficient profits to attract capital) and protecting the public from the potential abuses of a monopoly franchisee (in the form of high toll rates or limits on capacity).

California chose to grant the private toll roads exclusive franchises, delimiting territories within which the state promised not to build competing facilities and to use its best efforts to persuade local governments from doing so as well. Backers of private projects have not requested similar protections in most other states, however, probably because they think improvements to parallel facilities were unlikely on budgetary and environmental grounds.

All the states which have authorized private toll roads have decided to regulate toll rates, returns on investment or both. Three different approaches have emerged, however, with the first three states to experiment with modern toll roads. Virginia adopted conventional rate-of-return regulation by the state public utility commission (PUC) that also regulates electricity, telephone, gas and other utility rates. California selected a contractual approach setting the ceiling for the rates of return allowed over the life of the project in each franchise agreement. California's private toll road operators are free to set their own toll rates, so long as they stay within their established ceiling returns, set out in the franchise contract. Puerto Rico also adopted a contractual approach controlling the rate of return, but provides for the state to share in the profits when the returns reach certain levels rather than capping the return altogether. The owners of the San Jose Lagoon bridge can keep all profits until they earn a 19% return on equity; returns above 19% and but below 22% are shared 60/40 with the state; returns in excess of 22% are shared 85/15 with the state.

The three schemes have different advantages and disadvantages. Virginia's PUC model has more history in the United States, and thus may be more acceptable to financial markets. On the other hand, the PUC approach may leave investors more subject to the vagaries of future political developments (although Virginia's regulators agreed to protect investors to some degree by establishing an account in which the unpaid earnings from the early and riskiest years of the project accumulate as liabilities for later repayment out of earnings). Moreover, the PUC approach requires burdensome rate-of-return investigations whenever the franchisee requests a toll increase.

California and Puerto Rico's one-time contractual approach ostensibly fixes rates of return for the life of the project, thus protecting investors from changes in the political climate and from the burden of periodic investigations of the adequacy of returns. Whether the state will stick to the terms of the agreement is unclear, however; California's contract does not specify the compensation required in an event of a state default and promises only that Caltrans will use its best efforts to persuade the legislature to appropriate funds for compensation. Either the operator or the state will probably try to modify the agreement in the future, moreover, since it is unlikely that a contract signed in the early 1990s can anticipate and cover every contingency through the 2030s (when most of these franchises will expire). Thus some exposure to the vagaries of the political climate may be unavoidable.

Puerto Rico's system of rate sharing seems to offer advantages over California's system of rate caps in that the concessionaire no longer has incentives to operate the concession efficiently (or at all) once returns reach a cap. Moreover, the Puerto Rican scheme provides an easy and understandable way for sharing risks and returns. The Puerto Rican government invented the scheme after Dragados pressed them to guarantee that traffic would not fall below certain forecast levels. If the Commonwealth was to assume some of the downside risks, officials reasoned, then it should also share in the upside rewards.

Projects have been successfully financed under all three schemes, but the California approach appears more popular with private toll road investors than Virginia's. Washington adopted California's one-time approach, for example. Arizona's road privatization law provided something of a test of investor preferences in that it allowed for two franchises to be granted with contracts modelled after California's and two with PUC style regulation like Virginia's. Nine of the ten responses to the solicitation requested California contract agreements, although two of these indicated the PUC option was also acceptable.

The Arizona results may reflect the possibility that California's negotiators were too generous in the ceiling caps they allowed as well as (or rather than) investor preferences for the contractual approach. California agreed to fix ceiling rates of return on combined debt and equity of between 17% and 21.5% over the 35-year lives of each project (each of the four projects has a different fixed cap). By contrast, Virginia's PUC set a ceiling return of only 14% and only for the first six years, while Puerto Rico allowed 19% but on equity only.

Whether or not California's higher rates were necessary to attract capital is unclear. On the one hand, it might be argued that the Virginia PUC, unaccustomed to dealing with infant industries, may not recognize the potential risks of pioneering a private toll road. Virginia's Greenway project is also arguably less risky than some of the California projects, particularly Midstate and SR-57. On the other hand, Virginia's 14% rate was the rate that the Greenway's backers had requested and ultimately proved adequate. Moreover, the California ceiling caps seem overly sensitive to the scenarios that were assumed in their calculation. For example, in doing the calculations undue weight may have been placed on the hazard of permits being denied at the very last minute. In the real world such adverse possibilities should be evident well before, so that private sponsors could pull out before they lost all potential development expenses.[12]

In any event, although both state officials and private road developers profess to be satisfied with the various arrangements they have made, regulatory issues are likely to become controversial in the future. The discrepancy between California's returns and those allowed by most PUC's may become more visible if one of the California franchises proves exceptionally profitable. And the franchises are so long lived that California and Puerto Rico's contracts will probably have to be renegotiated at some stage.

18.5.   The Practical Advantages of Private Provision

The US experience also provides a test of the advantages claimed by proponents of private toll roads. Interestingly, there is only limited evidence to support two claims often made: that privatization will stimulate aggregate investment in roads and that private toll roads will be built more cheaply and faster than public toll roads. In the US context, the advantages of private provision seem to lie more in its ability to stimulate innovation in road design and operating practices.

Added Investment

Privatization is often alleged to increase overall highway investment above levels possible with limited public budgets by tapping a new source of funds: private capital markets. There are two theoretical objections to this argument. First, public toll roads could tap private capital markets too by issuing revenue or general obligation bonds; private operators would have an advantage only if overall public debt was somehow constrained or if tolling (needed to secure revenue bonds) was more politically acceptable when done by a private rather than a public toll road operator. Second, in a full or near full employment economy any added investment in highways would likely come at the expense of other forms of private investment since privatization does not automatically increase the pool of private savings on which private capital markets draw. Publicly provided highways, by contrast, might increase total investments (in highways and all else) to the extent that the public highway projects were funded by current taxes or highway user charges rather than debt and these taxes or charges were borne in part by a reduction in private consumption rather than private saving.

In practice, the US experience suggests that private provision may add to aggregate highway investment. Most of the states that adopted privatization did so only after opportunities for raising taxes were exhausted (at least politically). Some of the states that have franchised private toll roads, such as California, also have very few public toll roads which implies that tolling may sometimes be more acceptable when done by private rather than public road operators. If higher taxes or public tolls are not possibilities, then it is also less likely that the public sector could have financed more highways by tapping into private capital markets or by reducing consumption rather than savings.

Any increase in aggregate highway investment is likely to be minimal, however, given the various barriers to private toll roads noted earlier. Indeed, it is striking that only one private bridge and two private roads have been built or are under construction after nearly a decade of debate over private roads.

Cheaper and Faster

The US experience does not provide definitive evidence as to whether private road construction or operation is cheaper than public, in part because only one bridge has been completed and placed in service. Even when more private roads are completed it will be difficult to tell whether there were savings because most roads and bridges have unique features and problems, so identifying comparable public projects will be difficult.

The only explicit pre-construction comparison of public and private costs was made in Virginia, where the state's PUC was required by law to compare public and private costs and timeliness before issuing a certificate to a private road developer. The PUC staff comparison claimed that a toll road built by the Virginia Department of Transportation (VDOT) would cost motorists only $0.9 billion over 40 years, while the private Greenway proposal would cost $3.5 billion. The Greenway would cost users more, according to the PUC, because it was to be financed with a sale-leaseback scheme with an effective annual interest rate of 10% while the VDOT road could be financed by combination of 7% tax-free state bonds supplemented by surpluses from the existing state-owned Dulles Toll Road (to cover debt payments in early years, before traffic built up). Greenway costs were also higher because the private road operator would have to pay federal and state income taxes, local property taxes, as well as dividends to its equity investors.

As the PUC eventually recognized, however, such simple cost comparisons are misleading in that the reported differences in VDOT and Greenway costs mostly do not represent fundamental savings to society or the economy as a whole but rather transfers of costs from one part of society to another. From the perspective of society as a whole, a private road would be less costly only if it required fewer physical resources, services or amenities to build or operate than a comparable public road. The private road might be less costly, for example, if it required less right-of-way, concrete, or labour to build because of more efficient design. The leftover land, labour and concrete could then be used for other projects, such as building another road or housing. Most of the claimed savings for VDOT were not of this fundamental type, however, but rather were transfers. The VDOT and Greenway designs, alignments and direct construction costs appeared fairly similar, for example. VDOT exhibited savings largely because it is tax exempt and because it proposed various financing gimmicks to shift risk from road investors and users to state taxpayers (see Gomez-Ibanez and Meyer, 1993, pp. 183–186).

The one real cost advantage claimed in the Greenway-VDOT debate was a Greenway argument that it could open the road sooner by starting construction earlier and building it faster. If true, this would represent a real saving to society as a whole. Starting sooner and building faster (all else being equal) reduces the amount of capital that must be tied up during the construction period and the time before the fruits of the investment are enjoyed. The Greenway's experience is somewhat discouraging, however, since the process of obtaining the necessary public approvals and searching for financing took seven years (from 1986 to 1993). Part of the delay is almost surely because it was a pioneering private toll road project in the United States, so there were few precedents to guide developers or public officials. Nevertheless, some tasks – such as negotiating with landowners for contributions or with Loudoun County for approvals – took far longer than the Greenway's backers expected.

More Innovative

The US experience does suggest that privatization can enhance the prospects for innovation, which may be at least as important as speed or cost. This is particularly apparent where states have allowed the private sector to nominate projects, most notably in the open competitions organized by California, Arizona and Washington.

Many of the proposals nominated in the California competition, for example, had been rejected, neglected, or overlooked by public highway authorities. The extension of SR-57 had been abandoned by Caltrans as too expensive in the 1970s, the southern segment of SR-125 was on state and county plans but was not to have been built for at least 10 or 20 years, while the Midstate alignment had not even occurred to public officials.

The designs and operating plans of the private projects are often innovative as well, perhaps because the private firms are less encumbered by past practice. The sponsors of SR-57 proposed an auto-only road, for example, to reduce the cost of building the viaduct and thus help make the expensive project financially viable. SR-91 is the first project in the United States that will allow toll-paying SOVs to use special HOV lanes, a concept that potentially provides a means not only of financing HOV lanes but of exploiting the often underused capacity of these facilities as well. Another idea being pioneered or advanced by many private projects is varying toll rates with time-of-day or levels of congestion. Peak-hour or congestion pricing is a key element in the plans for many congestion-relieving roads, such as SR-57 and SR-91, and is being considered by several developmental roads as well. It is striking that no US public toll road has ever adopted time-of-day or congestion pricing, despite the advantages often cited by economists and widespread use of such schemes in airlines, telecommunications, power or other industries whose service demands vary seasonally or hourly.

The potential importance of innovation has implications for the design of privatization programmes. Some have suggested, for example, that state governments should assume the responsibility for conducting environmental studies and winning local permissions, since raising the venture capital needed poses such problems for private road promoters. The approved projects would then be turned over to private interests for consummation. This clearly would make private investment more attractive, but it would also reduce the opportunities for innovative projects. Virginia, California, Arizona and Washington's strategies of allowing the private sector to identify and propose projects exposes the firms to more developmental risks, but provides the flexibility and incentive to develop new ideas.

Promoting innovation may also conflict with efforts to encourage privatizations by getting state and local governments to share a part of the costs of marginally profitable projects. Cost sharing has been difficult in part because of concerns about favouritism, corruption or simple naivety on the part of public officials negotiating the franchises. The traditional solution for such concerns – competitive contracting – is simplest, however, when the project to be bid is fairly clearly specified in advance. In short, competitive contracting may be necessary to increase the number of projects that can be privatized but may also reduce one of privatization's key advantages: the enhanced possibility of innovation.

18.6. PROSPECTS

What do these experiences suggest about the opportunities for private sector toll roads in the other states? To start, they indicate that development roads may have a slightly better chance of being privately developed than congestion relievers, although much depends on very local or site specific considerations. Development roads have the advantage of being in situations where tolling is more likely to be politically acceptable and probably can be done at costs that are not so exorbitant that they cannot be recovered from tolls. The congestion relievers, by contrast, are almost by definition (with SR-91 being an exception that proves the rule) very high cost facilities. Accordingly, congestion relievers often will need to tap into other sources of financing which will greatly complicate the task of establishing the political alliances and coalitions needed for implementation. Furthermore, the congestion relievers, since they go through already built-up areas, will have fewer opportunities than the development roads to tap into the most obvious source of outside financing, that of donations from private developers holding large nearby vacant land holdings.

A far more robust generalization, however, is that private toll roads probably will not be built in very large numbers in the United States given the constraints of financial feasibility and political acceptance. The most important limitation on the building of private toll roads is the sheer size of the existing US road system, which means that many of the potential opportunities for profitable toll roads have already been pre-empted, adding to the difficulties of attracting landowner contributions or government aid to supplement tolls. Tolling may also not be politically acceptable in some situations and the high costs of delays for private investors will make them avoid roads with significant environmental or siting opposition.

Nevertheless, private toll roads may make a contribution by stimulating innovation and by generally serving as a benchmark against which the performance of public highway authorities can be measured and stimulated. The principal advantages are not likely to be in lower cost construction or operation or in bringing some roads on stream faster than the public sector could, although these may sometimes prove to be the case. The main contribution of private toll roads is more likely to be their willingness to be more innovative, to explore new technologies and techniques. These potential contributions, while no solution to all highway problems, are also not trivial; they certainly merit further consideration and experimentation with highway privatization.

Notes

1. This chapter updates and expands upon our earlier review of the U.S. experience with private toll roads originally published at Jose A. Gomez-Ibanez and John R. Meyer, *Going Private: The International Experience with Transport Privatization* (Washington, DC: Brookings Institution, 1993), pp. 164–193.

2. For an account of the French and Spanish experiences see Gomez-Ibanez and Meyer, *Going Private* 1993, pp. 107–144.

3. For a more detailed account of the Dulles Greenway see Reinhardt, 1994*a*. and Gomez-Ibanez and Meyer, 1991, pp. 21–65.

4. Teams of Caltrans experts ranked the proposals on criteria that included the importance of the transportation need served, the ease of implementation (includ-

ing local support and environmental or right-of-way acquisition obstacles), the experience of the consortium, the extent to which the project would promote economic development, and the degree to which the project incorporated innovative ideas. For further more detailed descriptions of the California programme see Reinhardt, 1990; or Gomez-Ibanez and Meyer, 1991, pp. 67–106.

5.   The private company can charge HOV3s half the regular toll if the project fails to meet certain financial targets.

6.   There had been some exceptions previously, although these were confined to the approximately 2,500 miles of older toll expressways that were grandfathered into the Interstate System, unusually expensive tunnels and bridges, and a pilot programme of projects in 9 states begun in 1987; see U.S. General Accounting Office, 1990.

7.   Almost ten concessions were applied for under the old law before it was repealed. Most of these are apparently not very active, including four made by the same Perot interests that had won the SR-57 concession in California. The one project which is active and stands the greatest chance of being built is a truck road to the Mexican border near Laredo.

8.   The tenth was for a road on the California border, for a description of the projects see Anon, 1992.

9.   For descriptions of the Washington experience see. Reinhardt, 1994b; and Anon, 1994.

10.   The land was valued at $60 million in 1991, around the time of donation. At that time other development costs were estimated at $300 million; by the close of financing in 1993 these costs had been estimated at $360 million.

11.   In 1994, after construction had begun, Riverside County officials reportedly changed their minds about the equity of tolling Riverside residents and sued to stop the project. The suit was based on environmental objections, since the County had already agreed to tolling, and is thought unlikely to succeed.

12.   California's incentive returns are likely to become another source of controversy. All four private roads can earn up to 6 percentage points above their allowed ceiling rates of return if they meet certain public objectives, including increasing average vehicle occupancy, reducing toll road operating costs, or reducing accident rates. One problem is whether incentives for such purposes are necessary. The case for vehicle occupancy or road operating cost incentives seems the most plausible, since increasing occupancy or reducing operating costs is arguably more in the interests of the general public than the private operator. By contrast, in the case of operating cost reductions, the extra incentive should only be needed when the private operator is already earning the ceiling rate of return. Similarly, safety is in the operator's interest, but it may also be largely beyond his control. An even more troubling problem is whether the incentives are too generous. Operating expenses are a small proportion of total roadway costs, for example, and the vehicle occupancy targets may be only too easily met. Raising the average rate of return on total capital by 6 percentage points could increase returns to equity investors several fold, moreover, since all the increased earnings are likely to go to equity (rather than debt). See Gomez-Ibanez and Meyer, 1991, pp. 97–100, 201–202.

References

Anon (1992) Special Report: Arizona draws strong interest in public-private road projects. *Public Works Financing*, May, pp. 1–7.

Anon (1994) Washington State attracts top developers to test its new public-private initiative. *Public Works Financing*, 74, May, pp. 15–28.

Donahue, John D. (1989) *The Privatization Decision: Public Ends, Private Means.* New York: Basic Books.

Gomez-Ibanez, Jose A. and Meyer, John R. (1991) Private Toll Roads in the United States: The Early experience of California and Virginia. Report to the Region One University Transportation Center and to the U.S. Department of Government Transportation, prepared at the Taubman Center for State and Local Government, Kennedy School of Government, Harvard University, Cambridge, Massachusetts.

Gomez-Ibanez, Jose A. and Meyer, John, R. (1993) *Going Private: The International Experience with Transport Privatization.* Washington, DC: Brookings Institution.

Reinhardt, William G. (1990) AB 680 Special Report: Infrastructure entrepreneurs pioneer private toll roads, *Public Works Financing,* October.

Reinhardt, William G. (1994a) Virginia's Dulles Greenway: First U.S. private startup toll road is financed and under construction. *Public Works Financing*, 70, January, pp. 1–8.

Reinhardt, William G. (1994b) Next test for U.S. private roads: Washington State. *Public Works Financing*, 71, February, pp. 23–25.

U.S. General Accounting Office (1990) *Participating States benefit under Toll Facilities Pilot Program.* Washington, DC: U.S. Government Printing Office.

CHAPTER 19

PRIVATE SECTOR INVESTMENT IN ROADS: THE RHETORIC AND THE REALITY

David Banister

The conclusions reached in Gomez-Ibanez and Meyer's chapter on the potential for substantial private sector involvement in the financing of road construction are not optimistic. The US experience suggests that 'toll roads are unlikely to be a very promising area for privatization' as there are few new possibilities for viable investment opportunities. All the potentially profitable roads have already been built. There is greater potential for the private sector in roads built for *development reasons* as there is likely to be less opposition, the costs are lower and the potential for development is higher. Roads built to relieve *congestion* require more complicated packages as costs are higher and there is likely to be greater opposition. Consequently, private sector interest is lower. The main role for the private sector may be as innovators – the benchmark against which the performance of public authorities can be measured and stimulated. Examples here would include new methods of charging by time of day or levels of congestion, or by maximizing capacity through charging single occupancy vehicles for using high occupancy vehicle lanes.

The experience of the United States provides an informative reference point against which to judge road investment decisions in Europe. In Western Europe as a whole, there are some 40,000 km of motorways, of which 13,500 km are tolled. Over 90% of the tolled motorways are in France, Italy and Spain. In 1991, the annual revenue from tolls ranged from £500 million in Spain to over £1 billion in Italy and around £2 billion in France (DOT, 1993). France has the best developed system of toll motorways, constructed through letting concessions to semi-public bodies (Société d'Economie Mixte – SEM) which are contracted to build particular sections of road. Legislation has also been passed to allow private companies to build certain roads. In all cases the state has implicitly supported the private sector by providing financial support through low or zero interest cash advances, guaranteed loans or the provision of related infrastructure. At present, France has seven autoroute SEMs, one private autoroute concessionaire (COFIROUTE), and two tunnel SEMs (DOT, 1993). The SEMs and COFIROUTE keep the revenues from the tolls which can then be used for road maintenance and the construction of new autoroutes.

Elsewhere, private sector funding has mainly been directed at very specific links, such as bridges and airport roads. These new links often duplicate existing routes where capacity is limited, and they are not constructed for development reasons. This places them in Gomez-Ibanez and Meyer's more difficult category. The main difference from the US situation is that the public sector allows the private sector to take over the operation of the existing congested link. This 'deal' places the private sector in a virtual monopoly position, particularly where there are no alternative routes. If growth in demand is expected and the scale of investment modest, then the interest of the private sector is substantial. In the UK, the two best examples are the Queen Elizabeth II bridge across the river Thames, which duplicates the existing Dartford Tunnels on the M25 London orbital motorway, and the second Severn Bridge across the river Severn between Avon in England and Gwent in Wales. In both cases the private sector construction company has taken over the existing tunnel or bridge (table 19.1).

Table 19.1.   The Dartford river crossing on the M25 London orbital motorway.

1963	Two lane bored tunnel at Dartford – 12,000 vehicles per day.
1980	Second two lane tunnel – joint capacity 65,000 vehicles per day.
1986	M25 completed and demand now 79,000 vehicles per day.
1986	Trafalgar House consortium wins bid to build a new bridge. £86 million (1986 prices). Dartford River Crossing Limited set up.

Dartford River Crossing Limited has taken over the outstanding debt on the existing Dartford Tunnels from Kent and Essex County Councils and operates both the tunnels and the new bridge as toll facilities. The bridge provides 4 lanes for southbound traffic and the existing tunnels provide for the 4 lanes of northbound traffic. The Company has a maximum of 20 years to recoup its costs and to make a profit. Tolls must not be increased in real terms above the levels prevailing at 1 January 1986.

1988	Construction started.
1991	Bridge opened.

Dartford River Crossing Limited funded by two subordinated loan stocks, a syndicated bank loan and the toll revenue from the existing tunnels and the new bridge. Current estimate of the payback period is 14 years of the available 20 years.

Apart from these notable exceptions, the private sector interest in road infrastructure projects has been distinctly lukewarm. Transport projects have always been subject to cost overruns and delays. These factors, together with optimistic forecasts of future levels of demand, technical deficiencies in construction and high maintenance costs, lengthy planning procedures and high land acquisition costs, have all resulted in low levels of interest.

Underlying all of the debate, both in the US and in Europe, is the question of risk. Private sector capital is available, but investment in transport infrastructure is seen as having a higher risk than investment in other types of projects. Projects often take a considerable time to come online (table 19.2). The Birmingham Northern Relief Road may be the first section of privately funded road in the UK, and it will duplicate a heavily congested section of the M6 to the north of Birmingham. Construction will probably start in 1996, after the second public inquiry has taken place. The competition for the right to design, build, finance and operate the new road took place in 1989 and added two years to the development process. Although Midland Expressway Limited (MEL) have strong indications from the international financing community that the project will be financed, uncertainty over the public inquiry process together with the market conditions has meant that no finance has actually been committed as yet. The promoters (Trafalgar House and Iritecna) have funded all MEL's costs so far (Carlile, 1994), and it will only be in 1995 that MEL will be clear as to whether the project can be funded.

Table 19.2.   The Birmingham Northern Relief Road.

1980	Plans for the Birmingham Northern Relief Road (BNRR) announced.
1987	After extensive consultations, Draft Orders were published for a 53 km motorway from the M54 at Featherstone to the M6 near Coleshill.
1988	A Public Inquiry was held.
1989	The Government announced a competition to design, build, finance and operate (DBFO) the BNRR as the first purpose built inland tolled motorway in Britain.
1991	Midland Expressway Limited (MEL) a joint venture between Trafalgar House and Iritecna was announced as the winner.
1992	A Concession Agreement signed for 53 years. The revised preferred route was published in March 1992.
1993	Draft compulsory purchase Orders authorizing the acquisition of land published.
1994	Objections heard at a Second Public Inquiry.
1996	Construction scheduled to commence.
1998	Road to be opened.

The total cost of the new road estimated at £270 million (1990 prices).

Source: Based on Banister, Andersen and Barrett (1995).

A substantial part of the risk and the preconstruction costs has been transferred to the private sector, yet there is no guarantee that the finance will be available for the new road or whether construction will actually take place. This high level of uncertainty, in a situation where the other conditions for private sector involvement are promising, may suggest that this form of road building has limited prospects.

In addition to the lengthy planning procedures, capital cost outlays are high at the beginning of any project, whilst the revenues only accrue over a long period after opening. There are also substantial sunk costs, and it is costly and difficult to reverse a decision once it has been made. Road projects require long amortization periods (53 years for the BNRR), and this contrasts with many private sector projects where payback periods are made in the medium term (about 15 years). The net result has been limited interest from the private sector unless the perceived risks have been reduced through part of the costs being underwritten by the public sector (as in French motorways), or through the private sector obtaining monopoly control over competing routes (as in the UK bridges).

Given the experience in the US and Europe, the conclusion might be that there is no role for the private sector. This is not the case. There are well established processes for the involvement of the public sector in road construction and the private sector may only have a limited role where development is completely in the private sector (table 19.3).

Where there is much greater potential is in joint funding opportunities where the risks and returns are enjoyed by both the private and the public sectors. The principal role for the public sector is in the planning and design stages of the road. These lengthy procedures, including public

Table 19.3.   Examples of Private Sector Funded Road Projects in the European Union.

Road Infrastructure Already Open
1.   The Mont-Blanc, St Bernard and Frejus tunnels in the Alps
2.   The Cadi Pyrenean tunnel
3.   The tunnel under the Schelde at Antwerp
4.   The Tancarville bridge over the estuary of the Seine
5.   The Dartford bridge over the Thames
6.   A bridge on the Dublin ring road

Road Infrastructure Under Construction or as Proposals
1.   The bridge over the Great Belt
2.   The North Birmingham Relief Road
3.   The Normandy bridge
4.   The second Severn bridge
5.   The Puymorens tunnel
6.   Toll roads in Marseilles and Lyons

inquiries, land acquisition and compulsory purchase rights, can best be undertaken by the public sector. The private sector would then undertake the construction and operation of the road, after a competitive tendering stage. Finance may come from the private sector or from both the public and private sectors. If the road is to relieve congestion, then most of the revenues would come from tolls. But if the road was built for development reasons, then returns would come primarily from the development rights associated with the land adjacent to the road. There are also investigations in the UK into the possibilities of shadow tolls for motorways. The private sector would finance, construct and operate the motorway, and they would be paid a charge according to the numbers and the mix of vehicles using the route. It seems that there are many possible arrangements for public and private sector partnership, but few seem to have been adopted in either the US or in Europe. Yet it is through joint funding opportunities that most major new road projects will be funded, particularly where expected levels of demand are modest or where development objectives are paramount.

In Europe, these issues are now a major concern with respect to the Trans European Networks (TEN) which are to be constructed across all European Union countries. This major infrastructure investment programme (road and rail) will be financed in part by the European Investment Bank through the European Infrastructure Fund set up at the Edinburgh Summit in December 1992. The Trans European Networks consist of 54,000 km of road, of which about 40,000 km is in use at present. This means that 14,000 km is to be completed by 2002, and a further 5,000 km needs to be upgraded at a total cost of over 120 billion Ecus – £90 billion (CEC, 1993). However, complementary funding is also required from other sources including innovative forms of tolling, other user charges and investment from the private sector.

Both the theoretical arguments and the practical experience from Europe and the US seem to raise the main questions, but not to resolve the issues. Private sector investment is possible for well defined small scale projects where the risks are low and the returns guaranteed. For larger scale, higher risk projects with longer payback periods, the public sector is still the main agent, perhaps with greater assistance from the private sector to promote innovation. More generally, the crucial questions facing governments are over the appropriate transport policy for the end of the millennium and the role that road investment might have in that strategy. There is considerable pressure to reduce levels of public expenditure on road infrastructure and the belief that investment can be linked with economic growth is still unproven. Other arguments, such as environmental impacts of new roads and whether the pricing of the infrastructure is appropriate, seem to dominate. Similarly, the claims for public sector budget constraints and inefficiency, and higher levels of private sector productivity are also unclear. These complex issues may never be resolved, but the raising of new sources of finance for roads needs clear answers now. Joint ventures between the public and private sectors with a sharing of the risks and the rewards must be seen as a major opportunity for releasing more capital for the funding of road infrastructure projects.

References

Banister, D., Andersen, B. and Barrett, S. (1995) Private sector investment in transport infrastructure in Europe, in Banister, D., Capello, R. and Nijkamp, P. (eds.) *European Transport and Communications Networks: Policy Evolution and Change*. London: Belhaven.

Carlile, J.L. (1994) Private funding of public highway projects. *Proceedings of the Institution of Civil Engineers*, **105**, February, pp. 53–63.

Commission of the European Communities (1993) *Trans European Networks – Towards a Masterplan for the Road Network and Road Traffic*. Brussels: CEC Directorate General for Transport, Report of the Motorway Working Group.

Department of Transport (1993) *Paying for Better Motorways: Issues for Discussion*. London: HMSO.

Chapter 20

Summary and Conclusions

Peter Hall and David Banister

20.1. Introduction

For many years there has been an implicit assumption that there is a link between transport and development, and in many cases this link has been seen as a positive and causal one. Those countries, regions or cities which attract a high proportion of transport investment will have a competitive advantage over those locations which have been less successful in obtaining investment. These arguments certainly go back to the 1960s with the debates over whether transport was a prerequisite for economic development (Rostow, 1960) or whether it was a consequence of development (Fogel, 1964). The debate is still raging and the chapters in this book have given a strong flavour of the latest thinking on the issues. The focus of the debate has moved away from the macroeconomic arguments over economic growth at the national and regional scale towards the more local scale urban effects of transport investment. In the introduction, ten key issues were identified as questions and issues for debate (table 20.1). All of these issues can be subsumed under the four headings which form the main conclusions from this book. In the summary we discuss each of them in turn – accessibility (table 20.1, points 1, 2 and 3); the importance of transport in the development process (table 20.1, point 4); financing of infrastructure (table 20.1, points 5 and 6); and forecasting and evaluation (table 20.1, points 7, 8 and 9). The final issue on technological change cuts across all of these issues.

20.2. Accessibility

Underlying much of the argument over increased development resulting from transport investment is the change in accessibility, or the ease with which people can travel to and from a particular location. Traditionally,

Table 20.1.   The ten key questions and issues for debate.

1. Impact on total economy and the development potential of an area.
2. Regional development effects and improved accessibility.
3. Accessible locations and interchanges which allow maximum development potential.
4. Importance of transport costs in the total production costs of firms.
5. Balance between private and public sector funding.
6. Influence of fiscal and taxation policies on the land development process.
7. Allocation of resources between different modes of transport.
8. Different theories which have been used to link land use, development and transport.
9. The treatment of time in analysis, the links between cause and effect, and establishing what would have happened in the absence of investment.
10. The role of technological change in reinforcing or breaking the links between transport and urban development.

improvements in accessibility have been viewed as a benefit to the local area as it becomes more attractive as a location to live and work in, and as property and land values rise. However, the empirical evidence now suggests that the accessibility changes are relatively small, particularly in a dense urban network of routes, and that the impacts are highly localized around the new facility (e.g. rail station or airport). A new investment may give a short-term relief to urban congestion, but the additional capacity resulting from the reallocation of travel from existing congested links will quickly be absorbed as a new congested equilibrium is reached. The changes in accessibility resulting from new investment in an already dense and congested network will not be of a sufficient scale to have a major long-term impact on the local economy. They are unlikely to be of a sufficient scale to attract major new employment into the city. Their impact may encourage longer distance travel out of the city as the new investment will make other locations more accessible; accessibility works in both directions. There seems to be a scale element here, as the investment must be of a sufficient scale and located in an area with particularly poor accessibility to have a measurable impact. It must have a demonstration effect as well as an accessibility effect. In this way it may increase one location's accessibility, relative to another area's accessibility (table 20.1, points 1 and 2). But such cases may be rare in the developed world where transport infrastructure is fairly ubiquitous. It is only in the developing countries that the changes in accessibility resulting from investment in new infrastructure will have a major impact on regional and local development.

Where accessibility does seem to have an impact is at the interchange locations between modes, particularly if there is extensive land available for development (table 20.1, point 3). But even here, the evidence is conflicting. Joint development schemes around transit stations in the United States (Cervero and Landis, this volume) have yielded miniscule returns, largely because the public agencies were relatively inexperienced, but also because the effects were being vitiated by simultaneous large-scale road investments. Ballston in Virginia, one of the more successful large-scale examples, is still overshadowed by the speculative highway-based Tysons Corner scheme a few miles away.

Yet in France (at Euralille – see Ampe, this volume) there is an expectation that major public and private investment in the new rail facility at Lille will regenerate the local and regional economy, with the city becoming a European hub on the high speed rail network. The intended effect here is different from that of a suburban node like Ballston, as its purpose is to enhance Lille's role as the regional centre of the Trans-Manche region.

This debate relates to the complementarity found within networks. Accessibility tends to be viewed as the impact of one new link on the network as a whole. However, many investments are strongly complementary and they do not need to be consumed in fixed proportions as they form systems. Competition is really taking place between systems and not individual products. So accessibility should not only be viewed as the changes in one particular system (e.g. rail), but the new competitive position of that system in relation to other systems (e.g. road). Lille is again a good example, as Euralille provides an interchange between international Eurostar services, national TGV, regional rail and local VAL and tramway systems, as well as the national Autoroute system. The real value of improvements in the quality of the network is that it provides the opportunity to take part in the network, even if they choose not to. There is an optionality benefit. The value of membership to one user is positively affected when another user joins and enlarges the network (see Katz and Schapiro, 1994). New concepts of networks and accessibility are required to determine under what conditions the competitive position of one network will be changed as compared with another on at least three dimensions – to influence expectations, to facilitate coordination and to ensure compatibility.

20.3. The Importance of Transport in the Development Process

Much of the debate in this book has questioned the importance of transport in the urban development process, particularly in cities and regions which already have a high quality and dense network of road and rail routes. As already noted, the changes in accessibility are likely to be small and not of a sufficient scale to influence location. Transport costs as a proportion of total production costs in many industries are relatively small (table 20.1, point 4) and other factors such as skilled labour, suitable sites, availability of government grants and a quality environment are all more important than transport. However, these conclusions are derived largely from manufacturing rather than from advanced services where the effects are subtle and difficult to measure. The new forms of manufacturing and employment may require a reassessment of these traditional locational factors as the globalization of production has resulted in one centre supplying an international market. For example, the Johnson Matthey factory has been built in Belgium (1990) to produce catalytic converters for the whole of the European car industry. It cost £30 million to build and produces over 5 million units a year, and there are clear economies of scale in concentrating production at one central point, but inevitably the transport costs form an increasing proportion of total production costs.

It seems that new arguments are required to account for the location factors which determine service industries. By definition, some need to be located near to their markets, but others can be provided remotely. For example, in the telephone enquiry service the person actually answering your question need not be in close proximity. Provided that the call is charged at a local rate, it makes economic sense to locate that person at a terminal in a location where suitable (cheap) labour is available. Telecommunications has made notions of distance irrelevant in the provision of many services. High quality transport and telecommunications infrastructure have allowed a greater flexibility in the location of many services.

Growth will only take place where conditions are actually already evident and transport investment may increase the rate of growth, but only in already vibrant local economies. If this is the case, then transport investment may contribute to greater variation in local economic growth. It may increase regional and local disparities rather than reduce them. However, if this is the case, how can new locations evolve or develop? The understanding of the dynamics of the development process and the role that transport might have as an agent to accelerate or slow it down is not well known. The effects may lie in the subjective psychology of perception, rather than in objective, measurable cost reductions. The image of a particular area may form an important part of the decision to locate.

The conceptual framework is weak, and it is difficult to identify exactly what is being measured, either in terms of change in development or the performance of the transport system. Even then, it is difficult to claim causality (table 20.1, points 8 and 9). There seems to be a rich area of theoretical, methodological and empirical analysis waiting to be explored. One of the main messages from this book is that little progress in any of these areas has taken place, but that we now have long-term monitoring data (e.g. BART) and shorter-term data (e.g. Supertram) available for analysis.

A new impetus has been given to the research by a series of new studies at the macro economic level on the links between economic growth and transport infrastructure investment (e.g. Aschauer, 1989 and Munnell, 1993, table 20.1, point 8). This has reflected the increased concern about shifting public resources from consumption to investment, and it is now argued that there is a significant relationship over time between public capital and private sector output. Yet, even in this recent debate, the methods used have been questioned and the direction of the claimed causality is unclear. Economists are now arguing for prices which reflect full marginal costs rather than more investment.

20.4.   FINANCING OF INFRASTRUCTURE

During much of the twentieth century, transport infrastructure has been funded by the public sector, but with pressures on public budgets new sources of funding have been sought, particularly from the private sector. Most potential seems to be in forms of joint funding of projects, but there are many different agencies involved in the investment process and they have not always related to each other closely or amicably – state agencies, quangos, private companies, and some mixed entities. To achieve success in financing, there will have to be combinations of such agencies. Some combinations will have a measure of monopoly power, either brought about through market forces where there are substantial scale economies (e.g. in airport investment), or through artificial institutional arrangements (e.g. funding high speed rail investment in Europe). Competition will come from other modes (e.g. rail and air) or even the same modes (e.g. toll and free roads), but governments may find it very difficult to reduce the monopolistic tendency but at the same time maintaining the interest of the private sector. The British government has had to tackle this problem in its rail privatization plans.

The major problem in trying to inject private capital concerns the sharing of risk. The projects in question tend to be big and controversial. They involve front-end risks in handling political opposition, for instance through protracted public inquiries, and in dealing with possibly expensive mitigation measures. Governments have tended to caution here by sheltering possible private partners from risk, though the Channel Tunnel Rail Link incorporates an ingenious new formula for risk-sharing (see Vickerman, this volume). The problem here is that the ground rules can change, and with them the potential downside risks. Consider, for instance, the effect of airline deregulation on the potential for a new competing high-speed rail line. And, reinforcing all this, there is the brutal fact that the underlying arithmetic is difficult. To move from a Treasury-approved rate of return for public sector projects, typically 8%, to the typical private-sector rate including profit, typically 12–13%, will demand very substantial productivity gains. This is why – as in the case of the British signalmen's strikes of Summer 1994 – radical productivity agreements may be at the core of any attempt to privatize.

These problems are not insuperable, but they require ingenious innovative solutions, both in the form of cost cutting, already being developed by public agencies in the more entrepreneurial climate of the 1980s and 1990s, and revenue sharing, by discriminating between different classes of traffic and different times of day or week. The institutional learning capacity is rising rapidly. But the difficulties should not be underestimated.

The odd point about the transport investment-urban development nexus is that we did it, successfully, many years ago. American railroad magnates like Leland Stanford, Henry Huntingdon and F.E. 'Borax' Smith were supreme masters of the art; in London the Metropolitan Railway did it with their Surplus Lands Company; the Japanese financed scores of private railways around Tokyo and Osaka in this way. We find it difficult to emulate these examples today, for some good reasons. The most important is that, rightly or wrongly we have created rival pre-existing free facilities (more accurately, facilities financed out of general taxation, and free to the user at point of use) and facilities which are in part amortized and even subsidised, so that they provide a low-cost service. Roads are the prime example of the first, urban transit and commuter services of the second (table 20.1, point 7).

This gives immediate rise to some paradoxes. New investment can be coupled with new tolls, but only if new and superior facilities are also provided, as has happened in Oslo, and may shortly be introduced in Stockholm. This investment may risk further traffic congestion. If existing facilities are tolled as well, this may give rise to both technical problems (can all roads be tolled?) and problems of political acceptance. This still leaves a problem of free riders who return to the old untolled road system, incurring only minor time penalties as a result, but imposing severe environmental disbenefits on third parties who live along the old roads. Possibly, a very sophisticated system of smart cards would deal with this, but it would have to apply to all roads, not just a selected network. Further, planning controls coupled with local NIMBY pressures now make it difficult or impossible to achieve the simple equation between new transport facilities and new urban development that occurred so easily in the *laissez-faire* nineteenth century. We cannot simply build new Metrolands around London. Theoretically, perhaps, one could include environmental and other externalities in the toll, on the 'polluter pays' principle, but since the losers are unlikely to receive the compensation directly, this will not do much to lessen opposition (table 20.1, points 5 and 6). In the United Kingdom, several of the government's original list of possible private investments have been withdrawn, almost certainly because of lack of interest.

Yet all projects have a private and public sector context and no one sector has the total responsibility for investment. But for the private sector it is sometimes difficult to identify the direct benefits of financing infrastructure investment, particularly as their competitors may benefit as free riders. There are not many new opportunities for investments in cities as all options have been exhausted, and as it is notoriously difficult to build new infrastructure because of community resentment and legal obligations. Outside of cities there are more opportunities to open up new locations for development, but even here most attractive locations have already been taken. Again, it is difficult to recapture the benefits through agreements or exactions. A clearer understanding of the role of the private and public sectors, the exact impacts of the infrastructure investment, and the scale and nature of the benefits, including their distribution, would all help in devising new ways of funding investment, but this may require an evaluation by historians and not social scientists.

20.5.   FORECASTING AND EVALUATION

The final heading covers broader questions which have always returned to haunt transport analysis. It is extremely difficult to assess the direct transport impacts of a new investment, let alone the indirect or direct development effects. The work of people like Don Pickrell and Jonathan Richmond (Pickrell, 1992; Richmond, 1990) has shown just how great is the room for forecasting error, usually (for urban transit) in the form of gross over-estimation of future traffic. Beyond that, there is very limited experience of the urban development impacts, much of it not well assessed and certainly not well set in a rigorous comparative framework. The evidence is quite frequently somewhat pessimistic, but that could be because – as with any major investment, for instance in science parks or other technopole-type facilities – the returns tend to be long-term, while both politicians and private investors tend to look to short-term results.

The debate has again been complicated by the recent admission from the UK government that new roads are likely to generate more traffic (SACTRA, 1994). In the past, it has been assumed that new roads are built to accommodate expected increases in demand over time (traffic growth) and to attract existing traffic from parallel routes (traffic diversion). This has allowed traffic models to be based on fixed trip matrices. This official acceptance that new roads generate new traffic, which is common knowledge to all motorists, means that new methods of transport analysis will have to be developed which are based on variable trip matrices. The potential effects of different development patterns around the road is a major component of the expected generation of new trips, which in some cases may account for 20% of all trips along the new road.

Besides this, there are some critical conceptual and technical problems in making assessments. For example, there is the problem of avoiding double counting in evaluation where time benefits are then reflected in locational advantages; there is the problem of simultaneously evaluating externalities such as congestion and environmental impacts; and there is the problem of benefits and indeed costs that wash out beyond the immediate area where the investment is made. This is another version of the free rider problem, but this time applying to landowners outside the immediate ring fence, for instance just outside a special assessment district – one contributor referred to this as 'like herding frogs'. This last problem relates to the wider, continuing problem of reconciling private investment, and resulting private profit from urban development, with a system of planning and development control administered by the public sector. The obvious danger, appearing in many cases of 'planning gain' or 'development gain' in both Britain and the United States during the 1980s, was one of confusion between the roles, resulting in widespread grant of permission in order to capture gains for the public sector. In the United States it has clearly been very difficult to handle this relationship but in Europe, with its tradition of tighter land-use planning, it may still be possible.

Perhaps the forecasting and evaluation stages are the first point for researchers to start investigating whether this is carried out prior to projects being initiated (*ex ante*) or after completion (*ex post*). Here again, it is difficult to identify even the transport costs and benefits of a project, particularly if questions of funding sources, distributional and environmental impacts are also part of that evaluation. If the development impacts are to be evaluated, either as an integrated part of the justification for the project, or as part of the assessment of the wider social and economic factors, then clear criteria for judgement of the success of a particular project are required. What is required is a continuous process of monitoring, data collection, analysis and updating to understand the dynamics of change and the impacts of the project. Only then will the cause and effect factors be understood and isolated, together with the possibility of a clear assessment of the impact of the transport investment on urban development (table 20.1, points 8 and 9).

20.6. CONCLUSION

Much of this book has been concerned with the presentation of the methods together with appropriate case studies on the links between transport investment and urban development, but no clear message has emerged. Rather a complex assessment of the limitations of the research has been the main output, together with a clearer understanding of the importance of the issues. One great uncertainty is the role that technology will play (table 20.1, point 10). We are still constrained by a bundle of relatively ancient transport technologies, all of them – electric transit and commuter rail, the internal combustion engine, the airplane – developed between 1879 and 1903, with very little subsequent advance. One might argue that it was high time for a new bundle of technologies. High-speed rail, already developed, is one, Intelligent Vehicle Highway Systems, in course of development, another. The latter, in particular, offers the potential for a system superior to the conventional private car, but evolving out of it, and priced to reflect its superiority.

One question here is whether it is possible to read across, as British civil servants say, from one type of transport investment (for instance, airports) to another (for instance, high-speed trains). There are some obvious parallels where the investments serve similar markets and may be directly competitive; it has been argued for instance that high-speed train stations more closely resemble airports than they do conventional rail stations, but intermediate stations on such lines are not really like airports at all; and in any case, the critical threshold effects may be different. The position is further complicated if investments are complementary as well as competitive, as with an airport linked to a high-speed train station.

However much we build theory, the proof will come in experience. The most urgent need is to combine the two. To take the relatively few developments actually on the ground and about to start – in the UK this includes Manchester Metrolink, Sheffield Supertram, the Jubilee Line extension, the Channel Tunnel Rail Link – and subject them both to *ex ante* and *ex post* evaluations, determining the evaluation criteria before the *ex ante* stage and then embodying them into the design criteria; and then feeding the *ex post* results into the next *ex ante* study. In this way we would be able to build up a dossier of experience, progressively improving as we go. Because the UK in the mid-1990s is beginning on a whole series of such partnership ventures, it probably represents the best time and place to start.

Much of the analysis which has been carried out has tended to concentrate on the links between transport and urban development which can be established at one point in time. Very few cases actually have data over a period of time, and even in the most studied locations (e.g. BART in San Francisco) there are data at very few points. With the advent of a new generation of transport technologies, new patterns of working and leisure, and a wide range of new technologies in telecommunications, the identification of cause and effect in transport and urban development is likely to become even more difficult. The continuous monitoring of change over time, noted above, is one key to our understanding of the dynamics of the processes at work, but it is also necessary to have (simple) methods which can at least give us some indication of the scale of the expected impacts of transport on urban development. In addition to understanding the process of change and the scale of that change, it is also necessary to be aware of the range of changes which can now result from transport investment. Many of these are small in scale and may not all work in the same direction. The links between transport and urban development have interested researchers and policy-makers for many years, yet the explanations made have never quite matched expectations. Now there is a series of new challenges outlined in this book and perhaps this will give a new impetus to the study of this fascinating subject.

References

Aschauer, D. (1989) Is public expenditure productive? *Journal of Monetary Economics*, **23**(2), pp. 177–200.

Fogel, R.W. (1964) *Railroads and American Economic Growth: Essays in Econometric History*. Baltimore: Johns Hopkins University Press

Katz, M.L. and Schapiro, C. (1994) Systems competition and network effects. *Journal of Economic Perspectives*, **23**(2), pp. 177–200.

Munnell, A. (1993) An assessment of trends in and economic impacts of infrastructure investment, in OECD, *Infrastructure Policies for the 1990s*. Paris: OECD, pp. 21–54.

Pickrell, D. (1992) A desire named streetcar: Fantasy and fact in rail transit planning. *Journal of the American Planning Association*, **58**(2), pp. 158–176.

Richmond, J.E.D. (1990) Introducing philosophical theories to urban transportation planning: Or why all planners should practice bursting bubbles. *Systems Research*, **7**(1), pp. 47–56.

Rostow, W.W. (1960) *The Stages of Economic Growth*. Cambridge: MIT Press.

SACTRA (1994) *Trunk Roads and the Generation of Traffic*. Report of the Standing Advisory Committee on Trunk Road Appraisal. London: HMSO.

INDEX

Aberdeen 93
accessibility 3, 4, 13, 17, 25, 28, 29, 32,
    63, 80, 120, 125, 137, 157, 158, 159,
    170, 171, 184, 238, 278, 279
  accessible interchange point 5
  see mobility
Accountability 61
added investment 265
added value 5, 220
agglomeration economies 25, 188
agglomerations 66
aggregate impact analysis 208
air quality 40, 53
airport 130, 187, 188, 189, 214, 282,
    286
  airport competition 215
  airport roads 273
  see Charles de Gaulle, Heathrow,
    Manchester Airport, Schiphol
allocation of resources 6, 61
America 73
Amsterdam 68–9
Antwerp 132, 221, 223, 224, 228, 234
Arizona 253, 257
Ashford International 99, 117
  see Channel Tunnel
Atlanta 73, 136, 138, 149
Australia 73, 81
automated light rail 76
  see rail, trams, BART

backup land 225, 227
Barcelona 69

BART 12, 137–9, 140–3, 145–6, 150–1,
    153, 158, 286
  see rail, trams
Belfast 215
benefit assessment 153
  see cost benefit analysis
Bergen 71
Berlin 66
berth capacity 223
  see ports
Birmingham 65–66
  Birmingham Northern Relief Road
    274
Boston 136
Bristol 82
Britain 65
Bronx 27–28
Brooklyn 28
Brussels 69, 81, 126, 128, 129, 130, 132
Buffalo 140
business activity 170
  business impacts 174
  business travellers 198
busway 139

Calais 114, 132
California 137, 140, 151, 152, 153, 154,
    248, 250, 251, 257, 258, 259, 260,
    263, 264, 267
Caltrans 142, 267
  see California
Cambridge 93
capacity 228

capacity utilization 229
see ports
capital stock 24
    capital intensity 213
    capital markets 265
capitalization 142
    capitalization benefits 12
car parking 197
Channel Tunnel 11, 96–122, 128, 244,
    245
    Channel Tunnel Act 107
    Channel Tunnel Joint Consultative
        Committee 115
    Channel Tunnel Rail Link 104, 126,
        282, 286
    see Eurostar, Eurotunnel,
        Transmanche link
Charles de Gaulle Airport 100, 129,
    190
charter traffic 193, 204
citizens groups 46
city image 168, 172
classical location theory 6
Clean Air Act 37, 41
    Clean Air Act Amendments 37, 41,
        46
    see air quality
cohesion policy 119
Cologne 129
commercial office developments 150
    see business activity
compact cities 67, 74, 90, 92
    see density, sustainable
        development
competition 280
competitiveness 119
concession agreement 107
congestion 2, 40, 53, 100, 151, 186, 190,
    198, 245, 255, 260, 268, 272, 279,
    285
    Congestion Mitigation Air Quality
        40
    Congestion Mitigation Air Quality
        Program 39
    Congestion Management Systems
        41
    see air quality, Clean Air Act
connectivity 30
container 224
    container berths 226
    container ships 227
    see ports

containment 91
contestability 214
    see competition
contractual approach 263
Copenhagen 72
cost benefit analysis 30, 167, 177, 235,
    236
    cost benefit compensation 178
    see benefit assessment
cost function 24
    cost sharing 153, 268
    cost overruns 274
counter-factual 8, 14, 243
Croydon 82

decentralization 5, 11, 68, 91, 136, 159
    see suburbanization
demand management 53
demographic 50, 54
Dennis Plan 71
    see Stockholm
density 51, 67, 72, 90, 140, 143, 159,
    160
    see compact cities, sustainable
        development
deregulation 60
Detroit 148
development 272, 276
    development benefits 137
    development effects 189
    development gain 285
    development impacts 243
    development process 280
    development profits 126
    development roads 256
    see planning, land use
Didcot Parkway 70
distribution networks 8
distributional impacts 167
    see equity
dormitory town environment 153
    see suburbanization
Dortmund 65, 161
double counting 31, 32, 235, 285
    see benefit assessment
Dover 114

East Thames Corridor 84, 104, 126
East Kent Development Agency 115
economic benefits 32
    economic development 2, 62, 92,
        190, 199, 208, 241

economic growth 9, 17, 59, 62, 138,
    216, 282
economic impact 112, 197
economic location 241
economic linkages 201, 208
economic regeneration 165
economic rents 214
economies of scale 19, 182, 238
    see cost benefit analysis
economy 94
Edge City 84
efficiency 61
efficient city 74
    see compact cities, density
elasticity of costs 23
    see cost function
electronic data interchange 242
Employees Trip Reduction
    Programmes 42
employment 28, 138, 182, 185, 188,
    199, 202, 208, 234, 243
    employment growth 145
energy efficiency 74
    energy consumption 75, 90, 160
Enhancement Program 40
environmental 10, 94, 245, 285
    environmental costs 14
    environmental effects 189, 260
    environment friendly modes 160
    environmental groups 46, 104
    environmental impacts 159
    environmental issues 89
    environmental objectives 61
    Environmental Protection Agency
        41
    environmental standards 92
    see Clean Air Act
equity 20, 63
    see distributional impacts
Essen 69
Euralille 12, 132, 134, 135, 280
    see Lille, trams
Eurocity 135
Europe 60, 65, 68, 73, 80, 91, 125, 272
    European Coal and Steel
        Community 106, 109
    European Integration 119
    European Investment Bank 106, 109
    European Regional Development
        Fund 114
    European Union 61, 235
    see individual European countries

and cities
Eurostar 99
    see Channel Tunnel
Eurotunnel 101, 105, 106, 107, 108,
    109, 110, 115
    see Channel Tunnel
evaluation 284, 285
    see cost benefit analysis
evolution theory 7
externalities 20, 285
    see environmental

factor productivity 22
factor prices 31
fast-track design 107
finance-insurance-real estate 145
    see development
financing 55, 282
    see public-private partnerships
Florence 70
Florida 51, 54, 57
forecasting 284
    forecasting error 284
forecasts 274
France 65, 272
Franchise 256, 258
    see contractual approach
Frankfurt 65, 69, 75, 76, 126, 190
free rider 5, 283
freight traffic 97, 100, 118
full costs 245

Gatwick 190
Geographic Information Systems 55,
    140, 174, 176
Glasgow 66, 215
goods handler 232, 233
    see freight traffic
green belt 68, 152, 194
Grenoble 69
growth management 261
growth poles 201

Hague 73
handling capacity 224
    see ports
Hannover 69, 70
Heathrow 82, 85, 190
Hedonic model 140, 141, 174
High Occupancy Vehicle 42, 259, 260,
    267
    see single occupancy vehicles

high speed rail 5, 69, 70, 81, 85, 99, 282
  high speed train stations 286
  see Channel Tunnel, Shinkansen, TGV
high technology firms 241
hinterland connections 234
home values 140
housing 77
Houston 136
human activities 157

Ile-de-France 65, 81
impact analysis 64
  see cost benefit analysis
infrastructure investments 63
  see financing
innovation 267–9
  see technology
input-output tables 201
intangible benefits 212
  see externalities
intelligent vehicle highway 16, 36
  see high speed train stations, TGV stations
interchanges 241, 279
investment 17
  Investment analysis 53
  Investment effect 29
  see financing, public-private partnerships
inward investment 200
ISTEA 2, 10, 36–58, 59, 61, 62, 253, 257,
Italy 272

job search 171
  see employment
joint development 147–9, 280
  see public-private partnerships
just-in-time 242
  see logistic development, technology

Kent 97, 112
  Kent Impact Study 115
  Kent County Council 117
  see Channel Tunnel
Kyoto 83

labour 25–6
  labour market 62, 113, 170, 176

labour force 171, 182
  see employment
land assembly 261
land market 160
land use 15, 54, 75, 157, 196, 239
  land use changes 53
  land use planning 208
  land use system 158
  see planning
land values 125
Le Shuttle 97
  see Channel Tunnel, Eurotunnel
Leeds-Bradford 215
light rail 69, 139, 177
  see trams, Supertram
Lille 66, 69, 128–135
  see Euralille
Lisbon 223
Liverpool 201, 215
local economy 4, 169
local regeneration benefits 183
localization economies 201
location of activities 237
  location choices 208
  location factors 281
  see development
logistic development 237
logit model 151
London 65–7, 69–71, 73, 76, 81–2, 84–5, 100, 128–30, 132, 190, 273
  London-Dublin 215
Long Range Plan 37
Los Angeles 136, 148, 200, 260
loss of land 198
Lyon 66, 69, 82

macroeconomic indicators 20
Madrid 69
management systems 48
Manchester 66, 215
  Manchester Airport 13, 190–208, 212, 217, 242–3
  see airport
  Manchester Metrolink 96, 286
  see trams
Maritime Access 230
market failure 18, 216
market developments 238
Marseille 66, 69
MARTA 139, 148
Meadowhall Shopping Centre 164
  see Sheffield

Metropolitan Planning Organizations
    37–9
Miami 148
Milan 69–70
mixed use development 51, 150, 160
    see development
mobility 48, 137
    see accessibility
modal shifts 13
models 7
monitoring 285
    see forecasting
monopoly 262
    see competition
Montreal 138
multiplier analysis 13
Munich 69–70

Nagoya 83
Nantes 69, 83
National Ambient Air Quality
    Standards 40
    see Clean Air Act
National Environmental Policy Act 45
    see environmental
National Highway System 39, 43
Netherlands 77, 92, 160
networks 29, 280
New Jersey 56
New York 56, 148–9
noise 190, 198
    see externalities
non-motorized forms of transportation
    40, 48, 53
    see environmental
Nord-Pas de Calais 97, 112, 128
    see Channel Tunnel
Norwich 93

office development 145
    office parks 137
    office rents 147
    see development
optimum level of investment 125
    see financing
Oregon 51, 54, 56
Orlando 57
Osaka 83, 283
Oslo 69, 71, 283
output 21–2, 214

Paris 65–9, 73, 75–6, 83, 100, 128, 130,
    132, 190

park-and-ride 139, 169
parking 151
partnership ventures 286
    see public-private partnerships
passenger forecasts 192
    see forecasting
pedestrianization 70
people-mover systems 148
Peterborough 70
petrol prices 72
Philadelphia 138, 148
Phoenix 136
planning 68
    planning framework 9
    planning gain 285
    planning procedures 275
    see development, land use
political acceptance 257, 283
polluter pays 283
pollution 61, 167, 190, 198
    see externalities
population 65
    population distribution 80
ports   14
    port area 227
    port capacity 219, 227
    port competitiveness 14
    port development 219
    port investments 238
    port management 220
    port productivity 224
    port revenues 221
    port tariffs 218
Portland 56, 140
PPG13 92
    see planning
pricing 55, 60
    pricing mechanisms 213
    see full costs
private developers 262
    private investors 126
    private road 266
    private sector 96, 108, 115, 273, 276,
        284
    see development
privatization 60, 124, 214, 268, 282
production costs 5, 170
productivity 178
property developments 126
    property impacts 169
    property markets 124, 173
    property values 169
    see development

public capital stock 10
public capital 24–5
public expenditure 177, 276
public good 18
public inquiries 282
public investment 32
public-private partnerships 11, 276
public transport 69, 74, 90, 132, 149, 160, 184–5
Puerto Rico 248, 250, 252, 259, 263–4

quay length 233

rail 69
    rail investment 93
    rail transit 137
    rail systems 138
    see light rail, Supertram, trams
Randstad 65, 77, 81
rate-of-return 263, 283
rationality 123, 126
Reading 70, 82
real estate 150
regional development 4
    regional economy 198
    regional employment 21
    regional development 117
    regional impacts 118
Regional Express Transportation 132
regression 27
regulation 262
relocation of economic activity 96
    relocation decisions 170
    see development
residential location 143
responsibility 61
retail panel 175
Rhine-Ruhr 65, 81
ridership impacts 151
risk 120, 124, 126, 275, 282
    risk analysis 49
    see cost benefit analysis
road pricing 71
    see toll roads
roads generate new traffic 284
Rotterdam 69, 132, 220
runway capacity 191
    see airport

Sacramento 140
San Diego 260
San Francisco 56, 75–6, 138, 158
San Jose 140, 143, 151

satellite communities 74
scheduled traffic 193
Schiphol 94, 190
    see airport
sea locks 231
Seattle 56
self-financing project 255
    see financing
Sheffield 162–3, 168, 185–6
    Sheffield Supertram 96, 286
    see BART, Supertram, trams
Shin Yokohama 83–4
Shinkansen 81–2
    see high speed rail
Shirley Highway 139
simulation models 158
Single Occupant Vehicles 36, 41–2, 45–6, 49, 50, 53, 251, 259–60, 267
    see High Occupancy Vehicles
Single Market 120
social welfare 31, 169
social rate of return 177
Société d'Economie Mixte 272
South Hampshire 93
South Yorkshire Supertram 162–81, 183
    see Sheffield, Supertram
Spain 272
spatial behaviour 21
    spatial equilibrium model 25
    spatial impact multiplier 243
    see input-output models, models
State Implementation Plan 40
Stockholm 68–9, 71, 83, 152–3, 283
    see Dennis Plan
Stuttgart 69
suburbanization 2
    see decentralization
suburbs 75
sunk costs 275
Supertram 13, 184–5
    see light rail, Sheffield, trams
Surface Transportation Program 39–40
sustainable development 11, 90
sustainable patterns 76
    see compact cities, density
Sweden 83
Sydney 73

technological revolution 16
technology 286
telecommunications 286

telecommunications infrastructure
  281
telecommute 53–4
telephone survey 175
teleshop 53
terminals 231, 241–2
  see interchanges
TGV network 129
TGV station 83, 130, 132
Tokaido 81
Tokyo 82–3, 159, 283
toll roads 14, 248–71
  toll and free roads 282
  see pricing
tolls 55
Toronto 138
total production costs 280
Toulouse 69
town cramming 92
  see density
traffic calming 70
traffic diversion 284
traffic growth 284
trams 163
  see light rail
Trans European Networks 276
Transit Oriented Design 52
Transmanche Link 105
  see Channel Tunnel
transport costs 280
transport policy 119
transport technologies 15
Transportation Improvement Program
  37

Transportation Management Areas 41
travel behaviour 55
  see spatial behaviour
travel mode 29
travel time 32, 63
trip generation effects 167
Trondheim 71
Tyne-Wear Metro 169

unemployment 113, 176
unit intensity 202
United States 81
urban and regional development 17
  see regional development
urban development 165
urban environment 74
  see environmental
urban sustainability 73
  see sustainable development
urban transport 136
  see individual modes

value capture 12, 153
Vienna 69
Virginia 248, 250, 256, 258, 263–4
vitality of urban centres 182

Warwickshire 93
Washington 56, 137, 139, 149, 157,
  254, 257, 264
willingness to pay 185

Zürich 126